Praise for *Beneath*
by Marten J.

MW00941197

"I've known Marten for years, and our biggest common denominator is that we know a team's / athlete's culture is more important than their talent. No other book on the market gives a more full-spectrum, all-around approach to building a successful college athlete than *Beneath the College Jersey.* My suggestion is for every player on my team to read this, and more importantly, to heed the advice."
Mike Daly, Two-Time Men's Lacrosse NCAA National Champion Coach

"Marten elegantly depicts the true internal struggle that every college athlete goes through in understanding how every decision they make plays into the bigger picture that is their career. As an avid reader of health, fitness, and training literature, this is the first book I've read that truly stays neutral to its readers. It does not force a view or lifestyle on its audience, but rather, allows the reader to weigh the pros and cons in how they will live their college life for themselves."
Matt Witko, Professional MLL Midfield Lacrosse Player

"*Beneath the College Jersey* is a great resource for both current and aspiring college athletes. Marten has created a thoughtful analysis of how to be a healthier college athlete. He presents his premise in a well-written and enter-taining fashion, providing a road map for the reader to take necessary steps to a healthier experience. It changed the way I look at healthy living — thanks for keeping us focused on the big picture Marten — well done!"
John Casey, Vice President of the American Baseball Coaches Association

"Vandervelde has accurately identified lifestyle as the key to success in college sports and has given all athletes an understandable and indispensable guidebook to athletic achievement. *Beneath the College Jersey* contains indispensable tools for my student-athletes before, during, and after practice, and captures the essentials of healthy and successful athletic training."
Brad Snodgrass, Six-Time Diving NCAA National Champion Coach

"Marten's insights in *Beneath the College Jersey* could be used beyond the spectrum of college athletics — into both the military and business worlds to create a healthy answer to an ongoing issue. This book is a refreshing take on an overwhelmingly overlooked issue: health in college athletics. Marten nails it, and produces riveting science, self-help, and entertainment, all in one book."
Nick Falk, 1st Lieutenant United States Army, former collegiate football player

About the Author

MARTEN VANDERVELDE is originally from Green Lake, Wisconsin and now lives in Medford, Massachusetts. After graduating from Tufts University, he became certified as a Strength and Conditioning Specialist, started his own business, and took up employment in the Tufts Athletic Department as a Strength and Conditioning Coach.

BENEATH THE COLLEGE JERSEY

The Athlete's Guide to Healthier Nutrition, Habits, and Recovery Methods

Marten J. Vandervelde

Copyright © 2014 by Marten J. Vandervelde
All rights reserved.

This book is sold subject to the condition that it shall not, by way of trade or otherwise, be lent, resold, hired out, or otherwise circulated without the author's prior consent in any form of binding or cover other than that in which it is published and without a similar condition including this condition being imposed on the subsequent purchaser. No part of this publication may be copied, stored in a retrieval system, or transmitted in any form by any means — electronic, mechanical, recording, or otherwise — except brief extracts for the purpose of review, without the written permission of the author except as permitted under Sections 107 or 108 of the 1976 United States Copyright Act, or through payment of the appropriate per-copy fee.

The scanning, uploading, and distribution of this book via the Internet or via any other means without the permission of the publisher and author is illegal and punishable by law. Please purchase only authorized electronic editions, and do not participate in- or encourage electronic piracy of copyright materials. Your support of the author's hard work and legal rights is greatly appreciated.

ISBN-10: 1500344397
ISBN-13: 978-1500344399

Be advised although the author has taken all reasonable care in preparing this book, we make no warranty about the accuracy or completeness of its content and to the maximum extent permitted, disclaim all liability from its use including, but not limited to, any inconvenience, loss, or injury sustained by any person relying on information or advice in this book. Nothing written in this book should be viewed as a substitute for competent medical care. You should not undertake any changes in diet or exercise patterns without first consulting your physician, especially if you are currently being treated for any risk factor related to heart disease, high blood pressure or adult-onset diabetes. Now, enjoy the book.

Edited by my good friend Joe McManus
Cover design by Pixel Studio Banjaluka with help from Steve Gladstone

This book is dedicated to

College Athletes Everywhere,
I Truly Respect You

Foreword

Introduction

Part I
Changing the Paradigm

Unnecessary Confusion
Stereotypes...21
Where Hard Work Belongs...26
Defining Omnitect...28
Studying the Void..29
Ancient as the Greeks...31

168 Hours
Ideal Breakdown...35
Stress...37
Talent...40
Practical, Healthy, College Living...46
Broken Windows...48

(Non-Religious) Faith
Confirmation Bias...52
Buzz Words..57
Secret Knowledge 60
Mental Barriers...62
Delayed Gratification 66
Bringing the Focus Inwards...69

Part II
Nourishment

Real Food
A Brief History..75
The Source of Foods...80
The Crazy Stuff I've Witnessed about Nutrition.....................................83
Defining Food...88
Common Sense 94

Water's Significance
The Sheer Magnitude of It...101
Quick Fixes...103
Survival vs. Optimization..104

The Game of Nutrition

Rules...109
Body Image...112
Macronutrients: Carbs, Proteins, Fats...115
Post-Workout Nutrition..122
The Essential Supplementation..123
Pointers for Maintaining a College Food Budget..........................128

Alcohol and College Athletics

The Nonathlete / Athlete Comparison...132
Specific Concerns for Athletes..134
How We View College...136
How the Body Should Feel...138
If You Must...141

Part III
Training

Energy Systems

Why Learn Them?...149
Creatine Phosphate System: Strength...151
Glycolytic System: Speed..153
Oxidative System: Endurance..154
Comparing and Contrasting..155
Stop the LSD...157
Alternatives..161

The Imbalance of Sport

Sports are Dangerous..165
Sport's Effect on Posture..169
The Purpose of the Off-Season..174
Injured Person ≠ Wuss..177

Exercise Specifics

Fads..183
Three Reasons to Train...184
Understanding Exercise..185
Gambling..189
Form...192
Warm-Up...194

Sleep

Sine Qua Non..198
Circadian Clock..200
Strategies..203

Part IV
Progress

100% of Capacity
Horizontal Dependency...211
General Adaptation Syndrome...215
Six Benefits...218
Listening to Your Body..222

Healthy Habits How To
Svengali..227
How Habits Form..230
Impelling Habits...233
Changing Habits for the Better..239

Balancing Your Future
This is Your Responsibility..246
Lying to Yourself...249
Hope...251

Epilogue

Acknowledgements
Appendices

Appendix A — Seventy Major Points

Appendix B — Impelling Habits Checklist

Appendix C — The Soy Debacle

Appendix D — Cookbook

Appendix E — Qualitative Food Journal

Bibliography

Foreword

by Steve Buckley

ALL KINDS OF WONDERFUL, SCRAPBOOK-quality platitudes get delivered to any sportswriter who's willing to step up to the dais and say a few words at the Rotary Club luncheon or local sports-league banquet. We've been called story tellers ... raconteurs ... gatekeepers ... historians. We've even been called whistle blowers, though it's fair to say our whistles gathered plenty of dust in the early days of Major League Baseball's ever-growing dependence on performance-enhancing drugs.

We also get called "insiders." And there's a reason I've chosen to imprison this word, and not the others, in quotes. For while we who make a living as the chroniclers of sport are indeed story tellers, raconteurs, historians, etc., we can never, ever be true "insiders" — even though many of us are billed as such.

Consider the many times you've tuned in to some sports program and heard the host use these words to do a toss to the reporter down at the ballpark: "And here with more on the story is our very own baseball insider ... "

Insider? Really? In the nearly four decades I've been a sportswriter and columnist, on only one occasion have I been anything close to an insider. In late September of 1985, as the late, great Maine Mariners of the American Hockey League were preparing for the upcoming season, their coach, Tommy McVie, bestowed upon me a rare gift: For one week, he allowed me to practice with the team, travel with the team, dress with the team, and, for about five minutes one night, during an exhibition game against the Fredericton Express, actually play with the team.

The lesson I learned from this Pymptonian experience is that, once those doors close, once the sportswriters and the agents and the glad-handers are whisked away, once you must truly be inside to be an insider, everything changes. In the minutes leading up to a game — yes, even a preseason game that'll never get reflected in the standings — there's a mood swing that reveals that this is, after all, work. Away from the arena, I watched how athletes eat, how they drink, how they interact with each other and with the public. I'm happy to report that most of these minor-league hockey players took great pains to prepare their bodies and minds for the rigors of athletic competition; over the years, however, there's been enough anecdotal evidence to teach us this isn't always the case.

This is why Marten Vandervelde's first book, "Beneath the College Jersey: The Athlete's Guide to Healthier Nutrition, Habits, and Recovery Methods," is such an important tool for aspiring collegiate athletes and their parents. In terms of what it takes to train and prepare (and they're not the same, by the way) for college athletics, this book is about as inside as you can possibly get, and for the simple reason that Marten is, indeed, an insider.

I should stop here, I guess, and admit that when Marten first told me about this project the assumption was that it was going to be just another assembly-line, garden-variety, seen-one-seen-em-all Training Book. And you know exactly what I'm talking about: Lots of pages with lots of photos of well-built athletes doing dead lifts, curls and all kinds of other weight-lifting exercises whose specific names are lost on me.

"No, that's not it at all," Marten told me. "In athletics, some people still think training does everything. But there also needs to be focus away from the gym, and that's where things sometimes get complicated."

Or maybe not so complicated. Simply put, "Beneath the College Jersey" is packed with something that seems to be in short supply these days: Common sense. Some of it is stuff you may not have considered before, and some of it is stuff that'll make you want to say, "Well, duh!" But when it's all laid out — page after page, chapter after chapter — as a sort of road map for the college athlete, it's hard to imagine partaking in the experience without having Marten in your corner.

It's as though Marten has been surreptitiously writing this book for most of his life — as student, as athlete, as trainer, as mentor. He has combined his own life experiences with the teachings and writings of so many others, and he has taken the time to listen to the athletes with whom he has worked.

On those occasions when he writes about posing a certain question to a group of athletes, it's important to understand that this isn't being done in a laboratory. And the athletes aren't being lined up in front of a wall and grilled. The casualness of Marten's writing suggests this is all being done informally, and he comes out of these exchanges with valuable anecdotes that are easy to digest.

Marten teaches us that being a collegiate athlete is not complicated ... while teaching us that it is. In moving beyond the simplicity of college jocks combining God-given talent, arduous training and good coaching in their quest to make the team at dear old State U, Marten shows us that a healthy athlete isn't always a healthy student. And he wants to do something about that.

I'm not sure I agree with everything in this book. When Marten writes about the abuse of alcohol that is so prevalent on American college campuses, he feels the need to add an "If You Must" section that could be misconstrued as a how-to guide to go get soused and then make it to practice the next day on time.

Upon further review, however, Marten is simply being faithful to what this book should be all about. And what "Beneath the College Jersey" is all about is having a place to turn to for answers to ALL of your questions. After all, this is not a Boy Scout handbook; it's a book for young athletes, male and female, who are kneeling in the on-deck circle of adulthood. And they need all the help they can get.

Steve Buckley
June 2014

Steve Buckley has been a sportswriter since 1978, and has been a sports columnist with the Boston Herald since 1995. His last book, "Wicked Good Year: How the Red Sox, Patriots, and Celtics turned the Hub of the Universe into the Capital of Sports," was published by HarperCollins in 2009.

Introduction

"IF ONLY I KNEW THEN what I know now." That is how nearly every conversation with a former student-athlete goes. Once they leave the college environment and start cooking for themselves, sleeping better, drinking less, and working out in a safer way, they feel so much better to the point of regretting how they behaved in school. They wish they could go back to college, lead this healthier lifestyle, and be exponentially stronger and faster as a result. As their old strength and conditioning coach, they'll reach out to me and implore me to spend more time with my athletes teaching them about the benefits of a healthy lifestyle outside of the gym, as opposed to coaching them on how to squat and power clean.

My first couple years on the job, I more or less ignored these requests. My reasoning was simple: I've only got so many months with my athletes in the gym before sending them out onto their playing fields, and they need to squat and power clean in order to be stronger and faster than their opponents. What took me years to realize was that most student-athletes in college have habits outside the gym that hinder what they're capable of doing inside of it.

Contrary to popular belief, I know that the vast majority of varsity athletes want to be healthy and diligently attempt to do the right thing. The marketplace, however, views athletes as "dumb jocks" and diminishes the intellectual content of everything as if college students aren't smart enough, or interested enough, to learn about healthy living. Well, I strongly disagree, and I've spent four years on this book to help you in your four years of college.

After hearing all of the requests from alumni to teach more about general bodily health, I asked former athletes three questions: (1) Do you consider yourself healthier now or when you were in college? (2) Do you consider yourself in better shape now or when you were in college? (3) What would your advice to yourself in college be knowing what you know now? The results of this survey surprised me a lot and inspired me to write this book. A whopping 80 percent of former athletes reported they are healthier now, after college (ranging from three years out to as many as twenty years out), than they were during their collegiate years, and more than 50 percent of them claimed they were in better shape now than they were when they were college athletes. Their answers to the third question shaped the chapters of this book, and I tried to devote time to nearly every one of their suggestions.

This book is in four parts, each one revolving around a central thesis: college is an unhealthy place and athletes need to take care of their bodies outside of the gym in order to be successful inside of the gym and on their playing fields. This book won't be confusing or technical, because the very process of becoming a fine athlete isn't either. Part One is about changing the paradigm of how college is viewed as an unhealthy environment and a place to party. Part Two focuses on nourishing a competing athlete's body. Part Three delves into training and exercise, and provides important information about what working out should mean to college athletes. And finally, Part Four looks forward to progress, changing habits for the better, and further understanding how recovery methods may affect the body more than training itself.

I wrote this book to appeal to your intelligence in regard to health, not to your ability to follow a plan. Health is achieved by planning ahead and leading our lives one day at a time, one hour at a time, and one minute at a time, not by blindly following some sort of step by step regimen month to month. This book will help you cultivate strong principles that will turn all of your habits esemplastic, unifying them into a successful, unstoppable force.

The advice that follows is so critical to success in college today that without it you cannot be successful, but with it you cannot fail. The minute details are the most important ones, and without enough attention on them, student-athletes could be leading themselves right into the basement with no way out. Athletics, unlike other hobbies or careers, have no "fail safe" in place to save anyone if they have been doing something wrong for months or years. No one can bail you out should you show up to a competition grossly under- or overtrained.

This reminds me of my favorite expression, *deus ex machina. Deus ex machina* is an ancient expression that literally translates to "god from the machine." In the earliest days of Greek tragedies, before playwrights had developed story-writing skills, stage dramas often had poor conclusions. If a writer couldn't solve all the problems he had created by the end of his play, there was a convenient way out: he could employ a simple machine, typically a crane, and lower a god onto the stage. Hence, "god from the machine," *deus ex machina.* In effect, this god would wave his hand and proclaim all was well again, thereby ending the play in probably the laziest, most unimaginative way possible. So today, *deus ex machina* has become an expression for when a would-be unsolvable problem becomes miraculously solved by some contrived and often abrupt intervention.

Well, in life, as well as in good drama, there are no *deus ex machinas.* Unlike bad playwrights that write themselves into corners, we have no mechanisms in place to bail us out. We have to carry out our lives with our future goals dictating our present behaviors; if we don't, we will earn our just deserts. Every hour of every day you are writing your story, the only question is if you're thinking ahead to the conclusion. Know that if you aren't, no one is going to be able to bail you out. As the powerful members of academia wrote in the second Humanist Manifesto, "No deity will save us; we must save ourselves." Hence, *Non Deus ex Machina.*

Part I

Changing the Paradigm

1

Unnecessary Confusion

Stereotypes

THE COLLEGE ENVIRONMENT IS NEVER repeated. For four brief years, everyone is the same age, parties are abundant, laws are lenient, and competitive sports are accessible. College is also the final platform before no one is the same age, parties are at expensive clubs, laws are strict with severe consequences, and sports are rarely to be played again. College athletes truly have four years, and four years only, to make the most of their athletic prowess before it's too late. All student-athletes want to make the most out of this opportunity to be successful, but there are billions of dollars being spent every year to confuse them and dupe them into making poor choices. Sport-related companies have been attempting — and surely been succeeding — to complicate athletic preparedness. The more confusing exercise or supplement companies can make training and eating sound, the more there is for them to gain. Ben Goldacre, author of *Bad Science* puts it the most succinctly when he writes:

> Most people know what constitutes a healthy diet already. If you want to make money out of it, you have to make a space for yourself in the market, and to do this, you must overcomplicate it, attach your own dubious stamp.[1]

The irony is these nutrition and exercise companies aren't telling us it's confusing; rather, they're selling us on how easy it allegedly is! All we have to do, according to them, is follow this plan, or take this supplement, or eat this meal replacement, or perhaps all three. In turn, all these conflicting theories of "the easy way" muddy the waters and confuse consumers. Americans, especially college-aged ones, now perceive food and health the same way Winston Churchill described Russia: as "a riddle wrapped in a mystery inside an enigma."[2] And who can blame them? With the size of the industry backing all these health claims, it's nearly impossible not to be misled.

Being a strength coach, I get asked dozens of questions every day about which exercise is better for this, what is the correct form for that, what is the right food to eat for this, and is this supplement good for that. What's clear from the questions is that student-athletes want to be healthier, but several of them have fallen victim to the sleazy, deceitful marketplace. Many athletes think the answers to their questions lie within the confines of different shoes, more advanced supplementation, or better exercise regimens, and they'll spend their money in a manner congruent with those values. This is how we end up with two different camps of variables: those that people deem worthy of their time and money, and those that people overlook.

In the first camp of variables, we find the stuff that people love to discuss — most notably exercise, apparel, equipment, and supplements. These are the things for which we are seeing advertisements, and therefore what we typically deem most important. Almost everybody thinks this is where the secrets to success lie. Because of their popularity and appeal to businesses, let's call these marketable variables "commercial variables." Commercial variables are often promoted in tandem with "the latest research," and sold to us as if these new technologies are better than what we already have.

On the other hand, meal-to-meal nutrition, water consumption, sleep habits, recovery methods, posture, mood, intelligence, belief systems, environment, behavioral habits, and even level of maturity are all variables few people in the realm of college athletics address. When athletes, administrators, or coaches consider how an athlete might progress, most leave these variables off the table. They might still deem them important, but certainly these variables take a backseat to training, equipment, and supplements. Because these variables often go unmentioned, let's name them the "ineffables." The ineffables, by definition, are not to be spoken nor understood.

What is most interesting is how, in a discussion of athletic improvement, everyone can manage to walk around the ineffables. Almost no strength coaches, even fewer head coaches, hell, sometimes not even the athletes themselves are interested.   Most coaches and players alike just want to focus solely on training, leaving all matters regarding lifestyles unspoken, trusting that student-athletes will figure it out.   Well, as with anything that is unspoken, there is room for misinterpretation and confusion.   Athletes get the idea their habits don't matter to the coach, even if that is not true, and coaches get the idea the players' habits are sacrosanct.   If coaches did want to spend time with lifestyle interventions, it would undoubtedly eat up a lot of their usable time with athletes.   Best for coaches then to push this to the back burner and focus solely on exercise.   Obviously, it's going to be hard to convince coaches that training might need to take a backseat to lifestyle — or as Upton Sinclair said, "It is difficult to get a man to understand something when his salary depends on not understanding it."[3]   This has made us very skilled and astute when talking about training techniques, yet quite inept when talking about health's relationship to said training.   We can teach and learn the tangible elements of exercise very well, but when it comes to the important factors, like health, we have very little to say. Well, let's vow, from this day forth, to break that rule over and over again. The fact that the ineffables are essentially censored, especially in college, makes a "healthy student-athlete" an anomaly.   Half the people in college are 20 years old going on dead.   In light of how unhealthy most students are, the key to success can be very simple, thus the reason it is often missed: educated, dedicated, and well-planned **healthy living.**

There is this automatic tendency among athletes to believe that decisions about health — specifically diet and exercise — need to be difficult ones.   The simplicity of healthy living escapes them because it's not what their coaches are teaching them, it's not what is selling in magazines devoted to athletic performance, nor is it found on the shelves of a store claiming to be "for athletes."   Yet we must follow the words of Einstein when he said that everything should be made as simple as possible, but not simpler.   Yes, healthy living is simple, but that does not mean that it will necessarily be easy to carry out.   We will need help from our surrounding relationships, and unfortunately, college does not carry a reputation consistent with health.

There is a strong, societal system in college that allows, and even encourages, poor health.   As we drown in a sea of misinformation, college students become attached to the phrase, "It's college," to justify their unhealthy lifestyles, often deeming it implausible to attain health during these four years. This seemingly harmless clause, "It's college," is in fact extremely dangerous because those that say it are allowing themselves to be part of a stereotype. Researchers have found stereotype threat — "college students are unhealthy," for example — at work in nearly every situation where groups of people are depicted in negative ways.[4] Malcolm Gladwell, in his book *What the Dog Saw,* cites an example of a math test to portray this phenomenon. He writes that if a researcher prefaces a math test by presenting it simply as a research tool to the participants, a group of equally skilled men and women will test at the same level. If, however, the researcher distributes the test as a measure of their gender's quantitative ability, women will do much worse than men.[5] Because women have been stereotypically and unfairly labeled as poor mathematicians, they will fall victim to their stereotype threat when directly faced with it. By the same token, if you're constantly being told, or worse yet if you're telling yourself, that you can't be healthy in college, or that you're still not in "the real world" yet, it will be hard to move past that.

Somehow, college has adopted the stereotype of being the final stage of adolescence, as opposed to the first stage of adulthood. Only a few decades ago, the four years of college were widely considered the initial steps toward adulthood leading to people becoming "real adults" much sooner than now. In fact, if we were to define adulthood by the four characteristics of moving away from home, getting married, having children, and becoming financially independent, the trend in America is that it's taking us longer to become adults. In 1960, 70 percent of 30-year-old Americans had accomplished these things; by 2000, fewer than 40 percent had done the same.[6] One could attribute this to the concept of college being no longer the beginning of adult life, but rather the final party *before* adult life really begins. Because so many more people go to college now as did decades ago, college has become an extension of high school, as opposed to a mature decision one had to make instead of going immediately into the work force. In many ways, this is tremendously optimistic for our society, but in regard to the health of our college students, it's far from great.

We've got to change how college is viewed, not only to those within it, but perhaps even more importantly, to those outside of it. Most parents of college students still treat their kids the same way in college as they did in high school, only thereafter tightening the purse strings and threatening to cut them off. The personality adjustments of both the parents of students and the students themselves when they head off to college is negligible; they pretty much behave exactly the same way they did before. Parents will fly across the country to give their kids home-cooked brownies as if they're eight years old off to summer camp.

But once college is over, there is a very quick transition into adulthood, which can be seen with recent college graduates. The alumni that come back to campus merely a month or two after graduating are *completely* different people. Surely you've seen this with some of your friends. They've been out in the "real world" for a few weeks, and there is suddenly this aura of maturity about them that was not present before. They now view themselves as part of the "real world," then everybody else follows suit. Nothing happened to these alumni within those few weeks, it's just that they think now is the time to shape up as they're not children in school anymore.

A close friend of mine manifested this concept all too well after college. During his undergraduate years, he was undoubtedly intelligent and everyone knew he had the capacity to be a great student, but he was captain of the basketball team, and his obligation as a partier often superseded his duties as a student. Although he graduated cum laude, roughly in the top 30 percent of his class, he admits he was capable of doing better and often wished he applied himself more.   This is unsurprising, as he certainly was an adept student, but his balance of work and play was very typical of any undergraduate. As most inside and outside the bubble would recognize, while students are there primarily for an education, they're obviously looking for a good time as well. Ostensibly they want to be smart, but realistically they want to have fun.

My friend lived this "normal" college lifestyle, balancing his duties fairly well, and after graduation prepared himself for the next chapter of his life: law school. So here's a guy, undeniably popular and no stranger to partying, heading off to an environment far more difficult and competitive than his undergraduate education only three months after its completion.   I was not alone in wondering how he'd fare … Well, I wouldn't find out my answer until finals were over two semesters later, as he essentially dropped off the face of the earth. When asked about his disappearance into law school, he perfectly encapsulated the maturity of a college alumnus by stating, "I'm not an undergraduate anymore, I had to get serious about school." To his credit, after his first year of law school, he was ninth in his class of 250, the top five percent. His greater success in a more competitive environment only further demonstrates the manner in which the college bubble suppresses students, and how quickly alumni mature.

The only way to fix this is to convince people that change needs to happen after high school, four years earlier than it is currently. In college, everyone's always talking about "the real world," and how they don't know how they're going to manage within it, but guess what, this already is the real world.

Where Hard Work Belongs

THE COMMON THREAD AMONG MOST college athletes is they are willing to work really hard, but just aren't quite sure how. Even those that think they know what they're doing are often a little ill-advised. Almost all athletes are under this assumption that if they just put in more and more and more hard work in the gym and on the field, they will get better. Well, this is true, but only to a point. If athletes continue to push themselves to the extremes, then perpetually fuel their body with empty nutrition and in general disregard the ineffables, maybe they'll moderately improve, but they certainly will not excel. In short, many college athletes are creative and hard-working, but the manner in which they go about trying to achieve high success is often extremely inefficient.

My favorite metaphor of this was when I asked a college senior to make five copies of a 50-page document. He didn't know that copy machines were capable of sorting — where you put the entire document into a slot, and the machine copies one page after another then prints them in order — and so he went about copying each page independently. His strategy, therefore, was five copies of page one, make a small pile, five copies of page two, make a small pile, five copies of page three, make a small pile … all the way to fifty. When he didn't come back after about 15 minutes — three times longer than I thought it should've taken him — I went to check up on him. But it was too late. When I opened the door to the tiny copy room, all I saw was white. The room was covered, floor to ceiling, with small stacks of paper topped with sticky notes. In the midst of it all was a sweating, cursing 22-year old with an expression on his face somewhere between despair and frustration. After I calmed him down and showed him the better way to go about this in the future, I realized he was a great metaphor for unhealthy, yet semi-successful college athletes. While his system theoretically worked, it was far from efficient and, given the options available, made no sense. Once I showed him the better path, he realized how strange he must've looked to outsiders. Well, this is how I view life in college. Many people have trained and eaten in a very inefficient, strange manner, but still have been moderately successful. The only barrier to this student making smarter copies and a college athlete making healthier decisions is education.

Most people's minds are completely caught up and preoccupied with hard work, devoting very little effort to anything else. This is true for coaches and players alike, as they allocate 90% or more of their time in practice to physical labor, neglecting the other factors that carry the same weight. Now no one is suggesting that team practices routinely drop everything to talk about sleep and diet habits, but both coaches and players need to understand that the ineffables deserve their attention. These are critical variables that merit the same tenacity and commitment that the more popular, commercial variables have been given.

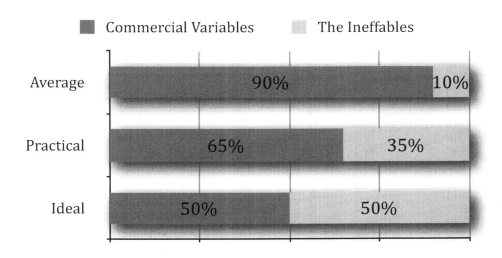

Understand that the chart above is not asking you to train half as much, it's merely showing you how your efforts should be more evenly distributed between these equally potent variables. Believing you can just train and train and train without ever dedicating any time or resources toward similarly important elements in your lifestyle shows a lack of appreciation for bodily health.

Defining Omnitect

WHAT FOCUS ON THE INEFFABLES will do is offer your body "synergism," which is defined as the interaction of elements that when combined produce a total effect that is greater than the sum of the individual contributions. This is what we're all about. Yes, chia seeds are good for you, but does that matter if you're a person who routinely eats burgers and french fries? Yes, protein is important for athletes, but if you don't eat fruits and vegetables, what's the point? Don't compartmentalize everything by scattering your variables and goals all pell-mell. Instead, lead a consistent, and driven life where every variable is <u>combined</u> to point in the same direction. This way, your body just thrives like nothing you've ever experienced.

Very few college athletes are training or performing at an optimal level, because very few of them are actually healthy. Those that perceive themselves to be healthy typically choose to define the word "health" as simply the absence of disease — that's it. Not being sick is good enough for them. Well, this is a deplorable definition of the word that truly misses the point of what health is supposed to be about. Health is not about eating a salad here and there and successfully avoiding the doctor, it's about a lifestyle of choices that create bountiful energy, deep sleep, and better moods. So while you may perceive yourself to be healthy, perhaps you will admit you're capable of doing better.

Your goal as an athlete should be to become an "omnitect" — a word specifically coined for our intents and purposes. The etymology of this word spotlights its significance: "omni-" comes from Latin meaning "all," while "-tect" is a Greek suffix meaning "worker." Put them together and you have someone who works at everything. To set yourself apart, you'll have to do a lot more than just work physically hard. Omnitects will have to constantly be inspired to pursue a healthier lifestyle that perpetually rewards them with more impressive performances.

Omnitects think about how they can make themselves better, even when they're outside the gym. Composer Igor Stravinsky once said that a real composer thinks about his work all the time, and even if he is not always conscious of it, he becomes aware of it later when he suddenly knows what to do. This is also true of real athletes. Successful athletes are the ones that think about their bodies all day, and even if they're not conscious of it, they become aware when they're offered something unhealthy to eat or asked to do something physical. This body awareness takes time to cultivate, and may be challenging for some, but in time everyone can succeed with a little hard work. And you will have to work at this.

Being on a losing team is fairly easy, come-as-you-are, but being on a winning team is stressful and requires its players to be mature and responsible. As Vince Lombardi said, living with success is more difficult than living with failure.[7] Omnitects will have to clean up their lifestyles based on their own values, make unpopular decisions with their friends, and consistently eat and sleep in conjunction with their athletic goals. This responsibility requires them to study the void.

Studying the Void

IF YOU WERE TO READ biographies or autobiographies of famous athletes, you would find page after page of training techniques and stories of epic comebacks. What you would not find would be anything mentioning their sleeping patterns, their habits, their water intake, or their daily food consumption — all about the commercial variables, nothing about the ineffables. Hard, physical labor has been the spotlight of athletic preparedness for centuries, and when people think about athletics, they tend to exclusively focus on the training aspect. This probably should not come as a surprise. After all, both exercise and practice are so highly variable, they lend themselves to be extensively studied and irregularly applied. A new coach looking to get hired will attempt to convince administrators that his/her way of training is *the right way*. If exercise and practice weren't so variable, if there was only *one* way to be a good basketball player for example, training would become so standardized and boring, coaches and players would find something else on which to focus. But because exercise is variable, a wide variety of styles can work. And if many styles of training can be effective, this makes the less popular, if not absent, variables ever more important. In the coming 300+ pages, you're going to study that powerfully auspicious absence.

The context of world history is only to learn about the winners, or at least those that have made themselves the most well known. While the Ancient Romans maintain incredible popularity, the villages, tribes, and civilizations they dismantled remain obscure, and to really learn the full story of Rome, one must study the less celebrated elements of their success. Well, the same is true in the arena of athletic preparation:

commercial variables have beaten out the ineffables to become the only variables athletes, coaches, and administrators alike deem worthy of their time and resources. Consider this: almost every college sport has at least two, if not seven or more, team coaches with an additional one to five strength and conditioning coaches. Very few have a sports nutritionist or lifestyle coach or sports psychologist. Training has dwarfed all other variables in perceived worthiness, especially at the administrative level.

The time has come to study the void athletes have been missing. Just because the Romans defeated the Carthaginians does not mean Carthage is then unimportant. Yes, history is certainly written by the victors, who are motivated to get over their wins quickly and give it closure, but it's the victims who have more to share and often go unnoticed. Exercise has won all the battles of today's society, but we must not forget about the significance health plays toward the potential of exercise, especially in an environment so corrupted by negligent advice, poor nutrition, deficient sleeping habits, an onslaught of alcohol, and a mindset devoted to overtraining.

Thanks to the emotion typically associated with diet and exercise, everyone tends to have a preconceived notion of what is best for them. No one is a blank sheet sliding into a typewriter, which is why it is sometimes hard to learn new things. In an effort to educate ourselves about meaningful decisions in life, we will turn to the Internet, the news, and entire sections of libraries to consistently find contradictory advice. As Sheena Iyengar, psychologist of choice, writes, "Even the most unbiased source can't promise that a new finding tomorrow won't reverse recommendations, so the more information we seek out, the more confused we become."[8] You have bought this book, no doubt, in the hopes it will serve as an unbiased source and not stand in opposition to anything you fervently believe. Although you are free from restrictions to information and have access to nearly every book ever written, sometimes your mind does not allow you to be free to take full advantage. After all, choice is only beneficial when it enhances people's self-control,[9] and given all the options on the subject of nutrition and exercise that openly contradict each other, it's easy to toss your hands in the air and give up.

We change this mindset by not allowing our lives to be affected by new "breakthroughs." If our lifestyles, in the way of diet and exercise, are carried out correctly, we will be immune to any bogus, hyped-up "breakthrough" that could come down the pike. We'll be living a life not controlled by any industry; rather, we'll control it with our high intelligence.

While the "good" and "bad" nutrients we cram into or take out of processed foods will forever be changing, *real food* will always be there. Simple plants and animals have kept our planet's species alive for millions of years before, and these real foods are capable of doing so for another couple million.

While the "good" and "bad" beverages will morph from fruit juices to vitamin drinks, *water* will always be there. While companies will try to profit from it in bottles, water is readily abundant and free right from your tap.

And while the "good" and "bad" training methods will shift each year, *simple practice* will always be there when everything else fails. The idea of practicing your craft in an effort to improve is as old as the Greeks, and has worked resoundingly well ever since.

The point is **training to become a good athlete is not complicated.** In fact, it is a really simple idea; the hard part is keeping it simple in a world so committed to you believing that is not the case. This is so important, yet it seems our focus has been on complicating things in recent years. With the upsurge of all the new types of training, or new supplements for athletes, there seems to be little room for the common sense things like real food and water and practice. Obviously, these things are far from new. Athletes have been properly eating and exercising since ancient times, and while we might like to think ancient forms of training are obsolete now, they actually have a lot to teach us.

Ancient as the Greeks

WHEN ONE STUDIES ANCIENT GREEK or Roman culture, it is easy to picture a dichotomy of brilliant philosophers with scholarly pursuits on one hand, and barbaric heathens with simple pleasures and vacuous principles on the other. One might imagine the original Olympic athletes to be rather unassuming creatures that knew very little about the ideal training environment of aspiring athletes. Turns out, even around the year A.D. 100, a wise philosopher by the name of Epictetus was giving lectures about that very subject, bridging the gap between the thinkers and the doers. What follows below are the colloquial notes of one of his followers, Arrian, most likely taken around the year A.D. 108:

With each work, consider the things that lead up to it, and the things that follow after it, and only then proceed with it. Otherwise, you will get to the first part eagerly enough, since you don't have the consequences in mind, but later when some difficulties turn up you will give it up shamefully. You want to be an Olympic athlete? Me too, by the gods — it's a dandy thing. But consider the things that lead up to it, and the things that follow after it, and only then come to grips with the work. You'll need discipline; you'll need to follow a diet, abstain from delicacies, do compulsory work-outs, on a fixed schedule, in the heat, in the cold. You can't drink cold water, or wine, except by orders — in general, you have to turn yourself over to your trainer as though following a doctor's orders. Then in the contest you'll need to dig in, and sometimes you'll sprain your wrist or twist an ankle. You'll swallow a lot of dust, and sometimes you'll get whipped. Oh, and after all that, you'll lose.

Take all this into consideration, and only then, if you still want to, proceed to be an athlete. Otherwise, you'll be behaving like children, who first play at being wrestlers, and then play gladiator, then play the trumpet, and then play in a tragedy. That's like you — now an athlete, now a gladiator, next a speechwriter, next a philosopher, but nothing with your whole soul. Whatever spectacle you see, you imitate, just like a monkey, and there's always something new to please you. You haven't proceeded to anything after due consideration or investigation, but randomly, and with a frigid desire.

Some people see a philosopher, or hear one speaking as Euphrates speaks (and no one can speak as well as he), and they want to be philosophers themselves. Friend, you should first consider what kind of thing it is. Next, get to know your own nature, to see if you can handle it. Do you want to be a pentathlete, or a wrestler? Take a look at your arms and thighs; get to know your back muscles. Different people are naturally good at different things. Do you think you can do it and still eat the same old way, still drink the same old way, still desire and get irritated? You've got to spend sleepless nights, you've got to do hard labour. You'll be away from your family; you'll be looked down on by the merest child, laughed at by everyone you meet. You'll get the worst of every situation — in reputation, political power, in law-suits, in every kind of business.   Look it all over, and see if you are willing to trade it for imperturbability, for freedom, for tranquility. And if not, then don't come near it. Don't act like children: first a philosopher, then a tax-collector, then a speech-writer, then a government official. These things don't go together. You've got to be one human being: either a good one, or a bad one. You've either got to work to develop your own mind, or external things; either devote your skill to what's inside, or to what's outside: in short, either maintain the rank of a philosopher, or of an ordinary person.[10]

After reading that, how far would you say we have really come since this was written? Truly, in 2,000 years, what progress have we made in the realm of athletic preparation? We certainly *think* we know a lot more, but the problems above are the exact same problems we're dealing with today. Whether it be devoting yourself entirely to your sport, following a sound nutritional plan, avoiding alcohol, trusting your coach, or simply the willingness to put in hard work, the athletes of the 21st century are no farther along than those of the 1st.

Perhaps the best part of the excerpt is near the end when Epictetus notes that we can't bounce around from being one thing then another with any chance at success. If you want to be an athlete, you have to behave like one even when you're not in the gym or out on the field. That doesn't mean you should be working out 24 hours every day, of course, but your decisions outside of your training need to be congruent with those being made in regard to the very training in question. Watching athletes kill themselves in the gym then feast on calzones provokes the question, "Are you athletes or not?" We need to sync up our lifestyles and our training, allotting more brain power to nutritional decisions and recovery methods.

If devoted athletes followed the advice of a philosopher from two millennia ago, they would already have plenty to worry about as it were. While there have been incredible leaps and bounds with regard to medical care and the general understanding of how our bodies work in the last 2,000 years, it will not aid in your development unless you have the basics down first.   As it happens, even the nutritional choices of antediluvian Olympic athletes were generally better than ours. According to one source, their diets were basically vegetarian, consisting of cereals, fruits, vegetables and legumes,[11] and we all know how ancient warriors used to supplement their diets by consuming very specific animal parts to confer strength, courage, and speed.   For thousands of years, athletes have known their diets and lifestyles needed to be better than average. This knowledge needs to be perpetuated into the 21st century.

Work hard in the gym and on the field, then come to grips with the end of your workout being just the beginning of your training. Commit yourself whole-heartedly, in every aspect of your life, and people will not only recognize your efforts now, they will remember you. This is what Epictetus and his ancient Greek friends would call "thumos," the desire of recognition not only now but for all time.[12]   All it takes is that you consider the things that lead up to it, and the things that follow after it, and only then proceed with it.

<u>Five Major Points</u>

- The college environment can be oppressive to athletes, but you do not have to participate in the stereotype.
- The ineffable variables are just as important as the commercial variables — if not more.
- Omnitects need to follow the etymology of the word and work hard at everything, not just training.
- Being healthy is not complicated, nor expensive, merely abnormal in this, the fattest country ever.
- 21st Century athletes are no different than 1st Century ones, and need not overthink their training.

2

Chapter Two

168 Hours

Ideal Breakdown

BECAUSE OF OUR SKEWED VIEW of the commercial and ineffable variables, some people create an overly developed sense of entitlement about exercise, as if it owed them something ... as if exercise leading to success was a fundamental right to be included in the United Nations Charter. The truth is that hard exercise and success are independent of each other — the presence of the former does not necessarily imply the presence of the latter. Let's not forget that training is just *one* variable, *one* part of the equation measuring into your success. There are 168 hours in a week, and even if you are working out in excess — three hours a day, six days a week: 18 hours — you still have barely put a dent in the week's total. Training owes you *nothing* if it isn't synergistically matched with the ineffables.

Thinking purely physically, in an impossibly ideal situation, your 168 hours would be limited to only three activities: eating, sleeping, and training. Of course, this is an unreasonable goal, but what you need to realize is that everything else you do over the course of your week has an effect on these big three. Every decision you make is going to tweak something about your food choices, sleeping pattern, training, or all of the above. Remember, the body is synergistic, not compartmentalized, and the same is true for your lifestyle. Everything is a variable, and the more of which you can control, the better off you are going to be.

Variables like the music to which you listen, the people with which you train, the time of day you exercise, who you're dating, or even how much you like your coach can all have great influences over how you eat, sleep, and train. Upon moving to college, you are suddenly thrown into all-you-can-eat dining halls, easy access to junk food, increased leisure time, and heavy alcohol use — not exactly the environment one would associate with health. In addition to that, studies have shown that college students' stress levels go up from academics and their peers, while at the same time coming down from their parents, and 70 percent of students claimed their relationships were a source of stress. With that in mind, it is no surprise that insufficient fruit and vegetable intake, high consumption of fried or fatty fast foods, and excessive binge drinking have been documented in this population. Within a short time of entering college, alcohol consumption jumps up 30 percent, workload and living conditions change for the worse, 80 percent of college freshmen gain weight, and 15 percent of students experience less happiness in their first year of school.[13]

If this is the kind of stuff that's happening in the other 150+ hours outside of the gym, who cares what's going on in the gym? When we zoom out to see the big picture, suddenly training doesn't seem like that big of a variable anymore. Every day, athletic trainers and strength coaches are being asked questions about things so minute, so inconceivably unimportant, it's remarkable. Athletes that haven't seen a vegetable in a week want to ask professionals about the differences between soy and whey protein powder. Athletes that drink four nights a week want to know if others believe in "spinal decompression." Athletes that haven't had a decent and/or sober night's sleep in a month question how coaches teach the squat. To borrow a line from Jerry Maguire, sometimes life with athletes is an "up-at-dawn, pride-swallowing seige."[14] We've gotten so homed in on the complex and elaborate elements of our lives without ever bothering to deal with the basic ones first. We need to zoom out.

One way to conceptualize this is to acknowledge how athletes view a day off from exercise. Most college athletes fear taking days off because they consider them signs of weakness, or they believe that one day is too important to be missed. Well certainly, in the *extreme* short term, skipping that one day is a big deal ... but if you zoom out and look at the big picture — like your week, month, or year — that one day becomes less and less significant. If you create a *lifestyle* of skipping days, then you've got a problem. The same is true of all variables: eat one ice cream sundae, no biggie; create a *lifestyle* of sundae eating, you're a fatso! Get four hours of sleep one night, you're tired for a day or two; create a *lifestyle* of four-hour nights, you're a zombie. The big picture will always matter more than the minute details.

Imagine you're flipping a coin. You've got a 50/50 shot of tails for each flip, and the probability of flipping tails ten times in a row is 0.5 to the tenth degree: 0.098%. Nearly impossible in ten flips. However, if you were to flip 30 times, instead of ten, your probability of 10 in a row becomes one percent. Flip it 50 times and you're up to two percent. The point is if your window of focus is too small, you fail to see what is really important. Eating, sleeping, and training will always be the biggest components factoring into your success, but you must remember that everything else you do will, directly or indirectly, affect your big three. And perhaps one of the biggest determinants in the way you eat, sleep, and train is stress.

Stress

As a college student, stress can present itself in a number of different ways: homework, homesickness, meeting new people, relationship issues, family problems, monetary trouble, complications finding employment, and so forth. Unfortunately, the college bubble is fairly prone to stressful situations. Even the things that are supposed to ease stress can create more! For example, one can hear the worry in students' voices when they say, "It's Halloween, I *gotta* go out tonight, but I have so much work to do first." The thought of missing an important night of partying can create a lot of anxiety in some students. Fall-sport athletes complain about being unable to attend Homecoming, while spring-sport athletes grumble about having to pass up Spring Break.

Heaven forbid.

Dan Millman, in his enlightening book *Way of the Peaceful Warrior* writes, "Stress happens when the mind resists what is."[15] Think about the grandeur and absolute truth of that sentence. Whenever you can't believe something is happening to you, you will begin to slowly come apart. "I can't believe we have a test already;" "I can't believe it's raining;" "I can't believe how hairy my arms are." The more you learn to accept your surroundings, or try to take control of them, the less stress you will encounter. Failure to do so can and will affect you in numerous ways, and over time, could actually kill you via massive coronary.

Scientists have actually confirmed that people who live with chronic stress can suffer cell loss in their hippocampus, lose memories of happy times, weaken their immune systems, depreciate the quality of their bones, and accumulate body fat more easily. Up to 18 months after working on an extremely stressful project (and even after a month-long vacation), engineers showed higher levels of cortisol and epinephrine, two chemicals associated with stress, in their bloodstreams.[16] Without question, the effects of stress can certainly be long-lasting and more destructive than we commonly believe.

In the short term, however, college's stresses will affect you a bit less perceivably. Maybe you'll mope about it, maybe you won't. Maybe you can internalize it, maybe you'll cry about it. No matter what, the inevitable stress of college is going to alter your mood, which is going to hinder your performance, how well you sleep, and/or what you choose to eat. Being crestfallen, maybe you'll reach for some junk food to try to ease your mind, but those fast-releasing simple sugars can create stress,[17] which only exacerbates your problem!

Our mood does matter and will have a lasting effect on us. We should learn to recognize the things we can and cannot control. Long nights of homework are probably going to happen no matter what, but consider this: weather can have a significant effect on people's lives. When asked on sunny days, people tend to say their lives are happy, yet on rainy days, their perspective on the world gets a little more negative and they report being less happy.[18] But why? Weather patterns, as Millman explains, are just random, "lawful displays of nature" — simple, unavoidable events.[19] Can our surroundings, even if unchangeable, affect us that much? Well, how about the fact that dressing up has been proven to inspire confidence?[20] Again, nothing about us has changed when we put on nice clothes, or when it's sunny outside, but somehow we let this stuff change us. Our surroundings should not, logically speaking, be a source of our moods, but we aren't exactly entirely rational, and thus our surroundings dramatically affect us. Our surroundings matter markedly, which is something we'll be talking about in great length later on.

With all this talk about our environment and our mindset, this is the all-important message: you have to sincerely *want* to live better in order to do so. If you stress about doing the "right thing," that *thing* is no longer right. You can't overlook the fact that if you are unhappy when you eat healthy, your body may not accept the nutrients with which you are attempting to provide it. Sadly, for some people, stress can be summoned just by *thinking* about a healthy lifestyle, nevertheless actually *doing* it. Thousands of people encounter this stress every day as they attempt new diet programs, and one would not be surprised to learn you're feeling some of the same stresses just *considering* a similar change in your lifestyle. Well first, understand healthy living is not hard. You still go to the grocery store, you still eat at the dining halls, and you still sleep in on the weekends. The important thing is to not overthink health and to not stress about it. That is why you truly have to *want* to change in order to be able to do so. You have to accept the idea, even love it, in order to prosper from it. The same can be said about your sport: if you don't love your sport, you're probably not going to do very well playing it.

Love is intangible. No one really knows how to describe love, as it is not really something to be understood, rather it must be experienced, but it matters when pertaining to sport. There is no better reason to play a sport than love, yet when asked, college athletes' answers as to why they are in their particular sport were surprising. Some real responses to that question include, "I was good in high school," "I couldn't make the team I really wanted to be on," "I'm just trying to keep in shape," "my parents pushed me into it," "my boyfriend told me I would look good in volleyball shorts," "I'm bored," "I just wanna be a lax bro, bro." Fewer people than expected actually answered, "I love the game," and that's a shame.

No one — not your friends, your parents, your coaches, nor anybody else — can force you to do anything. The decisions you make have to come from within. So if it's not *your* idea to train hard and live healthy, you will never fully subscribe to your coach's training regiment nor have an appreciation of quality living. No one ever got anywhere meaningful just following someone else's lead without any passion of their own. When people love what they do, it's much easier to put forth the effort necessary to succeed. Relate this idea back to childhood. Imagine forcing a kid that despises little league to go out to a diamond and hit balls off a tee. That poor lad would suffer through the excruciating minutia of every moment he was out there; hard work without pleasure might as well be a prison sentence. On the other hand, take a kid that lives for baseball — eats, sleeps, *breathes* baseball — and you could put him through extensive hours of drills and he would barely notice he was working hard. His athletic proficiency and future skill will simply be a by-product of his pleasure. This same concept applies to adults: it is a lot easier to convert fun into hard work than hard work into fun.   Make sure that your relationship to your sport, and your health, matters more than the results.

If you plan to be a good athlete, you have to find from where your stress develops.   Sometimes you have control over stressful situations (like choosing to wait until the last minute to finish a paper) and, of course, there are times when you don't, as we saw with the weather. But you are obligated to deal with your stress, and as you will learn later in the food chapters, when you stress, you use up valuable nutrients twice as fast as you would in a normal state.[21] In any event, the important thing to realize is that stress matters. Easily, and directly, stress will play a major role in your nutrition (via comfort food), rest (via up-all-night worrying), and training (via can't focus on the task at hand). Sadly, there are few environments in the world that have more potential for anxiety than college does. You are currently in a four-year bubble that radiates stress even when everything is going right!

Do not downplay the significance of nervous tension or unhappiness; you have every right to be anxious or depressed. But if you find that you are stressed about the idea of healthy living, something's gotta give. Just because you are in the bubble of college does not give you the right to be lazy or entitled about your lifestyle; you still need to engage with your environment.   The idea that you're in college and therefore it's unfair to expect you to eat reasonably well, drink less, and sleep more is risible. In no way is that a valid excuse. Coaches hear this every day and they need to dismiss it. The "Give me convenience or give me death" mentality will not fly, and if you're going to be stressed about your obligation to clean up your lifestyle, perhaps varsity sport is not for you.

Talent

GRANTED, TRAINING HARD AND LIVING healthy isn't always easy, and you may believe it comes easier to some than to others. Perhaps you look at those who are healthy and say, "Well, they like eating that stuff," or, "Weight management is just easier for her." Westerners, in general, tend to look at successful athletes as "naturals" — people who were just *born* to be great — and we view the arena of athletics not as a meritocracy, but as an aristocracy. To wit, it is common for us Americans to believe those that are born with the greatest abilities will organically rise to the top. The only problem with these notions is that they hold no weight when studied. As it turns out, the closer psychologists look at the careers of the gifted, in any and all fields, the smaller the role innate talent seems to play, and the bigger the role of preparation becomes.[22]

Studies fail to find "naturals" that effortlessly levitate to the top of their fields easily surpassing those that have worked much harder than them. Similarly, they rarely find "grinds," people who have practiced and labored longer than everyone else only to fall short because they "don't have what it takes."[23] Malcolm Gladwell, in his book *Outliers*, investigated highly successful people in many different fields, and found surprising results: success was never a product of god-given abilities. Instead, it was a result of at least 10,000 hours of practice with a distinct set of accumulative advantages. This is a widely-accepted theory of psychology, stating that to be an expert in any domain, whether it be at the violin, painting, or basketball, one must practice for about ten years, or 10,000 hours.[24]

Any expert or highly successful person could attest to this, but it is only starting to become acknowledged in the public domain. As early as 50 years ago, people viewed amateur bodybuilders and marathon runners as "gifted" — possessing innate abilities passed down to them through the generations. Then in the 1970s and 80s, when Arnold and the exercise wave hit America, the public began to realize a regular guy could train for either of these endeavors and succeed. Regular Joes and Jills came out of the woodwork and soon realized they too could obtain big muscles and run marathons. And while the exercise movement certainly helped the assumed potential of the average guy, to this day, most people still believe talent to be largely determined by birth. Sports fans will watch as generations of the same family come through the ranks of the professional leagues attesting one's gene pool is the best predictor of their future success. To this, researchers would point to the fact that because the parents were professional athletes, they held sports to such a high regard in the raising of their children, the kids easily had ten years of practice by the time they were entering high school giving them a huge advantage to the ones that were just picking the sport up for the first time.

As a society, we are far too generous to those who succeed and highly critical of those who fail. Yet, some people who could be world-renowned success stories are surrounded by failure starting the moment they are born. Their environments yielded them little opportunity and little chance of becoming great. Gladwell employs a great metaphor when he writes:

> The tallest oak in the forest is the tallest not just because it grew from the hardiest acorn; it is the tallest also because no other trees blocked its sunlight, the soil around it was deep and rich, no rabbit chewed through its bark as a sapling, and no lumberjack cut it down before it matured.[25]

No one is *destined* to be anything, all that matters is how hard one is willing to work and whether or not his or her environment is capable of cultivating success.

Perhaps the best example of this concept is found in the story of Todd Marinovich, an early-blooming quarterback ESPN documented in "The Marinovich Project." What's interesting about Todd is that he did not gain national attention just for his abilities, he became a household name due to the way he was raised. His father, Marv, was both a retired NFL player and one of the first Strength and Conditioning Coaches this nation ever employed. What this meant for young Todd was that his father was going to train him from birth to be the "perfect quarterback," ensuring he ate only the most nutritious foods and spent his free time as a young boy not romping around with friends, but lifting weights and studying the game of football. By his late teens, Todd was making national headlines as the "Robo QB," the man that was "bred to be a superstar." And it showed. Todd had an illustrious high school career, which brought him national attention, and a scholarship to USC — of course, one of the biggest football schools in this country. He started as a freshman and was awe-inspiring earning him an eventual first round draft pick into the NFL, ahead of Brett Favre.

Let's pause the story there and compare his young life to the aforementioned studies. According to what we learned earlier in this section, it takes 10,000 hours or 10 years to become an expert, and the majority of athletes are training in an environment counter-productive to their goals. Here's a kid that was famous for never having eaten at a fast food restaurant, and had essentially practiced to be a quarterback since he was old enough to walk; he is the paragon of the word omnitect. Although we could argue the morality of a father raising his son in this sort of the environment, what is not debatable is whether or not Todd's home life matched his goals for his athletic life. And so, unsurprisingly, Todd became an extraordinary quarterback at a very young age. By the time he was 14, he had already put in the obligatory 10,000 hours to become an expert. Sure his father was a former pro as well, but when one pauses to actually consider how Todd was raised, the prominence of Marv's history seems trivial.

Marv had made quite a project out of young Todd and both of their hard work was proving to be magnificently fruitful. However, as with any longterm project, there are many ways for the plan to fail, and although no one can ever be prepared for everything, the likelihood that *something* will go wrong in a big project is rather high. Todd's upbringing had made him an incredibly talented quarterback no doubt, but it had also ill-prepared him for the destructive college lifestyle that awaited him after high school. He had the obvious potential to be a megastar, but betting on potential is risky — there are a lot of variables out there capable of bringing people down. Todd's story essentially ends when he hits college for two reasons: one, he had become so talented by the time he entered college he began to care less about it, and two, college is an unhealthy place, a time away from parental guidance, and it took its toll on him, like it does so many great athletes.

First, Todd's lack of interest represents his "diminishing marginal utility," where the more of something you have, the less you care for extra. A good example of this would be to imagine you are planning two vacations, one that is two days long, another that is 16 days long. If, for both vacations, you were offered an extra day — to go from two to three and 16 to 17, respectively — the added day to the short vacation would mean a lot more when compared to the long vacation. This same rule applies to those who become extremely talented at a young age. For some, the more talented they become, the less they care about how much better they can get, so they stop working as hard as they used to. After all, why work so hard if you're already the best? This is sadly apparent in at least one person on almost every team in the country. Sometimes it's hard to stay motivated once you reach the top.

The other, and probably more impactful, cause of Todd's demise was the unwholesome lifestyle of college. Growing up under the attentive eye of his father, he'd had an amazing dietary record where he never ate anything processed, and the very idea of drugs and alcohol were not even on his radar. College, however, is sort of known for being a breeding ground for drugs and alcohol, and without the supervision of parents, the odds of young minds being corrupted is heightened. Unfortunately, forgivably, and one might dare to say unsurprisingly given the stress and level of expectation he experienced, Todd developed a drug habit in college that ruined his would-be future in the NFL.

Todd's story teaches us two important lessons: we all need to live in moderation (well, apart from drugs), and talent is earned, never given. So the next time you hear athletes using their genetics as an excuse, remind them of how hard we all have to practice to be great. No one was born to be an athlete. Some kids were instead thrown into sports by their parents at an early age and just so happened to enjoy it. Because they found so much pleasure in it, their practice time wasn't viewed as "hard work" but rather as play time, and before long, they had practiced so long and hard, they became decent at their sport. That's when their parents put them into a more competitive district, paid for personal coaches, and found them outlets to perpetually practice.

You see, their genetic make-up had little, if anything, to do with it. Sure, maybe some were born to be tall, or born to be muscular, but without the exposure to practice at a young age, would that matter at all? Environment matters! Did you know that history's fastest runners were born, on average, fourth in families of 4.6 children? Of the top-ten all-time NFL running backs in rushing yardage, they average 3.2 out of families of 4.4 kids.[26] Being born later, the theory goes, they had to work a little harder to keep up with their older siblings; it had nothing to do with their genetic blueprint. In fact, there are probably hundreds, if not thousands of people out there with the correct dimensions and genetic make-up to break the 100m-dash record. There are muscle fibers built for speed and strength, called "fast twitch," while others were built to endure, called "slow twitch." Everyone is born with a mixture of these fibers, however some have more of one than the other.[27] Think of all the people out there that are probably stock-piled with fast twitch muscle fibers that either don't want to train or haven't had the opportunity to do so. Potential means nothing without a conducive environment and a strong work ethic.

In college, it really comes down to who is willing to work the hardest and train the smartest. Because your competition is such a wide array of people all living in the same terribly unhealthy environment, you have huge potential to outwork and outsmart them. If you change your bad habits for the better, there is no way you can fail. This is reminiscent of an old Chinese proverb, "No one who can rise before dawn three hundred sixty days a year fails to make his family rich."[28] By the same logic, no one who practices long enough fails to become an expert, no matter what the activity. Have you ever seen that show *Dirty Jobs* on the Discovery Channel? Every week, host Mike Rowe goes to visit another group of people in another weird industry, but no matter where he goes or who he meets, one thing becomes obvious: these people are *experts* at what they do. Whether it's pumping toilets or making bricks, most of the people he meets have been practicing their craft for so long they have become so fast and efficient at it, sometimes it's mind-boggling. In the same way no one was predestined to become great at basketball or swimming, no one was born to be a toilet pumper or a brick maker either. With practice, we can all become experts; it just takes time, interest, and dedication.

You want to be able to play the guitar? Throw left-handed? Cook? All it takes is a little focused practice every day or so — getting yourself into a dedicated mindset and working hard at it for a half hour. With time, you can become an expert at anything, it will just take simple time and effort, not a genetic blueprint. After Michelangelo was referred to as a pure genius for creating the *Pietâ* at age twenty-four, he refuted the claims by stating, "If people knew how hard I had to work to gain my mastery, it would not seem so wonderful at all."[29] Use this as a guide to understand all you need to do is be your best, which takes more brains than anything else. If you work hard enough and smart enough, you will easily surpass those who might be genetically superior to you.

This applies to all variables of college athletics, too, not just exercise. Even if you couldn't put in the necessary work every day, think of the difference between one day a week and zero days a week. Imagine if you could only work out once a week, and picture how hard you'd work in that one session to try to catch yourself up to those who do it every day. You could still accomplish a lot even though it's only one day, the difference from zero to one being enormous. Apply this same idea to, say, recovery methods, or eating healthy.   If you have a history of never stretching or foam rolling, could you add it to your schedule one time each week? If you never cook for yourself, could you do it once, maybe on a Sunday?   You've got 168 hours every week, and clearing even a tiny opening for developmental habits will get you closer and closer to your goals. You can become great, it just requires some planning.

Perhaps Phil Jackson, arguably the most successful coach in history, said it best in his book *More than a Game,* "No matter how talented a player might be, there's always someone else who's just as talented."[30]   This is why we must never praise anyone, and you must never praise yourself, solely for his or her alleged innate talent. Multiple studies, mostly performed by world-renowned psychologist Carol Dweck, have shown how when people are praised for their talents, instead of for their efforts, their self-image drastically changes.   They begin to view themselves as only a product of their greatness, and do whatever it takes to maintain their image; they cannot risk making mistakes.[31]   When people define themselves by their supposed "talents," they have tremendous difficulties in the future when their self-image is threatened.[32]   Whereas those who only define themselves by the effort they are willing to exert are comfortable taking on challenging tasks, understanding mistakes will be part of the working process.[33]   Working hard to be that omnitect will get you pretty far in college sport, regardless of your genetic make-up.   You're just going to have to be smarter than everyone else in order to achieve the success you desire.

Practical, Healthy, College Living

YOU CAN'T CONTROL EVERYTHING, AND if you try, you'll go crazy. Of the 168 hours in the week, you should not expect perfection. If it were possible to control all the variables to which you'll be subjugated in a week, there would be a lot more Olympians out there. The very essence of life is not knowing what is coming next, which is exactly what makes it so exciting to live! Although the ideal athlete environment is "eat, sleep, train," no one in their right mind would *actually* prescribe such behavior, and this book is certainly *not* attempting to do so.

But when it comes to "eat, sleep, train," there are only two of those with which you need to concern yourself. Most athletes in college have little say over how they train; their coaches usually have them covered 12 months out of the year, which is why this book rarely discusses training tips. For the most part, people can't go wrong with training anyway. If they're working hard with experienced coaches, they should be fine. On the other hand, the ineffables are objectives college athletes must tackle on their own, and in regard to these topics, you must be relentless.

Our goal is always to find what is practical given your scenario. We should not be trying to turn the paradigm of college living on its head. What we should do, however, is be better. Everyone must understand what is optimal, what is practical, and what is lazy behavior.

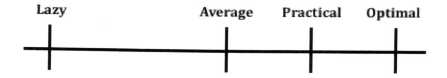

Practical goals include simple things like drinking 8-10 glasses of water per day, eating 5-10 servings of fruits and/or vegetables per day, sleeping 7-9 hours every night, and most importantly, viewing healthy living as a necessary element of your overall training. Those are all challenging, although practical goals you can achieve every single day, all of which bear minimal complications to being accomplished.

Of course, there is a lot more to a healthy lifestyle than those simple priorities, but they will be big steps in the right direction for most college students. Although, if you're not ready for any portion of it, don't force it on yourself. The thought alone is a little draconian, and pressuring yourself or someone else into health would create too much stress to be successful anyway. This is, and forever will be, *your* decision. But be forewarned, sports aren't what they used to be. Back in the 1960s when the Packers dominated the NFL, their best players were notorious for being the biggest partiers in the league.[34] Because the idea of healthy living was in its infancy, and they had one of the best NFL coaches of all time at their helm, they were able to out-train everyone else in the league. Well it's a different world now. So many coaches all over the world know everything there is to know about athletic performance, but many are still catching up to the idea of a healthy athlete.

Right now, you have a leg up on the majority of your competition. The vast majority of college athletes lead the typical college lifestyle: eat fried, chug booze, stress tons, sleep none. You are discovering in order to be successful, first you have to be educated about what is helping you and what is hindering you, because rarely will you find something in your life that isn't doing one or the other. Too often, athletes try to become superstars without doing all the foundational — read: educational — work first. As Robert Kiyosaki writes in *Rich Dad, Poor Dad*, people are trying to build the Empire State Building on a six-inch slab of foundation.[35] This is true for any facet of life, but especially for athleticism: the very first step of becoming successful is developing a strong, intelligent foundation from which to work. Without this firm base, the structures that you create off of your shoddy infrastructure will inevitably topple. In other words, those athletes uninterested in studying the educational components of their training will undoubtedly lead themselves to injury, failure, or both.

But meticulously scrutinizing your lifestyle is not beneficial. Counting calories, steps on a pedometer, stressing about what to eat … this is not health, and this is not what should be consuming your 168 hours. Health can be obtained in a countless number of ways, which is why education is the key. Intelligence can thwart any problem; thus, the key to success is to be "athletically literate." You must know your habits, your body, and their coexistence. Then, *and only then*, will you be able to make wise, rational decisions about your training.

Broken Windows

IN ORDER FOR THESE CHANGES to occur, you must create an environment in which they *can* occur. If you truly see yourself as a virtuous, committed person, these changes will happen organically. If you can send unconscious signals to yourself that you are a healthy, motivated individual, then you will naturally become one. On the flip side, surround yourself with messages that you are a slob and deserve to fail, you probably will. As we've already seen, outcomes are typically the result of environments.

Two researchers by the names of James Q. Wilson and George Kelling studied this phenomenon in some detail. Their findings have since become famous as the "Broken Windows Theory," and can offer us much insight in the realm of environment. Basically, what Wilson and Kelling argue is that crime is the inevitable result of disorder.[36] If a window is broken in some neighborhood, for example, and goes without repair for some time, people in the vicinity will get the idea no one cares. Before long, more windows break, and this sense of indifference will overrun the community sending the signal that anything goes. People that are otherwise good citizens get the apathetic message and alter their behavior for the worse.

What Wilson and Kelling discovered is that minor, seemingly insignificant deviations from order can quickly become tipping points that lead to exaggerated offenses. And, alternatively, these epidemics can be reversed by fiddling with the smallest of details![37] As Malcolm Gladwell writes in *The Tipping Point*:

> There are instances where you can take normal people from good schools and happy families and good neighborhoods and powerfully affect their behavior merely by changing the immediate details of their situation.[38]

There have been plenty of psychological studies that explicitly demonstrate this fact very well.

The point being, your behavior, the types of signals with which you surround yourself, how you view you current self, and most importantly, how you view your future self are all going to affect you. Studies have shown that what ignited progress the most in children was not any skill or gene; instead, it was the small, albeit powerful vision of their future. With the same amount of practice, a group of children who decided they were long-term committed outperformed their short-term commitment counterparts by 400 percent.[39]

So do you consider yourself in this for the long haul? Take a look around you. What do your surroundings say about your commitment? What do you hang on your walls? What TV shows are in your DVR? What books are on your bookshelf? How tidy do you keep your room? What is the background picture of your smartphone? If someone were to walk into your room, they could learn as much about you from one glance at your private space as they could from spending hours with you in conversation.[40]

If you think it's going to be hard to alter your lifestyle now, you'll be doing yourself no favors if you are unable to alter your surroundings as well. Your environment is half to blame for the lifestyle in the first place! Who your friends and families are as well as the town from which you came shaped the values you currently have. So if you're not pleased with that, get to work changing your environment. You want to eat more veggies? Change the background picture of your computer to a carrot. Hang a photo of a farm on your wall. Get a tattoo of you eating a salad … okay, maybe that one's extreme, but you get the gist. There can be no broken windows if you want to have a good chance at succeeding. By making all these small changes and surrounding yourself with success, you'll be able to tear down any mental blockages you previously held about your future. When you, or even the people near you, become successful, you start to believe that success is possible. Instead of being cloaked in failure, you recognize it's possible to do good.

Consider when the four-minute mile was broken. As with any record, the world record time had been gradually coming down over several decades. The performances had been nearing four minutes well before Roger Bannister and John Landy — the two men to eventually break four — hit the stage. In 1945, Sweden's Gunder Hägg set the world record at 4:01.3,[41] and there it stood for nine years. Many people deemed the four minute mile implausible; doctors even claimed it was humanly impossible, against the physics and chemistry of our bodies. For decades, the best middle-distance runners tried for it and failed, many coming within just two seconds. In the early 1950's, John Landy had ran a sub-4:03 mile more than five times, yet could not get under that four-minute barrier.[42] On January 21, 1954, during one of his most prolific attempts, he was on pace all the way up to 200 meters to go, but then unexplainably slowed to yet another sub-4:03.[43]

Finally, miraculously, and one might even say bravely, on May 6, 1954, Roger Bannister crossed the line in 3:59.4.[44] Bannister made very public he thought the only reason why no one had ran a sub-four mile before was because of the mental wall,[45] and sure enough, 46 days later, John Landy ran a 3:58.[46] With the mental barrier finally torn down, the flood gates opened. By the end of 1957, 16 more runners had broken four minutes as well.[47] Since then, the world record has continually gotten faster and faster, now bottoming out in the low 3:40s.[48]

Was it just a coincidence that all these other runners, especially in 1956 and '57, broke four minutes? Were all these runners just finally peaking over this same period in time? Of course not! When we can see that success is possible, and when we are surrounded by it, the very idea of it becomes much more tangible. This is why the best coaches in the world are rarely prolific geniuses bestowing upon their peasant followers the brilliance that is their wisdom. No. Instead, they are more closely related to careful farmers completely invested in the cultivation of their crops. Daniel Coyle studied these types of Master Coaches for many years and wrote about them in *The Talent Code.* What he noticed was that great coaches seldom gave inspiring speeches or doted out salient advice; rather, they had a knack for even the smallest of details. Every coach seemed to be extremely deliberate in the way they conducted business, never allowing any broken windows into their systems.

Franz Stampfl, Roger Bannister's coach, knew all too well the effects of a positive mindset, as he had been to hell and back during wartime and knew what faith could do to any individual. Stampfl applied this concept to his coaching, as he preached:

> Training is principally an act of faith. The athlete must believe in its efficacy: he must believe that through training his performance will improve and continue to improve indefinitely for as long as he continues to train to progressively stiff standards.[49]

And faith is exactly what we'll be studying in the next chapter.

Five Major Points

- There are 168 hours in a week, and whenever you aren't eating, sleeping, or training, you are still affecting those big three.
- Zoom out and look at the big picture more often.
- You have to *want* to be healthier in order to do so, otherwise you will simply be adding more stress to your already stressful life.
- Talent is not inbred. Everyone must work at least 10,000 hours to become an expert.
- Your surroundings matter, and you will inevitably become a product of them. Look around you.

Chapter Three

(Non-Religious) Faith

Confirmation Bias

WIDELY-ACCEPTED, BUT ERRONEOUS THEORIES envelop athletes' minds quite easily, and who can blame them? Understandably, athletes are willing to believe and try just about anything to become successful, thus making them a highly vulnerable group of consumers. By innocently wanting to win, they unknowingly allow themselves to be convinced there are tricks and secrets to success, even if these "tricks" are not governed by reason. Studies have shown that the more available a bit of information is, the faster we process it. The faster we process information, the more we believe it, and thus, the less likely we are to consider other bits of info.[50] So, if a workout or supplement sounds good to you or makes sense the first time you hear it, you will immediately create an affinity for it. This is why nearly every week health professionals find themselves in some form of a debate where they bring science and reason to the table to compete against what other people strongly *believe* to be true. Once people develop these convictions, they do not easily drop them, even if the evidence indisputably contradicts their core justifications for them. What's interesting is when asked why they believe what they do, or better yet to prove it, they can easily bounce from one rationale to another to preserve their ideology.

When people allow themselves to believe unknowingly inaccurate information, it can quickly snowball into a bias. Their future beliefs will be molded by what they presently think, resulting in what psychologists call the "confirmation bias." These partialities can sprout up quickly, or they can slowly develop over time into overwhelming biases. The quick ones are usually harmless, where people at racetracks feel way more confident about a horse's chance of victory after they've placed a bet on it.[51] The dangerous types of biases are the ones where people seek out information to confirm what they already hope to be true.

When people believe in something and want to find more information about it, they'll be looking for additional evidence to confirm the opinion to which they've already come, and of course, given the Internet, they will certainly find it. If we research something for which we feel emotion, new information we find that is consonant with our beliefs will be welcomed as well founded and useful. Conversely, if the evidence is dissonant, then we consider it biased or foolish.[52] What these emotions demonstrate is that we are a stubborn breed — once our minds are made up, we don't want to change them.[53] People's opinions are historically not the result of years of rational, objective analysis; instead, opinions are the result of years of paying attention to information that *confirmed* what we already believed, or hoped would be true, while ignoring any information that challenged our already-established positions.[54]

Faith, however, is not a reason. Just because you believe fervently in something does not make it true. Charlie Pierce, in his book *Idiot America*, points out that most discussions these days have slid from the brain to the gut. We no longer argue with thesis and antithesis; rather, people are pitting themselves against scientific research because they just *know* the truth. Intellect is being forced to duel against feeling. People want to treat training and nutrition like religion, where strong beliefs create unwavering emotional attachments that supersede all counterevidence. The problem is that unlike religion, diet and exercise are extraordinarily scientific, and what you believe matters little in an industry that has research-based, empirical evidence debunking unproven theories.

A football player once asked why I don't want my athletes to have a "conditioning base" — a very popular little phrase people like to toss around. I am, as he knew, strongly opposed to this idea of endurance training for athletes, and I was excited to share with him my reasonings, all the while thinking once he heard the argument, he'd jump on board.

First, I told him all about the science behind energy systems (discussed in Chapter Eight) and showed him the empirical evidence that proved this type of training was detrimental to speed athletes. Then, I figured, if that wasn't enough, I'd conclude by noting that his 60-minute sport never incorporated a single consecutive period of nonstop play longer than ten seconds.   He recognized that as fact … said he agreed with me. Subsequently, I asked him why, then, would he ever need to train for a "conditioning base?"   And this is where it gets intellectual. He truly did not have an answer, yet he still held strong to his ideals.

After agreeing with my point-by-point analysis, how could he still cling to his earlier beliefs? Is he an idiot? No. In fact, not at all. For starters, criticizing people for who they are rather than for what they did evokes a deep sense of shame and helplessness,[55] so calling him dumb or making him feel that way for one mistake is not constructive (remember this next time you're in a fight with your significant other). He had been educated through his experiences in high school to believe in a conditioning base, therefore he did. He had attained moderate success with these beliefs, so he saw himself as his own test subject, and his life as a reference point for debate. Therefore, asking him to change his mind in five minutes wasn't fair or even conscionable. So, he was told he had every right to believe what he wanted, but was asked to do his homework and find an article showing how important distance running is for football.

Well, he tried.

For two weeks.

Never found a single article.

He did, however, find an abundance of books, articles, and scientific journals scientifically debunking his firmly entrenched views. You might think that after all of this, he would come around … quite the opposite. He looked reality in the eye and denied it. Like most humans, he did not revise his first impression, he just found a way to become more confident that he was right.[56]   He essentially followed the teachings of Scientology's founder, L. Ron Hubbard, when he wrote, "What is true is what is true for you.   No one has any right to force data on you and command you to believe it or else. If it is not true for you, it isn't true."[57] This close-minded outlook of course sounds ridiculous, but this football player's mindset can teach us a lot about ourselves. We all like to think of ourselves as conscious, rational beings that make reasonable choices and decide how our lives will play out.   In reality, however, scientists are discovering our emotional selves are much more in control, and we often make judgments guided directly by feelings of liking or disliking.[58]

Sometimes, it is extremely efficient to let emotion take control, and perhaps it's worth noting. Take, for example, the decision of choosing a deodorant. With so many competing brands offering different odors, prices, qualities, and sizes, reason alone would get you nowhere. If you truly attempted to find the most logical deodorant to buy, you'd succumb to analysis paralysis and be locked into an unsolvable problem. People who have suffered damage to the emotional networks of their brains can rarely make simple decisions like what they want for lunch or what toothpaste to buy.[59] A purely emotional decision is sometimes warranted, but it's important to understand that the way you train is not one of them. The awareness that we often make decisions based solely on emotion is the first step in developing a defense against our own brain. Then, when we make a foolish decision based on emotion not reason, like our football player, it's possible for us not to be blind to our own blindness.

Our football player can't see his own blindness, or maybe he has wishful blindness. This is why it's obvious for us to see the flaw in his decision, yet it is nearly impossible for him. In this case, his blindness was due to something called the "sunk-cost bias."[60] Because of all the cost sunk into that belief — i.e. due to all the distance running he had done in previous years *because* of his belief in a conditioning base — his reality was skewed. Admitting he was wrong would have been admitting he had been wrong for years and would have compromised the confidence he had in his athleticism.

As the weeks and months went by, his stance on the issue did not change, nor was anyone expecting it to do so. Instead, he became more entrenched in his viewpoint and became more radical in his pursuit of proving science wrong. This is a perfect example of what Michael Shermer would call "belief-dependent realism." In his book *The Believing Brain*, Shermer explains how we all think our beliefs form after an onslaught of intellectual reasons, cogent arguments, and rational explanations, but more often than not, our beliefs come first, and explanations for beliefs follow.[61] Daniel Kahneman noticed the same patterns in his research, but went further to say that when emotion is involved, this behavior of concluding first and reasoning second is even more apparent.[62] We want to be right about how we see the world, so we seek out information that confirms our predetermined beliefs, while avoiding contradictory evidence and opinions.

There is something very psychologically intriguing about this reaction, and scientists have pinpointed it. The reasoning areas of the brain virtually shut down when people are confronted with dissonant information, and the emotion circuits of the brain light up happily when consonance is restored.[63] In fact, violations of normality are detected by one's brain with astonishing speed and subtlety.[64] This football player's brain didn't even allow him to look at contradictory data rationally — his emotion was simply too high. Psychologists have shown that most people, when directly confronted by evidence that they are wrong, do not change their point of view, but justify it even more tenaciously. Even irrefutable evidence is rarely enough to pierce their mental armor of self-justification.[65]

With this information, it would seem poor training, bad eating habits, lack of sleep, and alcohol are not the assassins of good athletes; rather, self-justification is. Self-justification is more potent and dangerous than just an explicit lie, because it allows people to convince themselves they are doing what's best, no matter how wrong they may be. Once people have devoted so much time and energy convincing themselves they are doing the right thing, so powerful is the need for consonance that when people are forced to look at disconfirming evidence, they will find a way to criticize, distort, or dismiss it so they can maintain or even strengthen their existing beliefs.[66]

Given that we all have some prejudices and preconceived notions, our greatest hope of self-correction lies in making sure we become educated, and we keep a few trusted naysayers in our lives. A little doubt and a couple sleepless nights are necessary to ensure we're not close-minded and unjustifiably overconfident, swayed by the illusory certainty of hindsight. We can't place too much faith in our intuitions, as we have come to some overconfident conclusions based on nothing more than statements coming from people we trust and like. Even something as arbitrary as the quality of the font in an article will have an effect on how we interpret it.[67] Jumping to conclusions on the basis of limited evidence is a huge part of our intuitive thinking.[68] This is why we need to find a way to be open, and accept that perhaps we have made some errors, for as JFK said, "An error does not become a mistake until you refuse to correct it."[69]

Buzz Words

THE ATHLETIC AND NUTRITIONAL ARENAS have so many little catchphrases and buzz words to which people adhere without ever fully understanding them. "Conditioning base" is an all-time favorite, but people will also talk about training their "core," gaining "functional strength," putting on "lean muscle" without becoming "muscle-bound," and the importance of "confusing" their "muscle memory!" Men are afraid of "bitch tits," while women are terrified of "bulking up." These little phrases are popular, reassuring, and wrong. They are just so catchily concise they conjure up a lot of emotion in those people who believe them, leaving little room or time for logic and reason to prevail. The reasonable part of your mind is rather slow and plodding, needing to make calculations and find rational answers. The emotional part is lightning-fast using only instinct and feeling to guide it.[70]

Since a whole chapter is devoted to "conditioning base" later in this book (Chapter Eight), and "bitch tits" is covered in Appendix C, the other buzz word worthy of some lampooning would be women's fear of "bulking up." Ladies, you have absolutely nothing to fear. Studies show us that, historically, anything that conjures fear will trump confusing statistics, but this is a time to let science and reason determine the truth. For starters, women generally have about a tenth of the testosterone as men (sometimes as little as one twentieth), which means their bodies are less capable of supporting rapid muscle growth.[71] That being said, it is not impossible for women to experience the same gains as men, and in fact research suggests that if men and women are put on the same exact program and forced to eat relatively the same, their improvements will be very comparable relative to their pretraining status.[72] **BUT**, few women are training like meatheads, and even less are eating like them. Muscle growth does not come solely from heavy, voluminous lifting: one also needs to be eating like a bodybuilder. No matter if we're talking about men or women, to "bulk up," or to become very muscular, people need to be grunting and screaming their way through excruciating lifts then going home to consume thousands upon thousands of calories daily with multiple protein supplements, and sometimes setting an alarm for the middle of the night just to cram another meal into the system ... the sort of things women are not known for doing. Of course one can gain muscle without going overboard like that, but no one is going to get unattractively bulky without an extremely high focus on hard lifting and heavy eating.

What *does* typically happen when women train hard, however, is their body composition changes. Because they, on average, have more body fat than men, for reproductive purposes,[73] as they lift, it's likely their percentage of body fat drops as they gain more muscle. Speaking merely logically, as one trades muscle for fat, it is probable she will gain weight on the scale, even if she in fact becomes smaller and looks better because of it. This is why if you're an athlete, male or female, your bodyweight matters *very* little. Sure, when you're older, it's a pretty good determinant of overall health, but as an athlete, you must accept your training will yield you a body conducive to excel in your sport. Worry little about the weight on the scale, because as you work hard to become great, all that matters are your skills out on the field.

People too often find erroneous correlations, like bodyweight to sport, and believe something is true by incorrectly pairing a cause and effect. As Michael Shermer writes in *The Believing Brain*, superstitions are "accidental forms of learning" where basically a coincidental relation exists between cause and effect.[74]   What Shermer discovered about superstitions and superstitious rituals is that they both rose with levels of uncertainty; uncertainty makes people anxious, and anxiety is related to magical thinking. A study found that if you show nervous parachute jumpers about to leap out of an airplane a photo of white noise, like "snow" on an out-of-service TV station, they are likely to attempt to make sense of it and find some nonexistent figure; the fear of their unknown future gives rise to their levels of mysticism.[75]

Well, in this field of diet and exercise, no one wants to feel as though they know nothing, so they look at the world around them and create a story that makes sense of it. We're storytelling creatures by nature, and while we may not always know exactly why we do the things we do, that doesn't stop us from creating perfectly logical-sounding reasons for our actions. One study demonstrated this particularly well. Psychologists lined up four identical socks and asked passersby which sock was superior. People voted, by and large, for the sock all the way on the right. When asked why, they often claimed it was of a better texture, color and/or quality, not knowing it was exactly the same as the ones to its left.[76] This just goes to show that we demand order in our lives, and we'll do whatever it takes, albeit sometimes subconsciously, to obtain it. We simply like to have reasons for what we do.

Often that means we'll make up answers on our own, like we saw with the socks. But if we can't make sense of something, the anxiety of the unknown makes us desperate for answers, which is when we seek out those who claim to have them. Given time, these desperate people will find some crackpot who claims to have *"the answer,"* and will follow him over the edge to insanity and irrationality. While true experts logically acknowledge their limitations and ignorance, this isn't what the general population wants to hear. Most people want someone who is more confident in their answers than truly rational, someone who at least *pretends* to have the knowledge they're seeking. Vividness of descriptions or information, even if it's wrong, can help persuade people to believe it.[77]

So, essentially, there are two camps of experts: those that study the field, strive to meet industry standards, and base their level of intellect against the top members of their respective field. The other group is composed of those that have picked up information along the way and base their level of expertise on how much more they know than their friends. What you may be recognizing here is the latter's clear embodiment of a classic narcissist. Because narcissists are overconfident, they tend to make their false claims with such conviction they can convince others, as well as themselves, rather easily. This explains how meatheads become strength coaches, how fitness buffs become personal trainers, and how every half-witted jock with less than ten percent body fat (guy or girl) can sell thousands of DVDs or books.

These people are able to sell their terrible advice to us because they, more often than not, have highly contagious personalities with a ton of charm and no lack of good looks. If they say something evenly moderately intriguing to us, we accept it more readily because of their strong character and aesthetically pleasing nature. Without question, good-looking people enjoy a huge cultural advantage. According to psychology professor Robert Cialdini, attractive people are better liked, more persuasive, more frequently helped, and are seen as possessing better personality traits and intellectual capabilities.[78] This is known as the "halo effect," where we try to match our view of all the qualities of a person to our judgment of a few attributes that are particularly noteworthy.[79] So if we think that someone is good-looking and affable, we are likely to think they are also intelligent and fair. We like when the world makes sense, so it's easier to think that good people are *all* good and bad people are *all* bad. A good way to conceptualize this is realize that you are rarely stumped over the course of an average day: we take those people we like and overlook their faults, then take those people we hate and overlook their strengths. The normal state of our minds is to have feelings and opinions about almost everything we see.[80]   In short, the human mind is not big on ambiguity.

Because we do not like ambiguity or uncertainty, we often believe whatever people say, given it comes from someone we like and they say it in a convincing manner. The famous Dutch philosopher Baruch Spinoza had a theory that the mere comprehension of a statement entailed the tacit acceptance of it being true, whereas disbelief required a subsequent process of rejection.[81]   In essence, belief is fast and natural, whereas skepticism is slow and unnatural — disbelieving is harder than it seems.[82]   Unless there is strong or obvious evidence to the contrary, we want to automatically believe whatever people say.[83]   That means our instincts are to trust, and given all the misinformation that's out there, this is a dangerous instinct.

Secret Knowledge

THE POINT IS SIMPLE.   HOW often do athletes read and/or hear complicated new strategies to make them faster or stronger? Whether it be from their friends, articles in magazines, or shows on TV, the amount of information on the subject of athletic prep, or exercise in general, is exorbitant. All Americans are bombarded with this stuff every single day of the week.   This overexposure to advertisements and celebrity endorsements eventually creates the "availability heuristic," which is the process of judging something by the ease with which instances come to mind.[84] So, because we are subjugated to this deluge of supplements and crazy workouts, that is what is always fresh in our minds; therefore, it is what most of us deem important.

The availability heuristic, however, defies what is true. A simple activity demonstrates this well. Think of the letter K. Is K more likely to appear as the first letter in a word or as the third letter? Take a minute. Think about it.

If you truly took the time to mull it over, you have probably concluded what most people do: you would say that K as the first letter appears about twice or maybe three times as often as K as the third letter, which puts the truth exactly backwards.[85] What you should have realized, by now, is that you relied on your availability heuristic to reach this decision — scanning your brain for words with K as the first and third letters, and sure enough you found way more for the former. As you can see, our availability heuristic makes judgments based solely on the ease with which examples come to mind, and therefore cannot be trusted.

This little psychological flaw is responsible for much of our erroneous mental baggage. Vincent Bugliosi, in his book *Reclaiming History* drives this phenomenon home as he discusses how 95 percent of the close to 1,000 books published about the John F. Kennedy assassination are *pro*-conspiracy.[86] Therefore, there is decidedly <u>no</u> surprise that 75 percent of Americans are convinced JFK was the victim of a massive scheme. People have a hard time believing that a man as charismatic and important as JFK could die at the hands of a single, deranged gunman. The same is true for people having a hard time following how athletic prowess could be as simple as a synergistic approach to health. For those of you who believe the JFK assassination was an elaborate scheme, think about how many documentaries you've seen, articles you've read, or anecdotes you've heard claiming it was a conspiracy. Probably quite a bit. Now, the real question is, have you ever read the Warren Report?

Or better yet, the Warren Commission?

Have you even *heard* of either of them?

There's nothing more fundamentally American than conspiracies and conspiracy theories. We always like to think there is secret knowledge out there, being kept hidden by someone, and we have to dig to find it. We tend to follow the advice of the rich and successful people who claim they have the secrets to becoming rich and successful. Bill Maher probably said it best when he claimed that everyone thinks there's some quick and easy secret we can obtain from these rich and successful people, but these people are only rich because they're robbing us![87] This is how diet and exercise fads get their start. A great salesman creates believers who throw all their money and hope into unwrapping the "secret" of diet and/or exercise. The problem is, there is no secret.

So many books are filled with fear and scare-tactic nonsense they become bestsellers. The authors promise everything you've heard before is wrong, then vehemently vilify one thing — whether it be an additive, a macronutrient, or a food, it doesn't matter. This has happened with dietary fat, fructose, sugar, gluten, carbohydrates, dairy, eggs, meat, GMOs, salt, mercury, saturated fat, palm oil ... the list could go on forever. As Dr. Katz, author of *Disease Proof* and probably the single best article contradicting these fad diets, wrote if any one of these arguments was truly valid, and their one food item is to blame for everything, well then it would prove all the other books are wrong. Fad followers sadly never catch on to that fact, and they drop one fad when it loses steam only to quickly sign on for the next. They are determined to find the "conspiracy of health:" the alleged secret knowledge some group is hiding. The truth is far less sexy, as there is no silver bullet to health.

Everybody finds conspiracies fascinating and intriguing the same way they find new exercises, especially if done by professional players, exciting and promising. Very few people care to find out what the most successful athletes are eating or drinking, because they don't believe the answers could be that easy. Most people just want to read about how crazy the workouts are, or how extreme their supplementation may be, not trusting the key to success could be as mundane as proper nutrition and an abundance of rest. This is why fad creators, the people who make up workouts allegedly based on what elite athletes do, make so much money.

We could easily sit here and point fingers at who's to blame, but the truth is we've done this to ourselves. For starters, when journalists or sports broadcasters speak with athletes about their lives, the only questions they're asking are in regard to their training. Second, Americans have such a high reverence for professional athletes, we take anyone who claims to be associated with them very seriously. We then put these self-proclaimed experts up on a pedestal as if they were intelligent arbiters dutifully carrying out their lives in some unabashed, irrepressible quest for perfection, when in reality, they are often vortexes of compromise. They're going to try to sell us on different workouts, tell us we *need* this video, or *need* this book, when we don't *need* to learn any more about how to train. We instead need to understand how other variables <u>allow</u> us to train.

Mental Barriers

OFTEN, THE BIGGEST PROBLEM IN those athletes willing to train the hardest is that they are entrenched in their personal views about what will make them better, no matter how ill-advised they may be. They set up this mental wall of what they think is best for them, and allow nothing else through. Blind faith in the status quo of athletic preparation — e.g. eating a whole carton of protein powder and exercising to utter exhaustion — leaves most people unwilling to be open-minded. The truth is that *everyone* has pre-conceived notions of what they believe to be best for them, and some never stray from those convictions. All one can ask of you is to sit down and contemplate from where you got your ideology.

Why do you believe what you do? Is it based in fact, or just something toward which you have a strong affinity? Have you ever tried anything different? Seriously, have you ever put the whole of your determination, will, and desire into something completely different than your normal routine? Are you at all open to the thought of change should counter-evidence to your position surmount itself?

A great example of people's stubbornness to adhere to the status quo and mental barriers can be seen with milk. We all grew up watching those original and creative advertisements about milk, and based on the maxim that an ad has to be seen at least six times before anyone will remember it,[88] we've probably all had a minimum exposure to the milk ads. Due to this overexposure, almost every American believes cow's milk makes strong, healthy bones and teeth — perhaps it's even "nature's most perfect food." What we never think about is how milk is species specific, with every mammal's milk being tailor-made for its own kind. We drink human milk when we're babies, then never touch the stuff again. The thought of drinking human milk as an adult is pretty revolting, is it not? Well all animals feel this way about their own milk; they grow up drinking their own species' milk, then never consider touching it again. No other animal drinks any other animal's milk (at least in adulthood), and even predatory animals that kill milk producers won't touch it.

So the very fact we drink milk *at all* is pretty interesting, but wait, it gets so much better. Of all the milk to be drank, why are we drinking *cow's* milk? Most people don't even question that fact nor find it strange they have never consumed the milk of another animal. Why aren't we drinking buffalo milk, bear milk, cat or dog milk? Hell, human milk is only 5 percent protein, while rat's milk is 45 percent![89] Most will cringe when they contemplate sipping on a glass of rat's milk, but why is cow's milk any better? You might answer "well because it's nature's most perfect food, of course," but the real answer is a bit more pessimistic. The meat and cattle industries in this country are absolutely gargantuan, and their connections to politics have been widely reported dating back to Nixon's infamous shady dealings. Whether or not the 1972 campaign contributions from the dairy industry led to illegal public acts from Nixon's administration remains partially shrouded, nevertheless it is interesting.

While you might be sniffing a conspiracy here, there is none. The most fascinating thing about milk is what you are reading here is all public information. No one, apart from maybe Nixon in the '70s, is trying to hide any of these details about milk's health, it's just that no one is out searching for them anymore. What is exciting, however, is that scientists do know an enormous amount about milk and health. Public opinion is just slow to catch up.

The most common public opinion about milk is that we need it for strong bones, which is what you are undoubtedly saying to yourself right now. Well, as it turns out, many studies have proven that the more animal protein we eat, the more calcium we lose.[90] While there is a lot of calcium in milk, it is not as "bioavailable," or usable by the body, as calcium from other sources such as brussels sprouts or broccoli (63.8 percent and 52.6 percent bioavailable, respectively, while cow's milk is 32 percent bioavailable).[91] Unsurprisingly, the more plant foods people eat, and the more people exercise, the stronger their bones will become, while eating a lot of animal products and skipping the gym can weaken bones.[92] This is not disputed in the scientific community. In fact, the countries with the highest consumption of dairy products are Finland, Sweden, the United States and England. Can you guess the countries with the highest rates of osteoporosis? Yeah: Finland, Sweden, the United States and England.[93] Of course, correlation is not causation, and diseases are rarely, if ever, a determinant of one variable, but it is compelling nevertheless.

Apart from the calcium plug, there are some other things people should know about milk. First, because of all the growth hormones and the way we raise our cattle in general, most American beef cannot be exported to the European Union.[94] In fact, Recombinant Bovine Growth Hormone (rBGH), with which we routinely inject our cattle, has been banned in Canada, New Zealand, Japan, Australia, and all 27 nations of the EU.[95] Consequently, they will not import our meat as they consider it dangerous for their populace. Rightly so, as milk from cows that have been injected with rBGH contains 2 to 10 times as much insulin-like growth factor (IGF-1) as normal cow's milk.[96] This is an important nugget of information as the risk of prostate cancer for men over 60 with high levels of this are eight times higher than men with low levels. Similarly for pre-menopausal women, the risk of breast cancer is seven times greater with high levels of IGF-1.[97]

Second, scientists have known for a long time that diets high in animal proteins have direct links to our most common cancers, especially three of our top four: breast, prostate, and colon. Turns out, countries that have low consumption rates of dairy, or the meat of dairy animals, also enjoy exceptionally low incidents of breast cancer, prostate cancer, and other hormone-related cancers.[98] The lowest cancer rates in the world are found in the Okinawans who consume no milk, but also consume the most soy.[99]   While high levels of plant protein have been proven safe in dramatically large amounts, animal proteins have not.[100] Most notable of the animal proteins linked to cancer is casein, milk's protein. Unbelievably, casein actually *promoted* all stages of the cancer process in tests with rats, and could *effectively turn cancer on* with moderate doses, 20 percent of subject's diet, or off with lower doses, five percent.[101]   What is important to note here is that the harmful dose of casein was a mere 20 percent of the subject's diet; our typical American diet often reaches and surpasses this amount! This, as you can see, is life-or-death information that is rarely acknowledged by Americans.

Finally, a milk promoter might say that milk is drank all over the world by billions of people and has been sustaining us since our primitive days. While it cannot be argued that animal milk — not only cow's milk, but also buffalo, horse, and other species — has been a factor in the past for the survival of our species, in the present day, things are different. To put it in perspective, go ahead and think about this question for a second: What percentage of adults worldwide drink milk? ... Got your number yet? Most Americans answer over 90 percent, but the actual answer will probably surprise you ...

Thirty-five percent.[102]   Thirty-five percent of adults worldwide actually drink the stuff. Why so low? *Newsflash*: cow's milk is not for humans! For starters, a lot of the world's population is actually lactose intolerant. Because there is no reasonable need to ever drink milk as an adult, from any animal, many bodies won't accept it. People of Asian descent are 90-100 percent lactose intolerant; Native Americans, 95 percent; those of African descent, 65 percent; Hispanic descent, 50 percent; Caucasian descent, only 10 percent.[103]

Now that your mind is blown (at least most people's are the first time they read this), let's bring this back to the point at hand. We all have mental barriers when it comes to diet and exercise, and the dangerous thing is that we often can't recognize them. Most people think milk is quite literally *the* greatest thing to put in one's body for nourishment, when in reality, it might be one of the worst (longterm at least). This is an incredibly menacing situation because no one is out there pushing onion rings on you, telling you they're healthy, because we all know that is ludicrous. There are, however, tons of advertisers, congresspeople, and mothers telling you milk is a necessity for all stages of the human aging process, among other things. Frequent repetition keeps driving this idea home, and psychologically speaking, familiarity is not easily distinguished from truth.[104]

     This fact makes the overabundant and endless barrage of ads for health definitively ominous. With promising commercials on television, convincing articles in newspapers, and pumped up beach babes in magazines, the hopeful, albeit susceptible, audience of overweight and overly "health-conscious" Americans prove to be easily persuaded by assessing the relative importance of an issue by the ease with which they can retrieve it from memory. In other words, frequently mentioned topics in the media make us believe something is important, and in turn, the media sees what's on our mind, and reports more on the subject to attract more viewers.[105] Like we've seen with milk, you can't always accept the status quo. There is no conspiracy selling us on health products, it is sometimes just our lack of good information that allows us to be duped. In order for you to be a success, in athletics, business, or life, it is your responsibility to become educated and make your decisions based in fact rather than opinion or what is popular.

Delayed Gratification

     WHEN YOU DO EDUCATE YOURSELF, you no longer need to guess at what is right or wrong. And this is such an important part of being an athlete, because when you truly understand what's best, you will have the ability to *believe* in your training, and therefore be patient with your progress. Being a good athlete truly is a practice of patience, or better yet, "delayed gratification."

     Delayed gratification is what has made humans prosperous. Since the dawn of man, cognitive foresight has separated us from the beasts. For example, all animals knew how to find the nearest water source, but only the early ancestors of humans thought of storing the water for future use. Later, more developed humans discovered they could farm and raise animals instead of hunting and gathering — an even more impressive example of delayed gratification. This is an extremely intelligent way of life, and one we must continue to carry out in this advanced stage of humanity.

     When we are born into this world as kicking, screaming babies, we enter as "instant gratifiers." We all live our pre-adolescent lives one step at a time, not caring (or even understanding) how our decisions might affect us in the future. When we're hungry, we demand food. When we're tired, we sleep. When we need to poop, we just go right ahead and do it.

Although it may seem that delayed gratification and patience are mature virtues, psychologists have shown how this idea of self-control in early stages of life can dramatically affect people's futures. Around 1970, a now famous psychological experiment was taking place at Stanford under Walter Mischel's supervision. He sat four-year-old subjects in a room and put a marshmallow on the table in front of them. He then proceeded to tell them they could eat the marshmallow right away, but if they waited until he returned, he would give them *two* marshmallows. As you can imagine, as soon as the kids were left alone, the agony of that marshmallow staring them in the face pleading with them to eat it made them kick and squirm and frustratingly bang their heads on the table (there are a lot of great videos online if you need a quick pick-me-up).

While this experiment may come across as harmlessly fun, the findings may surprise you. To quote David Brooks in his tremendous book *The Social Animal:*

> The kids who could wait several minutes subsequently did much better in school and had fewer behavioral problems than the kids who could wait only a few minutes. They had better social skills in middle school. The kids who could wait a full fifteen minutes had, thirteen years later, SAT scores that were 210 points higher than the kids who could wait only thirty seconds. (The marshmallow test turned out to be a better predictor of SAT scores than the IQ tests given to four-year-olds.) Twenty years later, they had much higher college-completion rates. The kids who could not wait at all had much higher incarceration rates. They were much more likely to suffer from drug- and alcohol-addiction problems.[106]

Basically, the self-controllers were healthier, wealthier, and wiser. So while you may think you have time to figure out how to be patient and learn how to control your impulses, the sooner you can become a delayed gratifier, the more you have to gain in life. As teenagers age, the most successful ones undergo a marked transformation into maturity, often yielding more delayed gratification. Where this change occurs along one's life continuum varies greatly, and can tell you a lot about a person; but as of late, this adaptation has been primarily occurring *after* college.

Most college students, especially in regard to the ineffables (most notably nutrition, sleep, and booze), are instant gratifiers, being more impulsive than reflective. They often make decisions in these realms of their lives that satisfy them in that moment. They'll eat food that makes them happy, but is awful for them (sometimes just *hearing* about their meals is enough to give a person diabetes); they'll often postpone sleep to study, party, have sex or just hang out; and they'll go out carousing several nights a week, lacking the foresight of having to deal with the hangover and crippling shame of hook ups gone wrong in the morning. Honestly, how many mornings have come and gone where you said, or heard someone else say, even if it was half-jokingly, "I'm never drinking again." That sentence encapsulates the battle of delayed versus instant gratification better than anything else imaginable. On those mornings, these people wake up and realize, "Oh my God, drinking hard sucks for so many reasons and yet I still *know* it won't be long 'til I am lured do it again."

Interestingly enough, college athletes seem to have delayed gratification down when it comes to education and exercise. Whether they're working in the library or in the gym, it's because they know that in the future, they will be better for it; so while they are hurting during their lifts or study groups, they know they will be gratified by their improvement in the weeks and months to come. The funny thing is this delayed gratification, as Daniel Coyle, author of *The Talent Code*, argues, is slightly irrational. Forgoing comfort now in order to work toward something bigger and better later on is a gamble. As he writes, "We speak of motivation as if it's a rational assessment of cause and effect, but in fact it's closer to a bet, and a highly uncertain one at that."[107] The fact that *any* of us are capable of delayed gratification at all is actually pretty impressive.

When the alarm clock rings, the mature little person in your head is telling you its in your best interest to get up, but the impulsive, instant gratifier in you is telling you to get more sleep, to metaphorically eat that marshmallow. Every single day you will be confronted with a litany of decisions where you must promptly weigh the instant versus delayed gratification: burger or salad, video games or stretch, soda or water, booze or sleep ...

So, are you the type of person that will wait for that second marshmallow?

Bringing the Focus Inwards

BELIEVING THAT HEALTHY LIVING IS the missing part of your equation is not an easy sell. You're in college, and Pandora's box of unhealthiness opened there long ago. The amazing thing is that modern science and the status quo have done everything to keep nutrition and lifestyle out of the spotlight. Every day you'll see an ad for a new supplement, pill, surgery, etc. that steals your focus away from where it is supposed to be: your lifestyle! If your habits were healthy, you wouldn't need supplements, pills, surgeries, or anything else to make you feel better or to even perform better. Unfortunately, logic fails. Our minds are all in the wrong places; we tend to focus on elements L-M-N-O-P, before we ever get by A-B- and C.

Few college athletes refute how their lifestyles exist in conflict with their goals, or that often their behavior defies all logic and the principle of a rational self-interest. Therefore, urging you to change your behavior solely based on logic and self-interest will probably be futile. What we have to do instead is create virtuous people: the *types* of people that care enough about their futures to show a little interest in the present; the *kinds* of people that recognize how lucky they are to be athletic and vow to not let it be in vain; the *sort* of people that others respect. College sports are calling on people who have their morals, virtues, and goals clear; people who have enough humility and courage to examine the self; people who recognize there is more to know. As the philosopher Bertrand Russell once said, "In the modern world the stupid are cocksure while the intelligent are full of doubt."[108] Fact is, if you can change your mindset, your behaviors will naturally follow, and unrivaled athleticism will be a happy byproduct of that achievement.

A lot of people fear adopting a healthy lifestyle because, sadly, it is not a part of American culture. Nothing in Western society really teaches us to be healthy, so what we tend to do is look at those people who seem to be the healthiest and ask them what is best. This is why Americans spend more than 33 billion dollars on various weight loss schemes and diet products every year.[109] Because we never bring our focus in to ourselves, we rarely process how unhealthy we are living in the first place.

Louis Pasteur said on his deathbed the host is more important than the invader.[110] For us, this means focusing inward, ensuring you are doing everything *you* can to improve, is much more important than what anyone else is doing. You'll notice that successful teams and individual athletes focus solely on themselves, rarely concerned about anyone else's skills, training regiments, or win-loss records. This is an absolutely vital characteristic of success in general: conquering yourself before you conquer others.

Nothing is more bothersome than when someone wants to know what other teams are doing for workouts, or better yet, what the Marines do. You shouldn't care one iota about what other people are doing, especially not the military. Their training is about learning how to *survive*, whereas your training is supposed to be about *optimization*. You have the luxury of choosing proper recovery, nutrition, water intake, stress relief, etc. They do not.

Having your mind focusing inward is essential to becoming an omnitect, because if you aren't trusting the potency of your training and lifestyle, your body will fail to capitalize. When you stop looking outside for answers, you'll be able to come to terms with yourself, your training, and your choices in regard to health. In the end, success in athletics cannot be bought nor stolen; it is one of the last honest professions left. Accepting that will help you realize how important health is, and you'll *want* to lead a better life.

One thing seems to be clear: your mind is the first thing we need to change. Only if you truly understand how important healthy living is will you be ready and eager to create a new lifestyle. To borrow a phrase from the early American writer Roger Williams, "a little key may open a box, where lies a bunch of keys."[111] The first key to athletic success in college is confidence that healthy living is your ticket to paradise; once that box opens, there lies all the other keys to your future success. Having that first key, you'll be more willing to eat healthier, more committed to water intake, more inclined to skip a night of drinking, more prepared to take a day off, etc., but first, you've got to have faith.

Five Major Points

- Faith is not a reason; ensure your principles are based in scientific fact, not powerful emotion.
- We often start with a belief then find ways to justify it after the fact, not the other way around.
- There is no secret to health, no conspiracies.
- Do not accept what is popular. If you are interested in a topic, do the obligatory research to discover for yourself the truth.
- Delayed Gratification is one of the best predictors of future success, not only in athletics, but in regard to health, happiness, and business as well.

Part II

Nourishment

Chapter Four

Real Food

A Brief History

IN MODERN AMERICA, CONSUMERS HAVE a wide variety of choices when mealtime arrives, especially those living on a college campus. On top of all the options of cooking for oneself, which few in college seem interested in doing, there are usually several, if not dozens of items waiting for them in the dining halls and at their local take-out places. Although this is obviously great for those searching for variety, with more options come more temptations and a higher probability of poor food being eaten. What most of us forget is that the very essence of eating is that it is supposed to *nourish* us. This connection between food and body used to be a given, but now it seems people's main goal with food is just to have it gratify them. We've successfully associated "comfort food" and "pleasure eating" with unhealthy foods, but who says nutritious, nourishing options don't taste good too? There are a lot of negative stigmas associated to healthy foods, most of which having to deal with inconvenience, cost, and taste, that cast a cynical shadow over attempting to eat well. As you'll discover in this chapter, eating healthy is not an arduous nor an expensive undertaking, and the typically convenient and cheap, albeit destructive, "pleasure foods" offer our bodies little but chubby bellies.

Finding a meal is the easiest it has ever been in the history of mankind, perhaps of any species ever. For the millions of years our species have been developing, food was never guaranteed, and starvation, or the consumption of rotten, diseased food, was a pretty normal occurrence. Our brains evolved in an environment nearly void of food (at least compared to today's standards), and whenever a high-calorie, high-fat, high-sugar, or high-sodium source presented itself, our natural inclination was to gorge ourselves on it.[112] This ancient instinct still exists within us, which is precisely the reason we have such weaknesses toward those types of foods. As an example, dark chocolate contains phenethylamine, which is the same chemical released in the brain when one falls in love or becomes infatuated.[113]

We have always had our instincts to tell us what to eat and how to eat. Until very recently, there was no philosophy of food, and no one claimed to be a vegetarian or vegan or anything. People simply ate what was for dinner. And what was for dinner typically constituted foods with only one ingredient, as it was just that one ingredient they were interested in eating! In such a simpler time, there were no "bad foods," unless they were poisonous, as everything that was edible nearby was consumed. Inevitably, the seasonality of foods dictated all things. I remember my grandmother telling me her favorite Christmas ever was when she was living in Iowa in the 1920s and got an orange in her stocking. While buying oranges in December seems like the most commonplace thing in the world now, back then it was a pretty ridiculous thought.

For the vast majority of our species' development, that was the norm. In general, all people of the world had been living more or less the same life until about a century ago. Since the dawn of civilization until about the time of Abraham Lincoln, technology had barely advanced. To transport an item or a message or a sick person, all anyone had was the speed of a horse or the speed of the wind (to carry a boat). Therefore, they were basically helpless in matters of health, and lived in constant fear of disease or plague or pandemic. The only thing that mattered was one's health, which was made evident when one studies letters of generations past: they typically begin and end with assurances of the good health of the writer and inquire about the health of the recipients and their families.[114] When faster modes of transportation made food a little easier to procure, life instantly improved. With these changes in technology came changes in lifestyle and people wanted to eat differently

— namely, they demanded to eat more meat. Between 1950 and 2000, world population doubled, and meat consumption increased five fold.[115]

Enter fast food. When fast food hit the streets in the early 20th Century, a dramatic change in our food production began. By the 1950s and '60s, when fast food was becoming the giant it is today, our lives began to change with it. As Eric Schlosser writes in *Fast Food Nation*, "What we eat has changed more in the last 40 years than in the previous 40 thousand," and while finding a cheap and easy meal is a readily available and tempting option today, our health suffers because of it.[116]

Our farmers and government officials have sacrificed much of the quality of our food in the interest of creating more at a cheaper option. They wanted to feed a nation and rid the people of starvation — a noble cause — but while they succeeded in increasing the scale, diversity of plants, and then ultimately our diets, declined. So while these officials and scientists were genuinely sincere at the onset, their good intentions have led to the irrevocably poor nutritional habits of our fat country only to be exacerbated by big business lobbyists fighting to keep the cheap, dangerous food in our marketplace.

Michael Pollan, one of the most renowned writers on the subject of American food, writes in his book *In Defense of Food* that our food has changed fundamentally in the last half century. We've gone from whole foods to refined, complex to simple, quality to quantity, leaves to seeds, and perhaps most importantly, food culture to food science.[117]   Think about it: for the entirety of human's existence, all we ate were things that were *minutes* old, of course with a few exceptions. Storing food was a luxury we now take for granted, as today, people can live their whole lives without ever eating something truly fresh, often eating items a week or month old or *older*!

Now, before we move on, let's be clear on something: this book is not pro food conspiracy. Sure, some companies are a little mammonistic in their pursuit of money, but certainly not all big businesses are evil, nor is the government out to get us by any means. That being said, it is clear most businesses are run with the bottom line driving decisions and you'll find a lot of government policies to be outdated. One such outdated and problematic policy is that the Food and Drug Administration does not offer independent, third-party evaluations of food products in our stores. Instead, the manufacturers themselves fund studies that then go on to the regulatory agencies; in other words, the FDA evaluates studies that the industry submits.[118]   This even applies to drug testing, where 90 percent of clinical trials, and 70 percent of trials reported in major medical journals are ones that are conducted or commissioned by the pharmaceutical industry themselves.[119] Of course it goes without saying, but there are huge biases and conflicts of interest here that affect what gets researched, how it gets researched, why it's researched in the first place, if results are reported, and if they are, how the data is eventually interpreted.

In light of that, nutrition remains a hot topic in Washington, and the politics are still highly and feverishly debated. What we sometimes forget is that our lawmakers live in the same environment we do, and therefore are prone to the same cognitive biases as the rest of us average citizens. We say we're a terribly misinformed country when it comes to nutrition, and we mustn't forget our senators and congresspeople watch the same news and read the same stories we do — some end up even more misguided than us! Remember when First Lady Michelle Obama laudably attempted to reform school lunches for the better only to have Sarah Palin fly in with dozens and dozens of cookies to distribute to the students in question? And if it's not politicians screwing things up, the citizens will do it to themselves. When Governor Arnold Schwarzenegger made a junk food ban in California, parents openly waited for their kids at the school fence to smuggle them candy bars. And when Cookie Monster tried to teach kids about eating vegetables, people picketed.[120]

If we can't look to the government for help, perhaps the best place to look is science. As we move more and more into a science-dominated world, it's worth noting what's happening in the realm of food science. When studying nutrition, it becomes plain that gaining any perspective of food through scientific means is extremely challenging; the scientific model is just too hard to apply to nutrition. Consider how most scientific studies are conducted: there is an experiment designed to minimize the effects of variables on two would-be identical groups, if it were not for an "independent variable" that is assigned to one group (the experimental), and not to the other (the control). So to study the effects of apples on one's health, we'd have to have two groups of people eating *exactly* the same stuff at *precisely* the same time, then add apples to the experimental group's diet. How plausible does that sound? Could you possibly get two people, never mind a large group of people, to eat *exactly* the same foods for a lengthy period of time? Not bloody likely! The only way to do a study like that effectively would be to lock all the participants up and force feed them at given intervals ... not going to happen.

How researchers inevitably attempt to get around this impossible problem is by some sort of other means that adds incredible potential for error, and often leaves the study more apt to discover "general trends" than specific numbers and information. Some ways to study food include, but are not limited to, the following:

- Animal testing — of course studying a food or nutrient's effect on animals then extrapolating the information out to humans has countless flaws.

- In vitro — this often examines the interactions between macro- and micronutrients on cells inside a laboratory. How the whole food, not just the nutrient, will react to the whole body, not just the cell, is impossible to study in a lab.

- Case studies — by looking at one person's history and observing their future (especially if they've developed some sort of disease) researchers try to connect the dots. Clearly this method is anecdotal at best.

- Cohort studies — these typically involve large numbers of people that scientists follow over the course of a lengthy period of time. By studying those who develop diseases against those who don't, researchers look for different lifestyle behaviors and link them to diseases.

- Randomized controlled trials — these attempt to involve an experimental group with a control group, but because no one can be force fed, the studies must rely on food journals and food frequency questionnaires.

Looking at all these methods, it's apparent how rife with problems the research of nutrition is; however, this is not to knock nutritional scientists and their lifelong efforts in extremely serious laboratories around the world. Clearly, these scientists have learned a ton about the relationship on certain foods to our bodies. The scary part about this is that these nutritional scientists are the *really good guys* when it comes to nutrition. These are the people breaking their backs to get potentially life-or-death information out to the public in a timely manner so that we can eat healthfully and be merry. Yet, because the science is nearly impossible to study, at least efficiently, even these world class scientists make mistakes and often cannot offer us anything better than educated guesses. In the end, anyone who expresses anything with *absolute certainty* in regard to diet and health is basically wrong, because the evidence has never come from a perfectly controlled study.

The Source of Foods

OUR HEALTH HAS STEADILY DECLINED in recent decades.[121]   More than half of all American adults and about one quarter of all American children are now obese or overweight,[122] and about 50 percent of Americans take some form of prescription drug.[123]   Sixty-two percent of calories come from processed foods in the American diet, while 25 percent come from animal products, and only five percent from fruits and vegetables.[124] According to the U.S. Surgeon General, of the 2.2 million Americans who die each year, 1.8 million of them die from diet-related diseases.[125]

Partially, this is because our food system depends on consumers not knowing anything about from where our food originates.   What's more than a little scary is that about 80 percent of globally traded food is controlled by five multi-international companies.[126]   Facts like these fly under the radar as price and taste are really the only things we judge. No surprise then that fast food is so popular, and that about 90% of the money Americans spend on food is used to buy processed food.[127] Nature organically provides a surplus of flavors and textures, but for some reason, most Americans still prefer the pre-packaged meals and fast food. What would happen if people knew more about their food?

Let's look at hamburger meat, as an example, and start with its origin: gargantuan, often diseased Concentrated Animal Feeding Operations (CAFOs).   These places are so tight with security, trying to visit one is like asking to sleep in the Lincoln Bedroom — probably with good reason. No one wants to see cows standing in several feet of their own fecal matter while being forced to eat corn (regardless of the fact their organs have been evolving for millions of years to eat grass), and no one wants to remember all the e-coli breakouts over the past several years. Hell, even Oprah got sued (unsuccessfully) just for saying she was done eating hamburgers!

Few people know a steak from a grain-fed, feedlot steer has more than double the total fat of a similar cut from a grass-fed steer.[128] Or how about this: did you know that the European Union refuses to serve American beef within the borders of their countries? They deem our beef so unfit for human consumption, they choose to pay the beef and cattle industry $150 million each year instead of importing the meat and making profits from it.[129] Shocking right? The strange thing is that it is pretty common for people to travel abroad and be afraid of the food over there, while most of us remain completely oblivious to the state of our food industry here.   In America, most cows have been taken off their regular diet of grass and given corn instead, due to cost. The effects of this have caused several outbreaks of e-coli, yet researchers discovered that providing the cattle with a diet of grass for only five days could result in an 80 percent eradication of the bacterium. That, however, was not a realistic answer for ranch owners. So, in addition to continuing to feed the cattle corn, they added chemicals to the processed meat that would attempt to wipe out e-coli *post*-production.[130] In fact, instead of correcting the filthy factory farm and slaughterhouse conditions that give rise to contamination in the first place, their answer is irradiation — the deliberate exposure of food to nuclear radiation — in order to kill pathogens. That's right, in order to *not* change the status quo, these businesses expose our food to radiation equivalent to 2.5 million chest X-rays.[131]

Incredibly, when I tell my friends, family, and athletes about how my life has changed due to the research I have done and the books I have read in regard to nutrition, their typical response is, "What books are you reading? … So I know to avoid them." Why do we *want* to be in the dark about this stuff? Some people truly choose to *not* know what's in their food. We certainly are not noble in reason and clearly need some help making better decisions, yet even that often isn't enough. To wit, health officials in New York made the assumption that if people could only see the calorie information on the boards at fast food restaurants, they'd eat a little better. *Wrong!* Diners actually ordered *more* calories after the law went into effect — a deplorable finding that seems to make obvious our lack of desire to know more about what we're eating.[132]

Perhaps it's not surprising then, that I'm the only person I know who has been to a slaughterhouse. In 2004, I went to a rural slaughterhouse in the boonies of Wisconsin. My tour group got to pick a cow out at pasture, watch it get shot in the face by one of those devices from *No Country for Old Men,* then bare witness to a gigantic man wearing overalls without a shirt saw its head off and place it on a pole. You think that's traumatic? It only gets worse. Once the headless, twitching cow was placed on its back on a table, four men came rushing in wielding saws to hurriedly chop the cow's meatless lower legs off. No more than five seconds had transpired before one of the poor sawing bastards caught a rogue, twitching hoof to his face. Yes, a decapitated cow booted the ever-living Christ out of this employee's lower mandible who then ran off bloody-faced and screaming while his buddies chortled and our tour group swallowed our vomit. After that, the rest of the tour carried on "as normal," at least as far as I could tell, and we watched previously slaughtered cows turn into steaks, T-bones, rib-eyes, patties, and ground round.   At the end of the tour, we were offered to buy some meat-style memorabilia of the cow we had just witnessed reap headless vengeance on the employees. If you're wondering, I just couldn't quite get myself to buy any of it (although many others on my tour did ... it was rural Wisconsin after all).

My experience there, albeit a little scarring, was so eye-opening that to this day I recommend it to all meat eaters.   Surprisingly, the slaughterhouse I went to was one of the most humane in the country, as it is very small, their cows are out in pastures not penned into stalls eating corn, and the employees deal with one cow at a time, all of them having several duties to perform on each animal. In large CAFOs, on the other hand, hundreds or thousands of cows await their death via assembly line in tiny spaces being force-fed grain to fatten them up faster.   The employees are often hired to perform one quick slice as dead cow, or sometimes a *should be* dead cow, passes by their station. Oh, and they don't invite the public on tours in those places. In fact, there have been agriculture gag bills proposed that would criminalize publishing photos of an industrial farm.[133] This is why I value my experience so much: it's rare.   What could be more important than knowing how your food is prepared and from where it originates?   My single half-day adventure changed my life profoundly and I wouldn't give that up for anything.

Knowing how your food arrives on your plate is important when you realize the kind of stuff that's happening out there. A single fast food hamburger could contain meat from dozens, or even hundreds of different cattle.[134]   This is how food poisoning outbreaks have turned from a localized event of bad cole slaw at a tailgate to a nation-wide spread of infection and disease in every city around the country.[135] And if the fear of illness isn't enough, how about the joy of better health? Scientists have questioned recently if eating red meat, long associated with cardio-vascular disease, is more about the animal in question or the animal's diet. The way animals are raised affects their bodies, obviously, and if we are eating them, shouldn't they be eating better too? We flat out *refuse* to drink a sip of water that is tainted a little brown, but we happily eat the meat of animals who have been drinking water with their own fecal matter in it.[136] This stuff matters! Today, you'd have to eat twenty supermarket eggs to get the same amount of omega-3s (healthy fats) that can be found in a single egg from a free range chicken.[137] Why wouldn't someone want to know that?

The Crazy Stuff I've Witnessed about Nutrition

THE IRRATIONAL BEHAVIOR OF NOT wanting to know what's in our food is not unwarranted, nor should we blame anyone for their theories about food. We do, in fact, live in a place where people have forgotten how or what to eat, and persistently look to experts to tell them what to do. The problem is for as many intelligent and caring nutritionists there are in this country trying to spread the word about a relatively easy, whole-foods diet, there are probably 20 times as many businessmen and women working hard to sell you their products under the guise of health. That's why we have so many people in America that truly believe they have it all together and are eating a perfect diet, while the reality of the situation is a bit more grim. Even though I hear it almost every day, I am still surprised when athletes tell me what they believe is healthy. Below is a list, an all too true list, of the crazy stuff I've heard come out of people's mouths that clearly demonstrates how brainwashed we are.

True Life Story Number One

Me: "How much soda do you drink in a day?"

Person 1: "Like four or five bottles. *But it's fine, because it's diet.*"

Whether it's zero calories or 5,000, soda is still an amalgamated and bastardized beverage consisting mainly of high fructose corn syrup that offers you nothing in terms of health. Yet, people get brainwashed into comparing only the diet to the regular instead of the soda itself to another drink such as water. Yes, the diet may be "better" than the regular, but that's like saying getting kicked in the shin is *better* than being kicked in the groin. Let's compare getting kicked in the shin to not getting kicked at all, and compare the diet soda to water! When you do that, suddenly there is no argument left to discuss.

True Life Story Number Two

I'm out to breakfast with a bodybuilding friend of mine who whole-heartedly subscribes to eating a whole-foods diet. Given the fact that most breakfast meal choices are versions of white bread and fried potatoes (french toast, pancakes, waffles, hash browns, american fries, etc.), he decided to order a vegetable omelette with no sides. As this 220-pound specimen of a man with less than 10% body fat is ordering a six-egg omelette with a copious amount of vegetables, I notice it is drawing the attention of our neighbors. After the waitress left, the most incredible thing happened: the man from the couple sitting next to us — both of whom, it's worth noting, were far from "fit" — leans over to say, and I quote, *"You know eggs are bad for you, right?   You should get your cholesterol checked."*

The two of us sat there dumbfounded for several seconds before we could even mumble any sort of a reply. Here is an overweight citizen with a plate of french toast, hashbrowns, sausage links, and bacon all covered in either maple syrup, ketchup, butter, or all three lecturing another man who competes in events *based* on athletic physique about the dangers of eating eggs. Yes, eggs are high in dietary cholesterol, an obviously well-known fact in this country, yet eggs are still natural, have only one ingredient, and offer many positive nutritional benefits to one's body, which is a lot more than our friend could say about his breakfast. And while I am certainly a proponent of eating more plants than animals, given our scenario and the options provided to us, I thought my friend made a great decision. People get so locked in to these news clippings and "scientific breakthroughs" about the quantitative values of their food, they forget how much the quality may matter.   Their beliefs are so steadfast and unwavering, they possess the courage and audacity to call out strangers on their nutritional choices!

True Life Story Number Three

So I'm perusing a menu at some god-awful place looking for something healthy to eat with protein in it. I have a hard time trusting the source of animal products when I'm out to eat, so I rarely, if ever, order any type of meat, with the exception of an occasional order of fish. With that in mind, it's obvious I'm going to be looking over the salads, especially when at some po-dunk diner in the middle of some crotchety town. Finally I land on it: a spinach salad topped with garbanzo beans, goat cheese, artichokes, pine nuts, and quinoa. An uppity menu item for a hole-in-the-wall kind of place, no doubt!

Anyway, I order that — called something like the "Beans Make Me Go Nuts Salad" — and the waitress looks at me defiantly, pauses contemplatively, and finally says, "What, no protein?" I mean I know I didn't order a steak or piece of chicken, but my choice still had a decent amount of protein in it. Let's run it down:

- Spinach: probably 30 leaves = 9 grams
- Garbanzo beans: half cup = 6 grams
- Goat cheese: quarter cup = 5 grams
- Artichokes: half cup = 2 grams
- Pine nuts: quarter cup = 4 grams
- Quinoa: half cup cooked = 5 grams

Add that all up and you get 31 grams of protein in my meal. Given a piece of chicken is something like 25 grams, I'd say I did pretty damn good! You don't *need* meat to obtain an adequate amount of protein.

True Life Story Number Four

This extremely large friend of mine asked me once about eating healthier. I was actually pretty excited when he asked me about it, because he was not one to give a damn about anything he ate. When I tried telling him that eating healthy wasn't complicated, it just required perhaps more plants than animals in one's diet, he got an inquisitive look on his face, like he didn't know what a plant was. So I started listing some fruits and vegetables to eat, and I happened to list avocado and banana in succession, after which I am interrupted by, "Wai- wai- wai- wait. I was told not to eat bananas or avocados because of their fat content." OH COME ON MAN! Yes it's true that both bananas and avocados have some fat — avocado much more so than bananas — but the fat is a) good for you and b) negligible compared to other foods in the average diet. The fact that a 400-pound individual can fear certain pieces of *fruit* is only further evidence our country is sadly misguided in regard to health and nutrition.

Some Good Real Life Quotes:

- "Grilled cheese is vegetarian, you know, so I've really been pushing the health conscious thing."
- "Yeah, could I have the Philly Cheesesteak, but instead of American cheese, do you guys have Cheese Whiz here instead?"
- "Uh, coach, after workouts should I just be eating a steak?"
- "Ooo this smells like bananas. I bet there's a lot of potassium in it."
- "You haven't made the mac and cheese yet?! Well it's too late *now*, let's make something easier."
- And the coup de grâce: "Eggs is dairy."

True Life Story Number Five (Last One)

Perhaps what inspired me most to write this book was when I was talking to a group of parents at a team dinner party. I had recently made a bet that I could dunk a basketball within six months, and to do so, I figured I needed to lose about 30 pounds — to go from 215 to 185 (I would also need to go from 5'10" to like 6'3" but that wasn't as easy to accomplish). To kickstart my weight loss, I went on a week-long vegan kick where I only allowed myself to eat raw fruits and vegetables with one plant protein supplement a day — a diet on which some people subsist for decades. Upon bringing up this idea to the group of parents, and let me preface this by saying this is by far the most astonishing thing I've ever heard in my life, one woman gasped and said, "Isn't that dangerous?!"

Here we are in America, a place where it is medically conservative to cut people open or prescribe pills with death as a potential side effect, yet I had to sit there and justify eating a well-balanced, vegan diet. John Robbins wrote of a similar travesty when someone who was diagnosed as a diabetic, and told she had to lose a leg, instead adopted a plant-based diet and reversed all the negative side effects of her diabetes. When she asked her doctor why he didn't recommend the strict diet instead of amputation, he responded by saying while the diet has proven effective, it was not a practical solution ... but cutting off her leg was.[138] I mean, it is the general consensus that the human race has been eating a predominantly vegetarian diet for *millions of years* with the occasional meal of meat or fish.[139]   Even Einstein said that nothing will benefit human health or increase our chances for survival as much as a vegetarian diet![140] That, however, is not what we are made to believe, nor is it what is being perpetuated by the media and the popular dogma of our time.

That sentence, "Isn't that dangerous?", cuts right to the core of what we're up against. Provided people, even if it's just *one* person, still think eating vegetables is dangerous, we're in serious trouble. This means the multi-billion dollar industry of food processors, pharmaceutical companies, and powerful lobbyists are winning the battle versus common sense. The sheer magnitude of this industry is terrifying and its power unfathomable. To put it in perspective, today the U.S. government can demand the nationwide recall of defective softball bats, sneakers, stuffed animals, and foam rubber toys, but it cannot order a meatpacking company to remove contaminated, potentially lethal beef from fast food kitchens and supermarket shelves.[141]   Recently, California citizens unconscionably voted down a bill that would have forced genetically-modified foods to be labeled as such. Can any rational person think of any reason why this shouldn't be the case? So how could it not pass? Of course, the only reason the bill failed is because the food industry lobbied hard on television and muddied the waters with their deep wallets. Unfortunately, looking to the food industry, or even the government for answers about food is like looking to the porn industry for answers about love.

That said, it's not all bad news. Eating healthy is easier than you might presume. You still go to the dining hall or grocery store, and you still prepare foods to take with you as snacks, it's just that your choices are more diligent, less random. You can't just go to the grocery store on a whim anymore, you need to prepare a healthy list of foods you plan to buy. This way, you'll be less likely to arrive at checkout with a cart full of junk you had no intention of buying when you left the house. Be on notice that grocers are sometimes against you, as they know that those who buy healthy stuff first will feel so uplifted they'll buy junk food later on in their trip.[142] Why do you think all those candy bars are staring you in the face at the checkout?

Often our nutritional choices are guided more by emotion and environment than by ratiocination and future goals. One example is found in the candy bar checkout line, yet another can be found in restaurants where people tend to eat more depending on the quantity of their company. Those eating with one other person eat 35 percent more than they do at home, while people in a party of four eat 75 percent more, and those dining with seven or more eat 96 percent more![143]

Clearly, our environment plays a significant role in our hunger, and our preferences change with our surroundings. We must stay ever vigilant or it is our environment that will dictate what we eat, not our brains. If you were asked what you wanted for lunch a week from now, a burger or a salad, most would answer the healthiest option. Yet, a week later, if the burger and salad were offered again, regardless of what you said a week prior, most are statistically likely to go for the burger.[144] The specific food choices for this example don't matter, the important thing to note is that most people *plan* to be healthy in the *future,* often leaving excuses for themselves in the present. They'll justify their bad choices in the moment by saying, "I'll do better next week."

Well, realize that today is "next week."   You have several opportunities *today* to make the right choices to propel you deeper into a healthy environment. Just do not feel as though healthy foods are limiting or distasteful. If you interpret healthy eating as negative, it's going to be very hard to promote it, even if the end result (improved health) is highly desirable.   Let's make logical decisions, like eating well in order to improve athletically.   This is a simple concept, and the specific food choices in your diet should be equally simple. All you need to do is eat "real food," which probably needs a definition.

The Real Food Pyramid

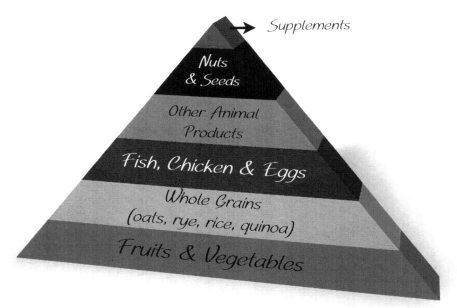

Defining Food

UNTIL A COUPLE CENTURIES AGO, our forefathers had spent millions of years hunting and gathering, then several thousand as agricultural farmers. As such, it's widely accepted that the human race has been eating a predominantly vegetarian diet for millions of years.[145] All their produce was naturally organic and resoundingly fresh making it more nutritious than most of our options today. Fruits and vegetables can only be as good as the soil in which they are grown,[146] and because modern farming relies so heavily on artificial fertilizers, our food pays the price, and ultimately, so do we. With all these developments of artificiality, the capacity of defining *real* food has become a challenge. While there are options out there that will make you feel full and may cost significantly less, some are not *real* food, they only *mimic* food. Attempting to navigate a grocery store or even a restaurant's menu in search of nutrient-rich foods can be discombobulating, which is why you should follow one elementary rule: eat food. Sounds simple right? Well, unfortunately, *real* food needs to be defined.

First and foremost, **food exists in nature**. Food grows on trees, comes out of the soil, or is attached to the bones of living creatures. Period. *Real* food cannot be forged or reinvented in the lab, and if a company sends out flyers stating, "We're reformulating our food to make it healthier" — which is a true advertisement from a fast food company — the "food" in question is clearly not real. Real foods are either plants or animals (and if we're getting technical, fungi too), and referring to your food as "plants" or "animals" keeps it as simple as possible.

Walking through the beautifully colorful whole foods section in the supermarket, one can easily forget from where that food originated. I once happened upon a woman in a grocery store making an energetic, vociferous scene in the produce section. As I tip-toed over to eavesdrop, I discovered the cause of her sickening display: there was dirt on the loose carrots.   Apparently this lady had forgotten from where carrots are harvested.

This little spectacle of lunacy provoked a question I am ashamed to answer, as I would guess you are too: when was the last time you had food that was only *minutes* old? How long has it been since you plucked an apple from the tree and ate it? Grabbed a tomato off the vine and cut it into a salad? Dug a carrot out of the dirt and bit into it moments later? I'll share with you my story of the last time I ate truly fresh food, if you'll allow the tangent:

Being a man with Greek heritage, I have been known to eat a fair share of "greek salads," which are nothing more than red onion, cucumber, tomato and feta cheese in a bowl — a harmonious bowl of deliciousness at that. The last time I traveled home to my parents' farm in rural Wisconsin, I went out to my mother's garden and found the three vegetables in their natural state, cut them from their source, chopped them up, added local feta cheese, and sat down with what had become my weekly, mundane salad. What I am about to say will sound contrived, but I don't mind telling you the truth: the first bite startled me. I had eaten that salad dozens, if not hundreds of times prior to that moment, but it had never tasted *nearly* that good.   I was instantly, and simultaneously, overjoyed to be eating something so delectable while also feeling a crushing embarrassment I had never eaten it so fresh before. How old are the vegetables I'm buying regularly at the store?

We think we have a plethora of fresh choices at the grocery store, but we are ultimately limited to what our culture suggests we eat, and what can be shipped to us. And when you really think about it, in the grand scheme of things, we can't eat that varied of a diet anyway. Most living biological matter on the Earth's land is in the form of wood and leaves, the lot of which humans are unable to digest.[147]   Of the plants we can eat, we actually consume very little of them. The Earth has countless varieties of fruits, vegetables, and meats to offer, yet we are restricted to "the norm:" apples, bananas, beef, and chicken.   In fact, only twelve species of plants — being wheat, corn, rice, barley, sorghum, soybean, potato, sweet potato, manioc, sugarcane, sugar beat, and banana — account for over 80 percent of the modern world's annual crop yields.[148]

This is why when you open the menu at a restaurant, you are very rarely surprised.   There are thousands of edible plants and meats out there, but if you read, "A Delectable, Rabbit Demi-Glace Seasoned and Served with the Finest Goatsbeard, Seaweed, and Cactus," you'd probably walk out of the restaurant. Our diets are a lot like our vocabularies, in the sense that even though there are a ton of options out there, we typically play it close to the vest, rarely venturing out of the boundaries of our comfort zone.   The most common one hundred words account for 60 percent of all conversations while the most common 4,000 words account for 98 percent of conversations.[149]   Whether it be in our word choice or food choice, we don't vary from the norm too often, and if you completed a simple week-long food journal (like the one found in Appendix E), you'd likely find similar data in regard to the variability of your food choices.

We might think we're relegated to apples, bananas, beef and chicken because those are the most nutritious for us, but it's more a product of tradition than anything else.   Why don't we eat quinoa as opposed to rice or pasta?   Quinoa is *way* better for us, just as easily purchased in the store, and takes about the same time and effort to cook as rice or pasta; the only difference is most of us weren't raised eating it, therefore we don't think of it.   Same deal with meats.   Why do we eat cows instead of rabbits or horses? Culture. As Jared Diamond writes in *Collapse,* the United States explicitly forbids the importation of kangaroo meat because, "we find the beasts cute, and a congressman's wife heard that kangaroos are endangered."[150]   While this is not suggesting we go out and picket congress to grill kangaroos, rabbits, and horses on the barbie, it is noteworthy to observe how policies can be created in this country, and how there's a lot more food out there than what we see in our stores.

Now, it doesn't matter where you live in the United States or if it's 50 below zero outside, you can still buy your apples, bananas, beef, and chicken. The seasonality of food has become a thing of the past, as one can get most fruits and vegetables most of the time. Because we aren't out there picking this food for ourselves, how do we know how old it is? If you buy a banana at the store, how long do you think it has been away from its leaf? In order to be ripe for you to eat, it must have been picked before its prime, boxed, shipped, stored in varying temperatures, handled by god knows how many people, laid on display for who knows how many days until you picked it up, then it sat on your shelf for another spell before you finally got around to eating it.

Due to these transportation challenges, the whole foods you buy in the store are below their true potential. Yet despite enduring all of that adversity and hardship, whole foods still outgun any manmade food ever created. No artificially produced food will ever be healthier or be able to offer more than real food, except for one key characteristic: shelf life. Because real food is not created by man, all real food goes bad in a finite period of time. **Food is only edible temporarily**, its ripeness coming and going with the seasons. While there have been substantial and impressive developments of processed food over the last several decades — one of which being a supplementation of shelf life — none of that applies to real food.

Another development in processed foods that doesn't apply to real food is their ability to be manipulated by science. Laboratories can shape foods to have all the right stats on paper — e.g. calories, protein, vitamins — yet, scientists still can't explain how whole foods prove to be more nutritious. Obviously, plants are more than they seem; they are not just the sum of their nutrient parts. They have synergistic properties that science can't measure ... But does it matter if plants' benefits are inexplicable? We don't need to understand why naturally-occurring food is better for us in order to prosper from it, much like we don't need to understand the combustible engine in order to start our cars.

The only question that remains, then, is if plants and animals are so superior to processed foods, why aren't we purchasing and consuming them more often? Maybe it has to do with the negative stigma of healthy foods being perceived as more expensive, which is only sometimes the case. This is a good segue to point number three: **food is worth money.** People will say they don't have the funds to purchase quality foods, and some certainly don't, but most are simply allocating their money elsewhere. Food should easily account for 15 to 20 percent of your expenses (I personally spend 30%), as it is greatly responsible for your well-being, your happiness, your alertness, your longevity, your athletic performance and your brain's functions. In fact, even though our brains account for only two percent of our bodyweight, they require 20 percent of our energy.[151] Therefore recently, and for good reason, more people have been choosing the better food options, hoping to avoid all the chemicals that rob our nutrition of its essential vitamins and minerals. Unfortunately, as you know, this can be the pricier option.

Realize, though, that only in the last century has our food become so readily-available and cheap. For the vast majority of humanity's (and currency's) existence, people have devoted most of their time in an effort to feed themselves. With the use of chemicals, a nation-wide endeavor to cease starvation, and the explosion of fast food in the past hundred years, our food has become *much* cheaper to the benefit of some. Those at the bottom of the health structure, i.e. those who were starving, benefitted greatly, but those at the top of it, athletes, have suffered.

People born in the last quarter century believe food is only worth five to ten percent of their income, so they constantly search, and sure enough find, those nutrient-deficient options that only cost them a few bucks. Americans spend less than ten percent of their disposable income on food, which not only marks the lowest percentage in human history, but also bodes poorly for the younger populace.[152] This dangerous precedent is one of the major reasons the current generation might not outlive the last.

Nutrient-rich foods — read: fruits and vegetables — are worth your money, especially if you are trying to get the most out of your body. No other variable can add to- or subtract from your potential, whether it be psychologically or physically, quite like food. More of an emphasis needs to be placed on this variable, especially when it comes to your wallet. At the end of Chapter Six, you'll find a section about how to support a healthy diet on a college budget, and at the end of this book there is a short cookbook dedicated to college athletes. Hopefully these mechanisms can inspire you to go to the grocery store and cook for yourself!

Regardless of what you are willing to spend, the most important thing is that you eat more whole foods. And when you're shopping, or perusing the buffet line, know that food should be eaten organic and raw more often. First, let's just use common sense to tackle the debate of organic vs. conventional farming. While there are plenty of books that state organic foods are more nutrient-dense than their chemically-grown twins, let's not even use that as a reason to shop organic. The movement back to organic foods is helping to minimize the damage of chemical pollution.[153] Also, a plant that is treated with pesticides loses its natural abilities to stave off insects, ipso facto losing some of its essential qualities that make it such a powerful food choice to begin with.

The organic revolution started as an incredible way to reclaim our vegetables and fruit by giving the power back to the local farmers. Yet now the movement has spread back into businesses that are using that word "organic" to delude us. As the American author Eric Hoffer once said, "Every great cause begins as a movement, becomes a business, and turns into a racket,"[154] and this is what is happening with organic foods. What used to simply be a better way to buy our plants has now become a way for companies to better market their frozen pizzas and candy bars. Just because these obviously nutrient-poor foods are labeled as "organic" does not mean they are not still frozen pizzas and candy bars!

While the organic movement is being swallowed up by the industry, the raw movement is still in its infancy. Although the advent of cooking saved our species and made us the world's greatest success, the cooking process tends to destroy enzymes, and the more refined, processed or cooked a fruit or vegetable is, the less nutrition it provides.[155] Thus, do your best to eat a robust salad every day, and snack on raw fruits between meals, as this is great for digestion.[156]

As a college student, maybe the organic request is a little quixotic, but one doesn't need to be a hemp-wearing hippie to benefit from the movement. In other words, not everything you buy and eat has to be organic or raw in order for you to occasionally prosper from consuming something that is. Eating organic and raw *more often* will be better for you and will add to your athletic prowess, which brings us to the final definition of food: **food is something that will supplement your success.** While processed foods can deliver some nourishment to an athletic body, every time you eat a combination of fresh, living foods — plants and animals — you are giving yourself a potent mixture of essential vitamins, minerals, antioxidants, phytochemicals, and whatever else modern science hasn't discovered yet. Everything is working synergistically in the plant, and it will continue to work synergistically in your body to promote your health.

If what you are consuming does not fall into these categories — exists in nature, has a short shelf life, is worth money, and will supplement your success — then you are not eating real food. There are many products out there that mimic food, but are in fact what Michael Pollan would refer to as edible food-like substances. They're food impostors. A few decades ago, these food-like creations that were made in labs had to be labeled "imitation,"[157] but now they are allowed to be on the shelf, degrading-label-free. Time and again, the argument is made that some of these processed foods are healthier because they contain the appropriate quantities of the "right" nutrients and lack all of the "wrong" ones. This is just nonsense, because a) the product is not a real food, and b) the "right" and "wrong" nutrients change as often as the tides, and although some vitamins and minerals are in the healthy spotlight now, that's likely to change in the future.

Common Sense

NO INTELLIGENT PERSON COULD EVER prescribe *what* to eat, because the possibilities are literally endless. Dictating one's food choices requires specificity, which, by its very nature, must be discriminative and exclusionary. A lot of athletes are actually looking for someone to take a clear stand against some foods while championing others, but there are far too many options available to be so particular. President Truman once asked for a "one-armed economist,"[158] as he was sick of people telling him one thing then immediately backtracking by saying, "On the other hand..." But the entire field of nutrition is one giant "on the other hand." For every terrible thing to eat out there, there are a few advantages (although sometimes solely psychological) to eating them.

Cake is bad for you, *on the other hand*, sometimes it's important to allow yourself to celebrate an occasion with food you enjoy! Every now and again, we need to treat ourselves to our guilty pleasures, allowing those foods to comfort us when we're stressed, or when we're celebrating. When we do indulge, it's vital to remember two things: 1) we can't make this an everyday occurrence, and 2) we need to *enjoy* the guilty pleasure while it's happening, not feel guilty about it the entire time. There is a lot of truth to the idea that stressing about what you're eating is more destructive than the bad food in itself. Michael Pollan calls this fear of eating poorly "orthorexia nervosa," which sheds light on the issue well.[159] If you're going to eat a sundae because you're stressed, well then enjoy it dammit!

This orthorexia nervosa makes some people scared to eat unhealthy food, and they will search high and low for research telling them which foods are good or bad. What we ate used to depend on who our mother was, but now all it takes is one crackpot scientist, one well written article, to set off a dangerous nutritional swing in this country.

Every few months, new research tells us that some nutrient is toxic, which leads people to run from it like it's the Bubonic Plague. We allow the nutrient to be vilified, scorn anyone associated with it, then unnecessarily avoid all sorts of foods. But we don't need science to tell us what's healthy and what's not. Even using nothing more than intuition is often enough to decide if a certain food is good for you.

Intuition can be powerful when it comes to making quick decisions. Alex Todorov and others at Princeton conducted a study about intuition where they showed their research subjects black-and-white photographs of the faces of rival political candidates, that they did not know, and were asked which of the candidates looked more competent. Amazingly, the candidates that were perceived as competent, even after only a second's glance, won 72 percent of the actual Senate races in which they were involved.[160] This is because intuition falls under our lightning-fast emotional system, which operates automatically and with little or no effort. In a heartbeat, it can deliver impressions that are surprisingly accurate.[161]

With this in mind, imagine you were shown flash cards of different foods. Do you think you would be able to identify them as healthy or not? Although we can't play with real flash cards, we can try it right here in prose form. You'll see a food, and as quickly as you can, say if it's healthy or not. Ready?!

Pizza.
Carrots.
Salmon.
Ice Cream.
Potato Chips.
Oatmeal.
Bacon.
Eggplants.
Brown Rice.

Okay, so how'd you do? Easy right? We all recognize those foods as healthy or unhealthy simply using intuition. Nobel laureate Herbert Simon wrote, "Intuition is nothing more and nothing less than recognition,"[162] which is why you did so well on the task above, you quickly recognized the foods.

This task could be done with any food in the world, and you'd have little problem quickly intuiting if it were good or bad for you. If, however, you stopped to envisage the pros and cons of each food, you would destroy your ability to use your lightning-fast insight. Similarly, we could ask scientists to conduct rigorous and thorough inspections of every aspect of a food, and these analyses would only find something we can already pick up instinctively. We Americans typically do a very good job seeking out as much extra information as we can about a subject, but more often than not — especially in the realm of diet and exercise — that extra information is corrupting and destructive. All it does is cloud the issue. Malcolm Gladwell wrote a book titled *Blink* that focuses precisely on this phenomenon. As he writes:

> [People] gather and consider far more information than is truly necessary because it makes them feel more confident ... the irony, though, is that that very desire for confidence is precisely what ends up undermining the accuracy of their decision. They feed the extra information into the already overcrowded equation they are building in their heads, and they get even more muddled.[163]

When it comes to thinking about what to eat, we don't need to make the decision harder than it is. We have virtually unlimited quantities of data available to us at all times, and we're always afraid of not knowing enough. But there is such a thing as having too much information. When we're constantly trying to find out if apples are still healthy for us, or what the latest news is on wheat, we're just going to be inundated with information. This is why Gladwell writes that the key to making good decisions is not always raw knowledge, it's *under-standing*.[164] We have all the knowledge we need to make smart nutritional choices, all we need to do now is understand that.

The fact that nearly every American can pinpoint if the aforementioned foods are good or bad does little to explain why we are the fattest nation in the history of the world[165] (although Mexico may have recently stolen that title). A quote from President Obama's second inaugural address perfectly applies here: "While these truths may be self-evident, they've never been self-executing." Although he was talking about our fundamental rights at the time, the words ring true in many facets of the American life, especially nutrition. The knowledge of fruits and vegetables being healthy is self-evident, but that doesn't mean anyone's going to do anything about it.

What this information shows us is that this country has an issue with velleity, volition in its weakest form. We all have a wish to be healthy, but often accompany that wish with little action. We want nice bodies, and certainly college athletes want to be really good at their sports, but we are not limited to perfectly reasoned solutions to problems. Both of these endeavors require us to train hard and to eat smart, but the vast majority of people in this country do not accomplish these goals. Most of the time we act without knowing full-well why we acted in the first place; it could be argued we're just being lazy most of the time. This might be why the single best predictor of whether or not a person is an organ donor is the designation of the default option that will be enacted without having to check a box.[166]   We better start examining our lives and better understanding our decisions; even Socrates reasoned that the unexamined life is not worth living.[167]   A lot of us certainly *think* we know what we're eating and how often we drink alcohol and how healthy we are, but few actually do. Until you truly stop to look, even write down what you're eating, how could you ever really know?

All we're talking about here is simple awareness. Pay attention to what you're eating, and **read nutritional labels.**   Find the ones on the back with all the information about the quantitative and qualitative elements of the food, *not* the ones on the front where it says in big bold letters "90% FAT FREE!"   Food companies are so creative with the way they frame their products, they can make anything look good on the *front* of the label. Truthfully, nearly every conceivable piece of information on a product, from the label to the packaging material itself, is tested. Marketing experts have found adding the tiniest signs of nature (e.g. a leaf or a sprig of parsley) or seemingly the simplest descriptive words (e.g. "fresh" or "wholesome") can seriously improve people's enjoyment of the food.[168]   Researchers are out there running tests like this in order to manipulate your impression of their product and dupe you into buying it. For reasons like this, you must try to remain objective to the package itself and flip it over to see the government-regulated ingredients list.

For example, if you are buying peanut butter, the ingredients should be peanuts. Period. Not hydrogenated oils, sugar, wheat germ, or any other additive; peanut butter should be made *solely* from peanuts (and organic peanuts at that!). Don't be concerned about what the label says on the front, the back, the top or the sides; none of that is regulated. Ingredients cannot lie, so check the label. Peanut butter's ingredients should read, "peanuts."   The same can be said for almost any other packaged food. You think that granola bar is healthy?   Check the ingredients and you'll typically find it more closely resembles a candy bar than oatmeal.

By these standards, there are several food-like creatures out there that should probably be avoided, because no matter what, they'll never even be close to real food.   Some examples include most (if not all) breakfast cereals, packaged desserts and candy (otherwise known as "junk food"), white bread, white pasta, fruit and cereal bars, frozen dinners and pizza, and of course, fast food. Comedian Jim Gaffigan would describe these foods as, "Momentary pleasures followed by incredible guilt eventually leading to cancer."

Yet these "momentary pleasures" are sometimes the staple foods coaches are feeding their athletes. If a team has a long road trip ahead of them, chances are they'll be stopping for fast food along the way, and if people get hungry between here and there, undoubtedly there will be some amalgamated granola and protein bars for their convenience. Convenience, by the way, is the only reason teams are eating this way, not because the coaching staff prefers it that way. If dedicated athletes were to broach the subject with their coaching staff and explain to them they would compete better with fresher and more natural snacks (fruit and vegetables, maybe even with the aforementioned peanut butter), could coaches really say no? That's a perfectly reasonable request, and with a little bit of campaigning, all rational coaches will make the necessary changes.

Although if they don't, that only serves as one final reminder: the best way to ensure you are eating the right stuff is to buy it and cook it yourself. Everyone believes they rarely have the time, energy, or supplies to prepare their own food. From the college student who never cooks to the parent that cooks every night, the common complaint is there is no time. But finding some time and preparing food yourself opens up many doors to which most college athletes thought they'd never have a key. Cooking for yourself allows you to buy organic, use wheat pasta and bread, control fat content of your meats, manage the use of butter and oils, and comprise a meal based entirely on what you want to eat, not just what is available that day in the dining halls. As a college student, it's understood that having a kitchen, money, and time to cook is atypical. However, if students wanted to make the effort to cook, even just once a week, they could find the resources. One way to start would be to flip through the College Athlete Cookbook found in Appendix D of this book.

Taking these steps toward your betterment *should* be easy ones, but for some reason, they are not. We, as Americans, have a values inversion. We'll quickly spend our money on video games, alcohol, and hot gadgets instead of the most scientifically proven superfoods. Michael

Pollan discovered that Americans spend only a fraction of their disposable income on food — about a tenth, down from a fifth in the 1950s. This suggests that Americans today spend less on food than any other people in the history of the world.[169] In fact, a generation ago, three quarters of the money used to buy food in the United States was spent to prepare meals at home. Today, about *half* the money we use to buy food is spent in restaurants, mainly fast food ones at that.[170] But quality food is worth the money, and cooking for yourself is worth the time.

Throughout your life, you will have an ongoing list of things you want to do, and those that you have to do. In order to go on vacation, you need to work first. In order to eat on clean plates, you need to do the dishes first. In order to excel at a sport, you need to fuel your body with healthy, sustaining nourishment first. Not willing to do so simply insinuates laziness. Numerous studies have demonstrated that our brains can assess the likelihood that a problem can be solved, provided it does not require an insight, with remarkable accuracy.[171] In other words, we can glance at a question and know instantaneously if the answer is within reach if only we put in the work. So, consider this question: can you eat healthier? Immediately, you have an answer to that question, and the rest of the equation is simply based on work ethic.

Eating healthy is not a painstaking challenge, nor does it require a whole lot of cognitive effort. Just eat plants and animals, and keep things varied. There is no better way to assure that you are getting all of your needed vitamins, minerals, micronutrients and macronutrients than from having a well-rounded, wide-ranging diet; when it comes to food, your body loves a variety.[172] This strategy requires a little time, money, and effort, but most of all, it demands planning. Making sure you have a heterogeneous array of meals over the course of the week forces you to think ahead and map out what and when you plan to eat. You can work your ass off in the gym all you want, but if you're not giving your body the appropriate nutrients to recovery properly, you have no shot at becoming successful.

That should be a fairly trite, common sense thing to tell people, but somehow it is not. We tend to think of advances in sport as a new drug, a powerful supplementation program, a persuasive coach, or something high tech and expensive. Believe it or not, however, it is the simple choices you make every hour — what to eat, what to drink, how to respond to stress — that make the powerful differences in your athletic body. This isn't a new, or even riveting idea, yet for some reason, all we seem to care about is the gym. Remember, there are 168 hours in the week, and eating real food will always be a more potent variable than exercise.

This idea is so simple, it's criminal; it's so comprehensive, yet so straightforward, it's mind-boggling more student-athletes haven't taken it seriously. Eat more of the good stuff, and eventually it's going to crowd out all the bad stuff. Just be healthy, and you'll find out for yourself; real food is the answer.

Five Major Points

- Trust your instincts when choosing foods to eat.
- Studying nutrition is very difficult, and most research is conducted by the food industry, so beware what you read.
- Learn more about the source of your foods by reading ingredients and shopping local.
- Focus more on the quality of your food than the quantities of nutrients within it. Cooking for yourself allows you to do this more regularly.
- "Real food" exists in nature, has a short shelf life, is worth money, and should be a conscious vote toward your improvement.

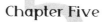

Chapter Five

Water's Significance

The Sheer Magnitude of It

SCIENTISTS NEARLY UNANIMOUSLY AGREE THAT life does not exist without water — here or anywhere else in the known universe. Any debate about life on neighboring planets will undoubtedly be cosmologists discussing the possibility of water on those distant lands. For as long as plants and animals have existed on this planet, they have been on a constant, endless, and painstaking odyssey in the pursuit of water. Read any book about the history of humans, or animals in general, and it will inevitably explore the ebbs and flows of nature producing droughts, yielding bad crop years, mass starvations, and extinctions, and floods that drown humans and animals, forcing the mass exodus of the remaining survivors. As 21st Century Americans, few of us experience those problems anymore. When nature throws a drought our way, most of us just turn on the faucet. No big deal.

Of course, not everyone lives like this and there are thousands of Americans that continue to make their living based highly on rainfall. But, for better or worse, most people in this country are disconnected from rural farmlands and those directly affected by droughts. Few of us ever need to consider a year, month, day, or even minute without easy access to water, the way our ancestors did. For now, the battles of obtaining potable water are behind us, and clean drinking water has become so abundant it is often overlooked. Many Americans take it so much for granted, they stop drinking it altogether!

Ask any scientist, however, and they'll tell you nothing lives without it, especially us. Dr. Fereydoon Batmanghelidj, or "Dr. B," recently discovered and wrote in his eye-opening book *Water: for Health, for Healing, for Life* that "chronic unintentional dehydration in the human body can manifest itself in as many ways as ... medicine has invented diseases."[173] When people feel down, slow, or off, doctors and trainers want to diagnose them with some sort of ailment and offer expensive treatments to cure. As Dr. B contends, often these people may simply be chronically dehydrated with a cure that is not only abundant, but cost-free: water. After all, the human body is about 75 percent water and 25 percent solid; in fact, the ideal pH of blood is 7.4, while water is a nearby 7.0![174]   Our society has programmed us to be reactive to our body's problems as opposed to proactive and preventative. We are pretty much only interested in body maintenance when we begin to suffer from a health problem. Unfortunately, you may not be able to appreciate your body's need for water until after you are suffering from a state of chronic dehydration that has lead to structural changes in your genetic blueprint.

To ensure this does not happen, you need to drink *water*, not to be confused with "fluids." Although composed mainly of water, coffee, alcohol, and manufactured beverages can rid the body of the water in which they are dissolved.[175] People like to believe that tea, coffee, energy drinks and juice will hydrate them well, but in fact these drinks are more apt to disrupt blood sugar balances than promote hydration.[176] To boot, these drinks provide calories with few nutrients — a definitive problem for our fat country. In fact, Americans now get 25 percent of their daily calories from liquids.[177]

One liquid that can be caloric, depending on how you drink it, is coffee. While the beverage itself only has one or two calories, coffee additives like half-and-half, sugar, whip cream, "mocha," caffe lattes, and cappuccinos can carry with them hundreds of calories; yet, almost everyone thinks they need this drink. Most interestingly, feeling tired without a plausible reason is a sign of dehydration, yet when most people feel groggy, what is it they typically want to drink?[178] Coffee. Caffeine is a natural diuretic, which means after the absorption of that coffee, consumers will be even more dehydrated than before. Unluckily for them, the caffeine will temporarily mask their bodies' indication of dehydration, further exacerbating their problem. Often times, drinking coffee makes people feel better simply because it relieves their symptoms of coffee withdrawal![179]   Of course coffee can serve a purpose, and you will probably continue to drink it when needed (after all, you are in college), but do yourself a favor: **drink two glasses of water before you reach for the coffee pot**.   Find out if you're simply dehydrated first, as even the food that is supposed to be a good source of energy has no real value until it is hydrolyzed by water, becoming energized in the process.[180]

Dr. Colgan of the Colgan Institute, an internationally renowned research center in California specializing in sports nutrition, marks the importance of water by stating, "the quality of your tissues, their performance, and their resistance to injury, is absolutely dependent on the quality and quantity of the water you drink."[181]   We'll get to the specific quantity requirements later, but what's important to note now is that the human body contains no mechanism to store water, therefore you must drink regularly throughout the day, every day.[182] This fact becomes important to you very quickly when you learn that **a muscle dehydrated by only three percent could cause about a ten percent loss of strength, and an eight percent loss of speed**.[183]   So here's the point: if you're not consistently getting enough water — on a daily and regular basis — you could be perpetually training and competing below your full potential.

Quick Fixes

WE EASILY SINK INTO THE mindset that if our knees hurt, we need surgery; if we feel tired, we need a coffee; if we feel pain, we need a painkiller.   People should realize that nothing the body tells them is without cause. Every signal of thirst or soreness or tiredness or pain has an immediate and direct connection to an imbalance in your current lifestyle.   Here is the all-important question: do you think if you were sleeping enough, providing your body with the nutrients it required, and keeping your stress levels low, you would ever *need* a coffee? Don't think so. Obviously, you will feel more alert after having a cup (even while your body's chemistry scrambles to produce hormones to restabilize your soaring blood sugar levels),[184] and caffeine certainly serves a purpose; however, it *should* be unnecessary.   We need to learn to listen to our bodies' warnings and threats, and provide them with the most natural healers we can before turning to drugs and medications.

In addition to the tired/caffeine relationship, another daily problem that could be ameliorated with water is in relation to pain. When most people feel chronic pain, they take a pain killer. As a strength coach, I am against the idea of regular pain killer usage, unless it's under grave situations, because when we're aching it's clear our bodies are trying to tell us something. Taking a pill to solve the problem just voids us of the responsibility of solving the real issue. And while twenty acetaminophen can kill you, one is extra work on the liver.[185] Aspirin can also thin the stomach lining, while healthy things like bananas thicken it.[186] So before you just pop a pain killer, investigate why you feel what you feel. Is there a natural way to remedy it? One way to try is to drink a healthy dose of water and see if perhaps you are simply dehydrated.

For our intents and purposes, in relation to the college athlete, the daily pains athletes encounter could almost always be solved with a little time to recover, better food, and likely a little extra water. Most athletic trainers would be wise to heed Voltaire's advice when he said the art of medicine consists of amusing the patient while nature cures the problem. Athletes need to conceptualize the reasoning behind their complications, not to just walk into an athletic trainer's office and say, "Fix me."

Survival vs. Optimization

WHEN INFORMATION LIKE THIS IS shared, the resistance one typically gets back is related to how far people have come without this knowledge, so why change now? Athletes have been successful drinking coffee and popping pain killers, and after all, water comes from many sources, so drinking it plain seems a bit redundant. This is partly true, actually. Almost everything you drink is water based, and most of the foods you eat, save some dense nuts, are composed of high percentages of water. Iceberg lettuce, for example, is almost solely water.[187]

So in short, yes, it is *probable* one could survive in today's America by consuming very little or no plain water. One could be sure many people do this on a regular, daily basis. Due to the water in most beverages and within most food, you could consume enough of it to continue breathing. Yes, one could possibly survive, it is conceivable. But of course, you're not trying to just *survive*, you're attempting to peak your body to its highest level of performance possible. While you can *get by* with sports drinks, energy drinks, juice and milk, your body does not require lemon-lime sugar water to survive, it *needs* water.

For starters, this miraculous substance acts as a lubricant and cushion around your joints.[188]   Leave your body in a perpetual state of dehydration, and that cushion will become less and less malleable. Many athletes encounter a confrontation with knee or shoulder pain eventually, and while the reason behind the discomfort could come from countless sources, one of the main contributors could be a lack of water in the joint. If you are experiencing joint pain, get started on a water campaign as soon as possible, but recognize this isn't something that you can remedy overnight. One must create a lasting environment of adequate amounts of water in order for the body to thrive off of its healing qualities.

You have probably heard that eight glasses of water a day is the typical allotment the body needs. Well, that's because the normal human body, in its constant metabolism and recycling processes, becomes short of about six to ten glasses of water each day, meaning that in order to reach a healthy homeostasis, six to ten glasses need to be consumed one way or another.[189] Now, if this is the case for the average human, imagine how much more *you* need! On the regular, you are extending your body to its limits, often sweating through your clothes. So, not only do you have to make that minimum mark of six glasses, you have to ensure that before, during, and after workouts, you are replacing what you lose to ensure you are at an optimal level.

During any sort of athletic activity, thirst signals come too late for people to feel or even comprehend. As such, athletes must be drinking water *during* training even if they don't feel thirst.[190] The message from research is pretty clear: **athletes should drink all the cold water they can during any extended event**.[191] They are losing more water than they could possibly drink during the bout, and are overheating to boot; ample amounts of cold water will help to deflate the negative effects of both ailments.

Some readers may see this and think back on all of the games they've played without drinking a lot of water. Undoubtedly, there are people that rarely drink water during training or games and still perform rather well. That may very well be true, but remember, even if you don't feel thirst, your body is still craving it. Every drip of sweat that comes off your body is another drip farther away from total hydration; ergo, every sip of water you can possibly consume in training or in competition should be taken.

By now, hopefully you're coming around to the significance of water, but perhaps you still have some curiosities about sports drinks such as Gatorade or Vitamin Water. Maybe after being bombarded with advertisements for the potency of Gatorade's effectiveness or the health-bestowing qualities of Vitamin Water, you are inclined to believe these products can offer you at least something in the way of health. Given the size of those advertising campaigns, you could be forgiven for that thought. What you probably haven't heard about is a lawsuit that took place in 2009 when the Center for Science in the Public Interest sued Coca-Cola for making "deceptive and unsubstantiated" health claims about Vitamin Water. How Coke's lawyers responded is truly remarkable. Their retort was that "no consumer could reasonably be misled into thinking vitaminwater [sic] was a healthy beverage."[192]   In essence, they were arguing no idiot could actually *believe* the things they were saying; according to Coke, that'd be unreasonable.

This case shined the light on beverages specially marketed to athletes, and although the suit did not get a lot of press time, the low impact it did have forced people to check the labels of their favorite sporty drinks. What they discovered — and what you surely will too once you look — is that these drinks are all just varieties of colored, sugary water. Call them what you want, nearly all of these beverages have somewhere between 20 and 40 grams of sugar, and the only natural substances listed in the ingredients are water, sugar, and salt.

If you want to save money, and more importantly be healthier, just skip the middle man and drink water! The only question that remains is how much an athlete should drink. We touched on the minimum (8+ glasses), so let's take a moment to study the maximum allowable intake. Yes, it's possible to overdose on water, but unless you are running a marathon or enduring some other ultra-long event, water intoxication, called hyponatremia, is extremely uncommon. Hyponatremia is basically a salt imbalance where a person either consumes far too much water or loses far too much salt to be healthy. For starters, most sports don't endure long enough for people to lose an amount of salt, through sweat, that would need to be replaced immediately. With shorter spurts of action, and the opportunity for brief rests, the vast majority of sports have no platform for an athlete to become hyponatremic. Endurance athletes, on the other hand, need to be rather concerned about the electrolytes they're losing — namely potassium, calcium, and sodium.[193] This is why sports drinks have salt in the ingredients and why marathon runners would require more than water to hydrate. Second, in regard to consuming too much water, the kidneys of a healthy adult can process more water than you are likely to drink in a day, given it is spaced out at somewhat of a regular interval. Therefore, provided you're not doing something extreme like marathon racing or chugging gallon after gallon of water, it will be very hard to drink too much.

The appropriate intake, as we discussed earlier, would be to consume the anecdotal eight glasses over the course of your day, and to supplement that depending on how hard you're working out. A great way to start the day would be to **chug two glasses right away in the morning**. We lose about that much water in our sleep through respiration and light perspiration over the course of the night, so to rectify our early onset of dehydration, two glasses must be consumed first thing in the morning.[194] This early act of hydration often nullifies one's interest in coffee! So not only do you start your day off on the right foot, but you also avoid unnecessary drugs.

The other noteworthy time to drink water is during workouts, especially if you are enduring through a long game or race. Water drank before exercise will help to have it available to sweat, during exercise will keep you as close to optimally hydrated as possible (thereby maintaining your strength and speed), and taken after exercise will aid in finally restoring all that you lost during your workout. Always remember that it is nearly impossible to keep up with how much water you are losing in a long athletic endeavor, so every ounce of water you can comfortably stomach should be drank.

Carry a water bottle with you everywhere you go to remind yourself to drink it regularly. Potable water is all around you, in every building. Most colleges have water fountains all over campus. There are places on this earth where people have no access to public water and have to travel miles before they can find drinkable water, and yet we live in a place where federal quality standards for tap water are more stringent and more strongly enforced than the standards for bottled water.[195] Even if we fear our water's quality, we can go out and buy any number of water purifying products and install them right to our tap or keep them in our personal fridges. We have absolutely no reason to fail in an attempt to drink more water, nor should we.

Realize, however, like anything, this regimented consumption of water will take practice. Don't wait for your big game to start this campaign of water intake: practice in your training to see what quantity makes you feel optimal. Staying hydrated is a constant, daily battle, but it is a necessary one. The question is how can one possibly succeed in something as rigorously complex and arduous as competitive sport if he or she can't do something elementary like drinking a couple glasses of water? Being healthy is not hard, nor does it require any more effort than the average lifestyle; water consumption is a great metaphor for that. We all know you're going to drink *something* at every meal, between classes and during games, so make the cheap, easy call, and make it water.

Five Major Points

- There is no mechanism in the body to store water. This makes water consumption a daily task.
- Thirst signals arrive too late, so drink cold water frequently during exercise and games.
- All body signals (e.g. pain, soreness, tiredness) have immediate and direct connections to imbalances, many of which can be alleviated with water intake.
- Drink two glasses of water upon waking up and before every energy drink or coffee you may want.
- Attempt to find natural solutions to aches and pains before taking medications or seeking specialists.

Chapter Six

The Game of Nutrition

Rules

FEELINGS OF CONTROL ARE ESSENTIAL for our well-being. We think clearer and make better decisions when we feel as though we are in control of our situations.[196] One fundamental way we can heighten our feeling of control is to learn as much as we can about a subject; knowledge is undoubtedly a potent form of control. So when athletes say they don't know *anything* about nutrition, red flags pop up. You see, every person out there knows enough about nutrition to eat moderately healthy and avoid junk food. That point is moot, however, if people don't *feel* as though they do. Believing themselves to be in the dark, average citizens then feel powerless against food lobbyists and advertising campaigns. When people are uncertain, they will simply look to others to decide how they themselves should act, and given the environment by which college students are surrounded, this is a scary thought.

But you can be assured, you already know just about everything you need to know. While there are an infinite number of scientific books and articles that have been published on the subject, the fact is you already know what's good for you and what isn't. You don't need to worry about caloric intakes, "low-fat" products, or even "high-protein" foods, because quantitative values do not represent health. Trust that if you are eating the right stuff, the qualities will always take care of the quantities.

And when you're thinking about eating better, you should not be conjuring up the idea of a restrictive diet. People often think of a "diet" as something that is ephemeral with a start and end date, but the word is simply supposed to mean the foods we habitually eat. If you picture a "diet" as having an end date, then you are doing nothing to change your lifestyle, you're simply biding your time. If you're one that loves and craves ice cream, then suddenly goes cold turkey, you'll have to have incredible willpower to avoid it in the future. Research tells us people see something as more desirable when it has recently become less available compared to when it has been scarce all along.[197] So instead of finding things to cut out of your diet, perhaps you should be dreaming about all the healthy choices you have available to you. Cutting out the ice cream will be come easier and easier as you continue to perceive yourself in a healthier light!

Nutrition is a game in itself, and learning how to play requires the same audacity, tenacity, and intelligence that one would apply to his or her sport. And while every sport has rights, wrongs, and areas of gray, so too does nutrition. Before we move on, we should start by clarifying that "rules of nutrition" is certainly *not* in reference to stuff like, "Do not eat after 8pm!" (If you're like other college students not going to bed until 2am, you certainly *need* to eat a late-night meal.) No, the rules in question are ones you will make for yourself based on what you know about nutrition and what you know about yourself. Do not think you need to understand the science behind protein and carbohydrates in order to eat right or to be healthy, you simply need to define food the way you learned in Chapter Four, and change your diet accordingly.

A study done in 1992, with a follow-up in 2001 yielding nearly identical results, showed that 76 percent of college varsity athletes believed vitamins contributed to energy; that 51 percent of athletes believe protein is the main source of energy; and that most responders displayed minimal knowledge of recommended dietary percentages of fat and protein.[198] While this data suggests college athletes do not know much about the science behind nutrition, is it important that they do? You don't need to know how to build a clock to tell the time, the same way you don't need to be a registered dietician to lay off the junk food. Making a rule that everything you eat will either be a plant or an animal, you will never have to think about food choices again, thereby avoiding stress, regret, and feelings of deprivation the next time you're buying groceries or stopped at a convenience store.

Of course, no one can be perfect all the time, and treating yourself to indulgences is part of life. Enjoy sweets now and again, and when you do choose to treat yourself, don't enter the meal with feelings of guilt. After all, the whole point of "treating yourself" is to do exactly that: *treat yourself!* There are definitely nutrient-rich foods, nutrient-poor foods, and those that are nutrient-empty; as long as your diet is *primarily* nutrient-rich foods (read: fruits and vegetables), and "treats" are treats, you can't go wrong. Don't forget, though, you are what you eat. And believe it or not, that sentence is almost literal. Experiments have shown that 98 percent of the human body is completely replaced each year; your blood, cells, structures, even your quads, biceps (or should we call them guns?), and six-pack abs are almost *entirely* composed of your nutritional decisions.[199]

Athletes must understand that for each food item they put into their bodies, they are submitting a vote. If your goals are to be the best, then every piece of nourishment you enter into your bloodstream should be a vote congruent with that goal. That stuff you're eating today is a part of your athletic structure for months to come. If you're one of those people who works really hard in the gym only to go home to fill your body with fast food and booze, you're acting as paradoxical as an arsonistic firefighter.

The advice I give most athletes is this: fill out a week-long food journal — there is one in Appendix E of this book, and a 12-week long one sold online in tandem with this book. The simple self-awareness food journaling can offer is typically all athletes need to change their diets. If, however, you do not think food journaling is possible, at least do one activity to promote awareness: take a picture of every meal you eat for three or four days. You don't have to do anything with the pictures, nor do you even have to save them or tweet them. Merely hold that picture up after you snap it and ponder, "*Would an athlete eat this?*"

You might be wondering why you have to take a picture instead of just looking down and reflecting on your choices as they sit in front of you. But you will not only be surprised by the difference a photograph makes, you will also be embarrassed with your own answers to the question. Of those that admit they've done this, most find it eerily eye-opening and realize they are not eating even what *they* perceive to be healthy.

Like anything one builds, if you are trying to create something impressive, you must first start with a high-quality base and add to it only the best elements. No matter how hard you work as an athlete, if you are refueling with garbage nutrition, you will never end up with a worthwhile product.

Some think eating for athletic performance does not correlate well with eating for enjoyment; they're quite confident they don't like "healthy" food. And if you're one of them, stop thinking that right now. There are *so many* healthy foods out there, and *millions* of recipes ... there is no room for excuses anymore. If you truly want to excel, you have little choice in the matter. Find the foods and recipes you enjoy and get to work. Make no mistake, you cannot out-train poor nutritional decisions.

Body Image

AROUND THE TIME OF THE 2008 Olympics, news of 8-time Gold medal winner — at those games alone — Michael Phelps' mammoth diet hit the headlines. Even Saturday Night Live parodied how this animal was mainlining up to 12,000 calories a day, not feeling bad about it.[200] Phelps and his coaches understood how aggressive his training sessions were, and forced the adequate amount of recovery, i.e. nourishment, back into his body. All other athletes take notice: **food/caloric intake must mimic intensity and duration of training bouts, as well as be consistent with the goals of the athlete**.

Although it really shouldn't be, counting calories is a very commonplace activity that millions of people do every day. No one should ever do it again — certainly no college athlete should. This being said, when determining how many calories you need, consider the following: weight gain and weight loss are completely determinant on caloric intake versus caloric expenditure, energy in vs. energy out. People tend to overthink this concept quite often despite its simplicity. If you are interested in weight loss, you plainly need to consume fewer calories than you use over the course of a day, a week, or a month, depending on how quickly you want to lose or gain the weight. One pound of body fat translates roughly to 3500 calories, which is an easy number to obtain in the long run whether you're trying to gain or lose weight, so do your best not to panic.[201]

While counting your caloric intake is a simple practice, discovering how many calories you are expending over the course of a day is a very different pursuit altogether. For starters, there are three ways your body expends energy, or uses calories:

1. *Basal Metabolic Rate* accounts for about two thirds of the energy an average person burns in a day, and this number varies considerably from person to person. For starters, lean tissue is metabolically more active than body fat, therefore the more athletic you get — i.e. the stronger and faster you become, and the more fat you lose — the more calories you inevitably burn, even at rest. This means that even as Michael Phelps sleeps, he is probably burning more calories than you while you're awake! Realize as your athletic year goes on, you *should* be getting stronger and developing more lean tissue; therefore, your nutrition needs will adapt. You will most likely need to eat more as you progress, even if your only interests are to maintain body weight.

2. *Thermic Effect of Food*, at most, accounts for only ten percent of one's overall caloric expenditure. Athletes need not concern themselves with this, but in the interest of thoroughness, a brief description is warranted: when a person eats, the gastro-intestinal tract speeds up and goes to work, absorbing about ten percent of the nutrients consumed.[202]

3. *Physical Activity* is the final contributor to energy expenditure, and as one would imagine, it varies immensely between sedentary and active people. The liberty has been taken that if you're reading this, you are probably fairly active, but even if you are extremely hard-working, the amount of energy you burn though exercise may only be 10-25 percent of your overall totals.[203] Much like one's basal metabolic rate, caloric needs fluctuate as the year goes on due to changes in training. As the competitive season starts and coaches demand two-a-days, athletes need to eat bountifully more to keep up with how much their workload has increased.

Which finally, gratefully, brings us to the point. Keeping the lifestyle of college students in mind, it is very likely the majority of athletes are undernourished. This, by no means, is stating athletes are under*fed*, rather, they are not getting enough of the nutrients they need to keep up with the demands they place on their bodies. This advice may be the opposite of what you personally believe or perhaps what you want to hear, but most athletes need to eat more. Remember that food is one of the major contributors to recovering from training, and the risk-to-benefit ratio of the eating more strategy is much more effective than the eating less one. Without the sufficient amount of nutrients, meaning not only calories, but vitamins, minerals, protein, carbohydrates, linoleic and alpha-linolenic fatty acids, branched-chain amino acids, etc., the active body fails to recover swiftly, ultimately leaving the body feeling drained and prone to injury.

This is why counting calories or anything quantitative is a silly endeavor: there's too much to count, making it a waste of time. Quality is the name of the game. **Do not count calories. Do not count grams. Count only plants and animals.**

Food represents one form of recovery from training bouts — as does sleep, stretching, and water — yet without adequate amounts of nutritious food, your body will not be able to recuperate to its optimal level before you train again. On the other hand, the worst thing that happens from *over*eating is a short influx of body fat, which is quickly detected by the individual who can immediately change dietary components to compensate. When examining your body for this, take time to consider and truly justify weight loss or gain. Two misperceptions that most athletes strongly hold deal with the same issue: body composition. Many male athletes want to gain weight believing that more mass will yield them more strength, and many female athletes wish to lose weight convinced it will make them faster. Obviously there is a large element of vanity in these desires, but nevertheless, they're out there.

No matter if your interest is in losing weight or gaining it, you need to tackle the issue intelligently by first understanding the typical male and female body composition. Average men have between 13 and 21 percent body fat, while average women, because of their greater quantity of essential fat required for reproduction, contain typically between 23 and 31 percent.[204] That being said, as athletes get stronger, their body composition remodels itself as old fat gives way to new muscle. As you probably already know, muscle weighs more than fat (or in better terms: muscle is heavier by volume than fat), so as you develop as an athlete, the scale may change in a direction you feared, despite everything going well, athletically speaking.

For men, this could mean they lose weight in lieu of their developing speed and loss of unnecessary fat, and for women this could mean they gain weight in response to their strength gains. Women in particular seem to be the most concerned about this, so let's make one thing abundantly clear: the worst misconception is to view such weight gain as dreadful, because to excel in your sport, you may actually have to be at a bodyweight you fear. What might happen to you could be an amazing transformation from a body with 25 percent body fat to one with only 15! You might be stronger, faster, and clearly better at your sport, while the scale fluctuates a couple pegs. Psychologically, you're going to have to accept that you are not training for vanity, you're training for performance; you'll have to get over it.

Whatever that shape may be, you should learn to love it. Worrying about what your body looks like does not only create unnecessary stress in your body, it can kill your possibilities with athletic performance. After your athletic career is over, you may want to concern yourself with washboard abs, but if your true goals are to excel in sport, you will welcome whatever type of body materializes as the result of your sport-specific training. And if you're doing everything you can to be an omnitect, you can be guaranteed you won't be disappointed.

Macronutrients: Carbs, Proteins, Fats

BEFORE YOU READ THIS SECTION, stop and remember your main focus in terms of nutrition should be to *eat food,* period. If, and only if you're mastering that, then what follows is your advanced lesson in sports nutrition. The primary goal here is to impart to you the essential knowledge of macronutrients without all the nonsense behind it, so understand what follows is certainly not an exhaustive list of macronutrients' benefits for athletes.

Between the three macronutrients, being carbohydrates, protein, and fat, you will probably eat more carbs than the others, so let's start there. Your body has three stores of glycogen — glycogen is a form of glucose, glucose is a form of sugar, sugar is a form of carbohydrate. One store is in your liver, another in your blood (as glucose), and then a third as direct storage in your muscles.[205] **That muscle glycogen is the most powerful energy source**, thus, during exercise, it gets depleted the most relative to the other stores of glycogen.[206] This information is worthwhile to know for two reasons:

1. *Having full muscle glycogen stores at the onset of exercise is what allows athletes to be powerful.* Studies have shown that elite athletes typically have nearly *twice* the resting muscle glycogen level than nonathletes.[207] Without this extra storage of glycogen, athletes would have no potential to be strong or fast. Accordingly, they must learn how to train their muscles to store as much glycogen as possible. Which leads us to number two.

2. *Muscle glycogen gets depleted so quickly (sometimes entirely) during exercise, that replacing it immediately post-workout becomes a critical component of becoming a successful athlete.* At maximum intensity

levels — such as heavy lifting and short sprints — carbs, specifically muscle glycogen, are the *exclusive* source of energy. As the duration of exercise prolongs, and the intensity inevitably lessens, carbohydrate usage can drop to 50 percent; however, carbs will still be the primary source of energy for *almost all* NCAA sports[208] (a detailed table can be found in Chapter Eight). Therefore, it is not a coincidence that low muscle glycogen levels, because of their association with premature fatigue, can be a major cause of overtraining.[209]

Carbohydrates By the Numbers

LBS	7 g/kg	8 g/kg
100	318 g	363 g
120	381 g	435 g
140	445 g	508 g
160	508 g	581 g
180	572 g	653 g
200	635 g	725 g
220	699 g	798 g
240	762 g	871 g
260	826 g	943 g
280	889 g	1016 g
300	953 g	1089 g

Food	Carbs in One Serving	Carbs Per Ounce
Raisins	65g (1/2 cup)	22 grams
Wheat Crackers	20g (5 big)	20 grams
Wheat Bread	14g (1 slice)	14 grams
Brown Rice	46g (7 oz.)	7 grams
Wheat Pasta	37g (5 oz.)	7 grams
Banana	31g (large)	6 grams
Sweet Potato	23g (medium)	6 grams
Beans	20g (1/2 cup)	6 grams
Quinoa	20g (1/2 cup)	6 grams
Oatmeal	35g (1 packet)	4 grams
Common Fruit	25g (large)	4 grams

With all this in mind, it's no surprise that carbohydrates should be a large component of athletes' diets. An especially good time to consume them would be right after exercise, as that is when glycogen stores are most depleted. The amount of carbohydrate intake necessary to maintain glycogen stores for hard-training athletes is usually above seven grams of carbohydrate per one kilogram of bodyweight for women, and eight grams per kilogram for men.[210] These quantitive values typically mean nothing, as if you sit down and do the math, you are extremely likely to be eating that much as it is (the tables on the previous page will demonstrate this more clearly).

The only question is to the quality of these foods. The best are probably brown rice, quinoa and oats, but no need to overthink this. Pastas, breads, sweet potatoes, and even apples, bananas, raisins and other dried fruit all count toward the total. One thing to keep in mind when buying pastas, breads, wraps, and the like, are to keep them whole wheat. Wheat has 25 nutrients removed in the refining process that turns it into white flour, and only four of them are replaced post-production; thus, it is imperative to find the wheat versions of your favorite foods.[211]

Carbohydrates are essential for athletic performance. Seven to eight grams of carbohydrate per kilogram of bodyweight is a ratio fairly unknown to most athletes, at least when compared to the popularity protein enjoys. When people think about athletes and nutrition, they tend to only focus on protein, but the Recommended Daily Allowance (RDA) for protein intake is 0.8 grams per kilogram of bodyweight,[212] which pales in comparison to carbohydrate!

Yet this isn't to say that protein intake isn't also vitally important to athletes. As it happens, that RDA of 0.8 grams per kilogram has been proven to actually limit muscle growth in strength-trained individuals.[213] *BUT!* Protein itself does nothing to stimulate muscle growth; no one ever got stronger by just wolfing protein supplements. Protein simply provides the building material for your body to utilize in order to cultivate strong muscles, much like wood is provided to a carpenter to build a solid house.[214] Supply a carpenter with an insufficient amount, or a poor quality of wood, and you'll get a sub-par house. Feed your body an equally inadequate quantity or quality of protein, and you'll end up with something short of an athletic body.

For these reasons, all athletes need to be eating a lot of protein. And while the average American diet may be proficient in carbohydrate intake, it is deficient in protein. Women, are you listening? Far too often, half the athletic population, primarily women, avoid protein supple-mentation because of an erroneous fear of it leading to a muscle-bound body. Hundreds of studies have shown that protein supplementation does not improve muscle growth or even performance, but rather it aids in the rebuilding processes. **What protein supplementation does is reduce muscle damage and soreness, thus allowing athletes to train hard on subsequent days.**[215]

College athletes need to understand this fact, and at the very least double the RDA in respect to their protein intake. Of course, how much protein your body needs for the specific demands you are insisting upon it will vary from sport to sport, person to person, and even season to season. If you are doing very intense, heavy-resisted work, your body could be calling for as much as two grams of protein per kilogram of bodyweight. If you are doing field sports, i.e. middle intensity work, your demands are around 1.7 grams per kilogram. Finally, if you are a distance athlete, your requirements are about 1.4 grams per kilogram.[216] While these recommendations are extremely specific (and the table below can help you with these calculations), the important thing to note is that regardless of who you are, you should be polishing off twice the RDA every day. Having trouble recovering or feel sore all the time? This could simply be a product of insufficient protein intake, with an equally simple solution.

Protein By the Numbers

LBS	1.4 g/kg	1.7 g/kg	2.0 g/kg
100	64 g	77 g	91 g
120	76 g	92 g	109 g
140	83 g	100 g	118 g
160	102 g	123 g	145 g
180	114 g	139 g	163 g
200	127 g	154 g	181 g
220	140 g	170 g	200 g
240	152 g	185 g	218 g
260	165 g	200 g	236 g
280	178 g	216 g	254 g
300	190 g	231 g	272 g

Food	Protein in One Serving	Protein Per Ounce
Chicken	25g (3 oz.)	8 grams
Fish	25g (3 oz.)	8 grams
Peanut Butter	7g (2 Tbsp.)	6 grams
Nuts	12g (1/2 cup)	5 grams
Wheat Pasta	7g (2 oz.)	3.5 grams
Eggs	6g (each)	3.5 grams
Oatmeal	5g (1 packet)	3 grams
Hummus	2g (2 Tbsp.)	2 grams
Beans	12g (1/2 cup)	1.5 grams
Quinoa	8g (1 cup)	1.2 grams
Spinach	5g (15 leaves)	1 gram

Before moving on, it's important to point out that this magic amount of protein comes from a lot of different sources in your diet. The biggest misinterpretation of protein is that it can only come from animal sources, but nearly every food on the shelf has *some* protein in it. Spending some time in the grocery store reading nutritional labels will help you deduce these foods for yourself, but the table on the previous page gives you a few good, healthy options, as well.

Apart from these whole foods, **every athlete should own protein powder**. There are a lot of varieties out there, so to shed a little light on the issue, first we have to think about the sources of these proteins. There are essentially three sources from which these protein supplements are made: whey, soy, or plant protein powder. An easy way to make the decision of which protein supplement to use would be to first think of where the products originate. Whey is from animal sources, soy is from soy beans, and plant is from varieties of plants, typically hemp, pea, rice, etc. If you were to be asked, or really any American was asked, what your diet is lacking most, would you answer meat, soy, or plants? To most people, this is an easy question with an equally easy answer, which is why it seems to make the most sense to supplement a plant protein powder over the other varieties. Between all the cheese, butter, meat, yogurt, and milk the average person consumes, if you're thinking about protein powders, you should probably refer to a Wisconsin license plate I once saw: NO WHEY!

While we're on the subject, we'd better stop for a moment and examine the fear some people, mostly men, have in regard to soy protein, soy milk, and other soy products. Nearly every time the word "soy" is mentioned to a group of male athletes, someone will inevitably bring up their concerns about "bitch tits" and "estrogen" and "nipple discharge" and "being turned into a chick." Go onto any bodybuilding forum and sure enough you'll find article after article about the dangers of the poisonous protein that is soy! So what I did was scroll to the bottom of these articles and look up every, single, last source from which these authors quoted. What amazed me was nearly every article cited was actually *pro*-soy, and what the authors of these anti-soy articles were doing was extracting partial-sentences that made their arguments sound legitimate. I will refer the reader to Appendix C where my findings can be read in explicit detail. What never makes any sense is when people will openly claim that a food is either healthy or has been shown to reduce risk of heart disease or cancer, but then attempt to vilify it when applying it to athletes. If a food is healthy, that's it. If it's good for people to eat to promote health, it's good for athletes.   No more information required as we are aware college athletes are in dire need of *more health.*

Whether it be soy, whey, hemp, plant, or what have you, an athletic body *requires* protein supplementation, and unless you are taking your protein content seriously at meal time, you will need this. Shopping around, one can find the companies that obtain their protein from healthy, even organic sources.   Realize, however, that these protein powders are nutritional *supplements*, not meal replacements.   The essence of the word "supplement" implies that it occurs in addition to something else, so be sure to *add* a scoop of this good stuff *on top of* your regular diet, not replace a meal because of it.

The final note on protein is to recognize the protein supplement marketplace is one of those environments where companies get off on confusing the hell out of their consumers. By advertising their protein powder as more than just a powder — including all sorts of extra "vital" supplements athletes supposedly *need* — people buy in. These bottles formerly filled with a simple macronutrient have gotten pretty complex, and picking one out from the store can be more confusing than trying to teach your grandma what e-mail is. Keep it simple: check the ingredients, and see which product is primarily composed of ingredients you recognize. Often times, it's easier to pick one out from a health food store than a supplement store.

Okay, so now that we're feeling comfortable with our carbohydrate and protein intake, we can start to pay attention to the fats. Fat, in recent decades, has gotten a pretty terrible rap from popular media, but make no mistake about it, fat in your body is crucial. Certain fats, omega 3's and 6's, in particular, are essential for the brain, nervous, immune, and cardiovascular systems, as well as the skin.[217] So, for those of you who aim to have 0% body fat, you will certainly die in the attempt before you achieve that goal.

The omega fats an athlete truly needs, linoleic and alpha-linoleic acids (a.k.a. omega 3 and 6), can be found in cold-water fish, e.g. salmon, sardines, mackerel, and trout; in nuts like walnuts; in seeds, e.g. flax, hemp, pumpkin, sunflower, and sesame; and in extra virgin olive oil.[218] Finding a way to work those foods into your diet a couple times a week is a necessity for fat intake, and if you live on a college campus, it could be challenging to find these foods. But, where there's a will there's a way, and if you make the choice to start snacking on nuts and seeds instead of chips and crackers, or to coat your bread/toast with extra virgin olive oil (EVOO) instead of butter, you'll be well on your way. As an aside, EVOO is the best "fat" with which to cook (over butter, margarine, and other oils) as it is a fruit-pressed liquid that never goes through a refinery. To make other corn or seed oils, they have to go through complicated refining processes, but "virgin" means it's not made by chemistry; it's simply pressed out of the fruit!

Now, it's not challenging to eat EVOO, nuts, or seeds: they're inexpensive, easily found in stores, and require little to no prep work before consumption. But what about fish you say? Between fearing the fish in the dining hall and not having the money to buy it off campus, college students certainly consider themselves up a creek when it comes to eating fish. Not so! While you may not be eating tuna steaks or sushi very often, you could be eating shrimp cocktails regularly, or at least some canned tuna or salmon. But if you don't see yourself doing this either, you need to go to your last hope: fish oil supplements. Supplementing fish oils, which are omega 3's and 6's, would be a great way to spend your money if you refuse to buy the actual food itself. The pills could easily be taken every day, or you could pour the actual oil into a protein shake or smoothie!

Notwithstanding, *most* of the fat in the American body is not the good fat, and serves little purpose. Someone with 15 percent body fat has enough energy potential from that fat to run up to 150 miles. Remember though, since most athletes use carbohydrates as their main energy source, they will rarely, if ever, find a purpose for their energy reserve of fat.[219]   When fat *is* used as a source however, the duration must be lengthy, and the intensity low, e.g. marathon running.[220] The reader again can be referred to the table in Chapter Eight.

One could safely say most college students are enjoying a surplus of the bad fat, while most likely being deficient in the good fats. Due to our ridiculous diet overwhelmed with fast food, Americans consistently eat too much saturated fat, the kind that kills, and too little of the essential fats, the kinds that heal. From now on, you will need to make better decisions and find a way to get those omega 3's and 6's into your body. Now, unless you are going out of your way to eat the right kinds of fat-rich foods, odds are you are not getting enough of the good fats, and supplementation may be necessary.

All three macronutrients are essential to your success, and promoting one over the other is unnecessary. By the same token, following a diet that urges you to void one of these macronutrients altogether is similarly unwise. Thankfully, the anti-fat campaign is nearing its death, and people are starting to eat healthy fats again.

Regretfully, however, the anti-grain campaign is starting to kick into full gear, and even some college athletes are becoming obsequious to its propaganda. But now at least *you* know you need all the macronutrients to prosper as an athlete.

Post-Workout Nutrition

AFTER A DISCUSSION OF MACRONUTRIENTS, it's worth noting now what should happen in a post-workout meal, as it primarily has to do with macronutrient intake. What happens when you exercise, as touched on earlier, is a loss of muscle glycogen; therefore, **immediately post-workout you need to be replenishing those stores by consuming carbohydrates as quickly as possible.** Yes, protein is important too, but replacing those carbs quickly will allow your muscles to better facilitate glycogen synthesis, thus enabling you to have even more energy for your next training session or game.[221] Ultimately, as you have learned, protein is what builds muscle, and protein synthesis is believed to be most prominent during your immediate recovery period as well.[222] Further-more, combining carbohydrates *and* proteins after exercise can promote glycogen resynthesis more effectively than by consuming either by itself.[223] This makes the message explicitly clear: **a good post-workout meal should include both carbohydrates and protein, and should be eaten as soon as possible.**

If you're wondering why the timing matters, it has to do with hormone responses during and after workouts. Exercise is "catabolic," meaning you are breaking muscle tissue down during a workout, and the only reason you get stronger or faster is because your "anabolic" system kicks in briefly after exercise is completed to help you recover.[224] We will get into this in much more detail later on, but for now, realize that what makes you stronger or faster is not the exercise itself, but the recovery from exercise. That short anabolic system you naturally get immediately after a workout is what's making you a good athlete!

Presumably, you've heard of anabolic steroids. What those do is put you in a constant state of anabolism, whereas naturally, your anabolic system is pretty brief. If you're not on 'roids, what happens is the second after you finish your last rep of the day, your anabolic hormones activate. The magnitude of their response depends on many factors — your age, gender, the type of training you did, and how much you accomplished — but either way, your anabolic cycle won't last long. Hormonal fluctuations occur quickly, then stabilize, as a hormone's duty is to simply send a signal to elicit an action in the body, and after that job is done, to quickly weave itself back into the woodwork.[225] This is the reason why you need to eat *something* immediately after you workout. You can help all of these processes along and you can make your body recover more efficiently — all you gotta do is eat!

Finally, you are probably asking *what* to eat post-workout. As you've read, both carbohydrates and protein are important, and you've learned some good sources of both, so the issue comes down to individualization. For those people that can't stomach real food after a training bout, there are a plethora of post-workout shakes and drinks out there. Read some nutritional labels, and find out for yourself if they have both carbs and protein. You'll eventually discover something you like, but just remember the essentials: eat *something* immediately after your workout, and ideally it should have both carbohydrates and proteins.

Hopefully your choice will be from the real food category, and then you won't have to concern yourself so much with the quantities of nutrients within it. Once, on television, a champion bodybuilder was being interviewed with an enormous shaker bottle next to him. Inside was some strangely semi-transparent, pink, viscous liquid. Finally, one of the interviewers asked him what was inside, and his answer was "boiled chicken and water, post-blender." This is not being brought up to encourage you to do the same, simply to show you that extremely successful athletes often go to the extremes in regard to their recovery as well. This particular bodybuilder wanted to supplement protein, but did not want to use any ingredient that was not real food. We all must learn the triumph of health lies not in the individual nutrients, but in the whole foods that contain them.

The Essential Supplementation

THE USE OF NONANABOLIC, AND certainly anabolic supplements in the interest of improving athletic abilities has become widespread in this country, and there are few athletes left that take no form of supplementation whatsoever. There are thousands of supplements in the marketplace that are directed specifically at athletes based on theoretical evidence derived from limited animal studies. Of course, no smart athletic trainer, strength coach, or physician would ever advise anyone to take any of these, but if athletes think they are safe, many are willing to try them to see if they are actually effective. Few, if any, have been proven in scientific research to be beneficial for athletes, and most have not gone under enough investigation to be deemed "healthy" for human consumption. Between all these weird supplements, the lack of sleep, and the abundance of alcohol, it's no wonder students are getting sick all the time.

Understand that health is nature's default. When and if you get sick, your body is trying to tell you that something about your current lifestyle is askew. Most of the time, especially in regard to hard-working athletes, being sick is a sign you are overworked and not receiving the adequate quantity or quality of nutrients to keep your immune system functioning at its optimal rate. You should rarely, if ever, get a long, debilitating cold if you are sufficiently nourished. In fact, a good judge of how healthy you are is measuring the duration of a cold. Immune-healthy people acquire no infections, thus their colds last about 24 hours; conversely, less healthy people can be immobile for a week.[226] (I haven't missed a day of work due to illness since I started living healthy seven years ago, and I work in one of the filthiest places a civilized community can offer: a gym! And although I would never pin any success or defeat on one variable, I do think I owe a lot of my continued health to my diet full of fruits and vegetables and void of junk foods.)

If you are one of those people who gets sick often, the first place to look is your diet. Are you supplying your body with enough nutrients for it to function optimally? If you are eating enough quality food, there really is no need to supplement much else at all, especially something that doesn't exist in nature. Too many items on the shelves of supplement stores are diabolical, man-made creations aimed to spike energy levels or overload our organs with unnatural drugs. So don't go into a vitamin store and ask if you need supplements — that's like going to a barber and asking if you need a haircut. While there are plenty of shiny, colorful "muscle-building" bottles of pills to entice you, the only real supplements anyone ever needs are the ones that might be lacking in their diet: vitamins, especially C, protein for athletes, and omega 3s and 6s such as fish oil.

Recently, studies have come out to say that multivitamin supplementation is "dangerous," and to avoid them at the cost of your very health and well-being. Soon thereafter, medical professionals started to be bombarded with questions regarding vitamin supple-mentation. What should be made clear, and in fact, what should be obvious, is that supplementation is not ideal. Your diet *should* be well-rounded, and it *should* include all of the macro- and micronutrients your body needs to stay healthy.

Be wary of these "scientific breakthroughs," as most of the time with food and health, there are different scientists conducting research that stands in complete opposition to each other. With regard to the scientific community and vitamin supplementation, there is something you should know. Vitamins are not drugs, therefore unlike medications, they come with little to no negative side effects, namely the lack of death. In fact, in the 25+ years they have been around, vitamins have allegedly killed ten people — a number that is highly contended by those in the community, but let's take it at its maximum number of ten.[227] While you may look at that number and scoff, when compared to the 225,000 people medications kill *every year,* it starts to look pretty good. In fact, pharmaceutical drugs could be pegged as the #3 cause of death in this country. For some reason, it seems that people have some sort of phobia when it comes to taking a multivitamin because they associate them with drugs, but vitamins are absolutely *nothing* like drugs. If something is therapeutically valuable, people think it is dangerous, because almost every pharmaceutical drug is, but this is not the case at all with multivitamins. Although they may be unnecessary to the average adult, they are certainly harmless and could help college students lead healthier lifestyles. With those numbers in mind, let's delve a little deeper into this issue so you can make an educated decision for yourself.

When most people consider how many vitamins and minerals their bodies need, they turn to the Recommended Daily Allowances (RDA) distributed by the government. RDAs, which are the numbers referred to when you see that a product has "25% RDA of Vitamin A," for example, are set by governments to prevent deficiency diseases;[228] they have *nothing* to do with optimal health. For example, if you take 90mg of Vitamin C, the current RDA, you are likely not to succumb to scurvy ... If you are more interested in optimal intakes however, those numbers are still highly debated, but you should know that with the exception of Vitamins A and D, levels 100 times greater than the RDA are likely to be safe for longterm ingestion[229] — not that anyone is advocating that, just stating a fact.

Studies have shown that the intake of nutrients associated with optimal health was often ten times higher than typical RDA levels. In fact, the combination of nutrients in high-quality, high-dosed multivitamins have proven, in hundreds of studies, to boost immunity, improve intellectual performance and resistance to infection, while also reducing the risk of birth defects, cancer, and heart disease.[230]

Before we move on, something really needs to be reiterated. Vitamin supplementation is *never* ideal. We were meant to receive all vital nutrients, in quality and quantity, from our daily intake of nutritious foods. All full-grown adults with salaries should never require vitamin supplementation, as they should be spending their money on the kinds of food that will provide them with ample nutrients. If there comes a time when they are malnourished, or deficient in certain vitamins, they need to look to their diets, not their supplementation regiment, to fix it.

Now, of course, we're not talking about salaried adults here, we're talking about college students, and because we're talking about college students, the advice needs to be altered. As we all recognize, college is unhealthy not only because of the physical habits people develop, but also the psychological ones. While students are there, they *view* themselves as unhealthy, and this negative mindset drives them to actions congruent with that outlook. What vitamin supplementation can offer is the aura of better health, thus providing students with a reason to believe they are healthy after all!

What has become apparent in recent years is those that take supplements are, in fact, healthier than those who do not. What's interesting, however, is that this may not be because vitamins are healthy in themselves. More likely, it's a combination of vitamins adding a moderate element of health to people who are already health conscious, have achieved a higher level of education, and who are likely more wealthy than the average citizen. But the point still remains that people who take vitamins tend to lead healthier lifestyles. For this reason, multivitamins could be helpful to a population of people who need all the assistance they can get in terms of healthy lifestyles: college students.

And for those of you who might fear the science behind what multivitamins actually are, maybe this will help: since the 1980s, more and more research has confirmed that many of the twentieth century's most common diseases are associated with shortages of antioxidant nutrients and helped by their supplementation.[231] Unfortunately, deficiencies in vitamins, minerals, and essential fats are not, despite popular belief, rare; many nutritionists believe that as few as one in ten people receive sufficient nutrients from their diets.[232] Without having the proper amount of vitamins and minerals circulating in your body, you will be unable to use the other nutrients you are consuming. For example, difficulty in building muscle is rarely due to a lack of protein intake;

rather, it is more often the result of not taking in adequate amounts of vitamins and minerals that help digest and use that protein.[233]

Finally, you might be asking which multivitamins to take. As you probably have seen, bottles of the stuff are available at huge discount retailers, pharmacies, sports equipment stores, and at vitamin shops. Some have pictures of farms on them with a vegetable stand and a sign reading, "Food-Based" or "Food-Grown" Vitamins making consumers feel comforted that these vitamins must have been taken right out of eggplants and plums and stuffed into little capsules! Well, even foods that have extremely high levels of certain vitamins do not yield enough of them to be used as a source in commercial vitamin products. So, essentially, almost all vitamins sold in bottles are the same.

But, you might be thinking, what about the organic ones?! What can be said about organic multivitamins and, in general, the brands that are sold at health food stores, is that they are likely more aware of animal testing, environmental impact, and things like vegetarianism than brands being sold at big-chained pharmacies. As far as the vitamins within the little pills go, the difference of organic to "regular" would be negligible.

That is not to say that vitamins from pills and vitamins from food are the same, however. $C_6H_8O_6$, or "ascorbic acid," may be relatively the same in all pill-form vitamins, but obtaining your $C_6H_8O_6$ from an orange is going to be more beneficial to your body than obtaining it from a pill. Remember, the body is not a machine, it is a complex, adaptive jungle where everything is interconnected. Your body will only adapt if all the circumstances are synergistically working together toward a common goal, and it helps to eat food that is synergistic as well — this means plants and animals! Considering the collegiate years may be somewhat lacking in that category, vitamin supplementation could be advisable to college athletes.

If you are not already on a daily multivitamin, know that one might help as every moment you spend stressed, whether it be mentally or physically, you use up valuable nutrients, as the body is consuming more energy than usual. Conservative estimates suggest that you can *double* your need for vitamins in a stressful state; so given your lifestyle of mental stress from class work and physical stress from exercise, you really need to eat right to perform well.[234] If not, it could be beneficial to take a multivitamin.

Apart from multivitamins, the good fats can also be challenging to mix into the diet. Considering you're in college, you might not have a lot of opportunity to eat fish, so you probably could benefit from supplementing fish oils into your daily routine. The good fats are responsible for high-quality brain function and keeping joints pliable, to name only a scarce amount of their advantages. There is absolutely no question that your body needs them to survive, and if you aren't ready to eat fish several times a week, supplementation is your only option. You can purchase fish oils in pill form, which can be quick and painless, or in liquid form, which is good to pour into smoothies or protein shakes!

This brings us to the last nutrient worthy of your supplementation: protein. Your body is being exposed to high levels of tissue breakdown, and without the proper amount of rest and adequate protein intake, you will never fully recover from your workouts. Being a college athlete implores your supplementation of protein; no matter what sport you play, what gender you are, or how much money you're willing to spend on supplementation, protein is vital.

Science has proven the advantages of regular supplementation of multis, omegas, and protein, while the superfluous supplements — e.g. nitrous oxide, "testosterone boosters" and all other pre-workout pump-ups or post-workout cocktails — remain only championed by each of their respective companies. Just about every day, I get asked for my opinion about one of these elixirs an athlete picked up from a vitamin store, and all I can offer is that college athletes' time and money would be *much* better spent buying real food over supplementation of any kind.

We can end the discussion of nutrition with a persuasive anecdote: what kind of people would be willing to sacrifice what they do for a sport — in other words, they give up time of day five days a week or more, all the pain of the weight room, the pain of the practice field, the problems with their coaches, the stresses if they're starting or even going to make the team, the laundry, all the money they spend on equipment — who would go through all that, but would not be willing to take a drink a protein shake … or drink ten glasses of water each day … or go to the grocery store …

Thinking about that can send your mind spinning.

Pointers for Maintaining a College Food Budget

Actually create a budget and track expenses. Attending college truly is a privilege, and most students attending a university have been fortunate enough to either receive scholarships or have wealthy parents. Anthony Carnevale and Stephen Rose surveyed the top 146 U.S. colleges and found that only three percent of students there came from families in the bottom economic quartile;[235] furthermore, only eight percent of students are unable to complete college for purely financial reasons.[236] The intention in making this note is to point to the fact the vast majority of college students have at least *some* money to burn. Maybe it's only a couple dollars here and there, but regardless, there's usually something for you to spend. The biggest complaint from athletes when discussing nutrition is that they have no money, consequently their options are limited. In spite of that, when asked how much money they can afford to squander on booze, they chuckle, "We-e-ell … you know … " One thing you could do is open up a spreadsheet, or buy one of the 10,000 apps on your smartphone dedicated to budgeting and finances, and map out how much money you have and/or make, and spread it out to all of your expenses. Set out to discover what kind of money you are blowing on non-necessities and move that over into your food budget. Tracking cash flow — income vs. expenses — is something that can benefit you the rest of your life, and something I do every day. Only after I did this did I realize I couldn't afford my favorite meal: sushi. But was I going to give it up? Hell no! By tracking my expenses, I realized if I gave up cable and internet, I could afford a giant sushi meal every week! And that's exactly what I did. I gave up cable for over a year so I could gorge myself on raw fish. Most of us have the money to do stuff like this, we just choose to allocate it where it doesn't *need* to be.

Go home as often as you can.   For some of you, this isn't a possibility, but you've got friends. Most parents are so delighted to see their sons or daughters come home, they are willing to cook up a storm for them! There really is something to be said about home-cooked meals. When something is prepared with love, not only is it probably more nutritious, it simply tastes better. Adults have much more control over what they eat than children, as they are the ones with all the money, and while you transition from old child to young adult, you need to take advantage where you can. Yes, that means using your parents and the parents of others every chance you get!

Cook with friends. There is just an endless supply of good reasons to cook with friends. First, it's cheaper. Trying to grill salmon by yourself can be pricey, but several people pitching in on a few choice salmon-steaks from a surplus store can really bring each individual cost way down. Second, you get to have lots of sides. Again, buying a bag of sweet potatoes by yourself for one meal is obnoxious, but when everyone chips in, suddenly this entrée has a side of roasted potato!   Third, it's fun.

Attempting to figure recipes out by yourself can make you want to put a bullet in your head, but with a bunch of your friends, anything you mess up is just a big joke. Finally, you are going to build cooking skills that you will use the rest of your life. Your spouse and children will thank you for it later. Check Appendix D at the back of this book for a few recipes that require very little time, money, experience, and equipment!

Drink water. Sports drinks, energy drinks, and juices can be pretty expensive, especially for those of you buying a lot of them. Water is, and always has been, free. If you think you are one of those people that drinks a lot of sports drinks, track your expenses with them for a month and find out how much you are throwing at those companies. If you drank water, not only would you be doing your body a favor, but you would have that much more money to ensure you could afford healthy food.

Recognize the cheap but beneficial food options:

- Eggs and egg whites could potentially be your best friend. Apart from being arguably the most versatile food ever, eggs are chock-full of protein with little fat, and cheap as anything you are likely to find. What's more, if you eat 30 grams of egg protein, your body will use 28 grams of it![237] This bioavailability is rare in foods.
- Whole wheat pasta, quinoa, and brown rice will forever be dirt cheap and good for you. Always, always, always buy whole wheat products instead of white.
- Canned tuna. What can a guy even say about canned tuna? Cheap, delicious, nutritious, and more versatile than Carl Lewis. One thing to look out for are sodium levels though, so shop for the low-sodium brands.
- Canned beans range from garbanzo to refried to black, all of which have an abundance of fiber and protein.
- Cooked shrimp, a.k.a. shrimp cocktail, is almost perpetually on sale in the supermarket. Shrimp is an excellent source of protein and is a versatile add-on to any meal, not to mention delicious on its own.
- Frozen assorted vegetables are a great side to any dinner and are really easy to throw in a pan to heat up and even easier to steam.
- Bananas are probably the most abundant fruit out there. Freeze them, then throw them in a blender with (soy or almond) milk, OJ, some protein powder, maybe even a little syrup or peanut butter for added flavor, next thing you know, you got a smoothie going!
- PB & J. If you've got the additional dollar, buy the organic peanut butter and the local jelly, as they taste a million times better, and are

abundantly more nutritious. And although this is typically a kid's meal, if you can buy the upscaled versions of the three ingredients (including bread), you can do okay for yourself.

- Chicken breasts in bulk. Very easy to slap onto a panini machine and cook through, then dip them into BBQ sauce, or whatever your preference is, and you've got a cheap, mega protein source.
- Cottage cheese is basically just protein. You know that watery stuff that hangs out on top of the curds? That's whey!
- Buy protein powder in the biggest tub you can find. Shop online if you have to, or go into a keg of it together with your friends. There's no reason for three close friends to each buy a two-pound supply every month when you can just as easily purchase a six-pound jug on the cheap.
- Finally, check out Appendix D at the end of this book for some really cheap and really fast recipes advisable to the college athlete!

Five Major Points

- Truly justify weight loss and gain. What is it you *really* want? Be specific.
- The RDA for protein will limit muscle growth. Refer to the tables and eat more food.
- Every athlete should own and use a bottle of protein powder every day. Between whey, soy, and plant, supplement the source your diet is lacking.
- A good post-workout meal should include both carbohydrates and protein, and should be eaten immediately.
- The only plausible supplements to take would be multivitamins, fish oils, and protein. Anything else is nearly unjustifiable.

Chapter Seven

Alcohol and College Athletics

The Nonathlete / Athlete Comparison

EVERYONE KNOWS HOW PREVALENT BINGE drinking is in college, and most know who the inveterate drinkers are: athletes. There seems to be two structures in place here: the sweater-wearing student-athlete and the nighttime economy of generic-brand liquors accompanied with intense displays of potvaliance. For whatever reason, the college athlete's way of life is somehow intertwined with alcohol. They live this paradoxical life with the health-promoting qualities of sports making them more susceptible to the health-compromising effects of consuming more alcohol. In fact, frequent binge drinking is not only more prevalent among college athletes, but even in former high school athletes that are currently attending college, yet not playing a varsity sport.[238] Alcohol remains the number one substance abused by teenagers, and by athletes everywhere — from junior high through the pros.[239]

In undergrad, I wrote my semester-long research paper with original data (wasn't called a thesis at the time) on fraternity drinking, and I'll never forget what a frat brother once said to me in passing, "Drunk people equals wilderness beasts." Oh how true that is. National Geographic could've included college students' pursuit of booze in their study of great migrations, for when there is word of a keg on campus, the underage congregate, like the fruit bats to Zambia, for a place at the drinking trough. Theme parties act as miraculous oases for college drunks, like the Mexican forests do for Monarch butterflies. And bystanders could set out lawn chairs and observe as flocks of the intoxicated migrate to Homecoming, like swallows to Capistrano, only to be seen hours later moribund in the ditch.

The question then becomes why athletes party harder than nonathletes. Is it the competitive nature of athletics spilling over into social activities, whereby athletes want to see how many or how fast they can drink? Is it their isolation from the rest of the student body? Is it that they're so popular they just keep getting roped into situations where alcohol is around? Or are athletes just bibulous people by nature? The answers are impossible to know. Regardless, college is typically the first time away from a close parental guide and all are ready to get rowdy. Alas, avoiding drinking excessively in college is like avoiding crabs in a dark-alley brothel. Many *outside* the bubble think men are to blame ... probably because they get the most rambunctious, cause the most fights, and are inevitably too ostentatious around girls. But everyone *in* the bubble knows women drink right alongside the men and are not immune to any of the harsh consequences of hard boozing: the loss of sleep, the hangovers, the risk of being considered a skank, and of course, waking up next to dragons which they forgot they took to bed. The morning after these raucous events, people are usually filled with so much self-loathing, they lie in bed late into the day cogitating on all the mistakes they've made that led to this deplorable moment. Nevertheless, they'll be back at it soon enough.

Nationwide, this alcohol abuse among college students has been responsible for around 1,400 student deaths, 500,000 unintentional injuries, and 600,000 assaults annually — not including sexual assaults.[240] But statistics like these do nothing to promote abstinence; alcohol is not going away from college. College students push a synonymous relationship between the words "drunk" and "fun," all the while positively knowing consuming alcohol is not good for them. Sadly, few realize how alcohol is affecting them and most don't know much they are actually drinking. This is why this book is not going to focus on teetotaling; instead, it's going to focus on responsibility and conse-quences.

Specific Concerns for Athletes

HOW MUCH ALCOHOL WOULD YOU say the average college student consumes in a week? Really, get a specific number in your head. Is it five drinks per week? Ten? What about 25?

Now, how much do *you* drink? Again, put a specific number in your head, and then compare it to your average.

Did you answer less for yourself than what you said was average? Most likely. This is a typical psychological phenomenon, whereby answering the question about the "average college student" allowed you to distance yourself from criticism and ultimately tell the truth about yourself without having to outright admit it (even if you were only admitting it to yourself). In a study conducted at Southern Methodist University, twenty percent of students surveyed reported drinking the previous night, yet they believe that over half the campus drank. Eight percent reported getting drunk, but they believed around a third of all students campus-wide did the same. Of those who drank, most reported only having a few drinks each week, yet they think the numbers for the average student ranged between ten and fifteen. And finally, 35 percent reported being abstainers, yet very few believed many of their peers were non-drinkers.[241]

I've asked these questions to students many times before and found there's a very quick response to the question of "the average college student," whereas when asked about themselves, people provide long-winded palavers ... liars like to embellish so they can believe their own fabrications. After all, psychologically-speaking, vivid descriptions are easier to believe.[242]

Regardless of how much you do or do not drink, the deleterious effects of even small amounts of alcohol will be experienced by your body. For starters, high alcohol users (in the 75th percentile) lived with significantly more anger and fatigue than did low alcohol users.[243] On top of this, more athletes report experiencing alcohol-related "harms" than nonathletes. These harms include, but are not limited to, missing class, blacking out, doing things they later regretted, having unplanned or unprotected sex, getting in trouble with campus police, and getting injured.[244]

To get even more specific to athletes, there is other surprising data. Alcohol consumption appears to have a causative effect in sports-related injury, with an injury incidence of 54.8% in drinkers compared with only a 23.5% in teetotalers. Perhaps this comes from the hangover effect of alcohol consumption, which has been shown to reduce athletic performance by at least 11 percent.[245]   Matthew Martens, a devoted researcher in reference to alcohol and college athletics, has extensively studied the alcohol/athlete relationship and wrote this in the Journal of Substance Abuse Treatment:

> Chronic, excessive alcohol use has considerable long-term consequences that are particularly problematic for athletes, including atrophy of Type II muscle fibers (those used in anaerobic exercise), reduced muscle mass, decreased dynamic and isokinetic exercise performance, and deleterious effects on the human immune response. The American College of Sports Medicine stated in its position statement on alcohol use and sport that acute alcohol consumption is associated with compromised psychomotor skills; decreased maximal oxygen consumption; decreased exercise capacity, muscular strength and cardiovascular endurance; and impaired body-temperature regulation system. Growing evidence also suggests that acute alcohol intake has direct consequences for athletic performance, such as reduced time to exhaustion among bicyclists and decreased endurance running performance. In addition, athletes who consumed alcohol once a week reported more than twice as many sport-related injuries as did nondrinkers. Finally, several studies have documented the detrimental effects of ingesting alcohol in the 24 hours before an athletic activity, such as decreased aerobic activity, and consuming alcohol after an athletic activity or competition (which may be particularly common among inter-collegiate athletes), such as worsened dehydration and overall impediments to physiological recovery.[246]

This specific data for athletes may not have been known before, but it usually comes as no surprise. No one is out there believing drinking alcohol is going to *improve* their performance, but most also believe it's fairly innocuous compared to the reality seen above.

Odds are if you're a college athlete, you're a drinker, and you are most likely unaware of how much you truly drink. Why? This way of life is invisible to college students; they are blind to the privileges life has handed them and justify their social position as one to which they are entitled.   As one lacrosse player perfectly epitomized in a few brief sentences, "I'm in college. College students drink. Transitive property." There is the bubble summed up in a few words. And while the bubble offers its fair share of benefits, probably the worst aspect of it all is not just in regard to how much alcohol is consumed, but about how much is socially accepted. While the amount in question may be coherent in the confines of college, drinking that much is unthinkable outside those walls.

How We View College

WHAT'S COMICAL IS THAT WHEN most, if not all college students hear the definition of an alcoholic, they chuckle and say, "Well what then? So we're all alcoholics?" Sadly yes. And if they weren't in college, they'd recognize it. Some of these definitions of alcoholism from the web might remind you of yourself or some buddies you know: "compulsive consumption of alcohol usually to the detriment of the drinker's health and personal relationships" (Wikipedia), "the person continues to drink even when he/she wants to stop because of his/her health and well-being," "the person feels guilty about drinking and feels as though he/she needs to cut down" (CAGE questionnaire), "for women and men, heavy drinking is typically defined as consuming an average of more than 1 or 2 drinks per day, respectively" (CDC.gov). A large number of college students have been there, heard those definitions, and exempted themselves from the findings. They laughed, much like you probably did, but the scary thing is, the moment you leave college, you get slapped in the face with the terrifying reality. Anyone that's graduated can tell you that.

What's actually *astonishing*, in every sense of the word, is how quickly recent graduates recognize how horrific their drinking habits in college were. Every year, I again experience firsthand evidence of how true this is. I have volunteered as a commencement assistant for several years, meaning every graduation day I am out on the quad assisting almost-alumni with seat assignments, building designations, and the like. As you can imagine, I see several of my former athletes donning cap and gown, and we'll often get to talking. What is shocking, unsettling, and distressing to hear is when they tell me, "I can't believe how much I used to drink in college. I'm so excited to get out of here so I can stop drinking!" *Oh the irony!* And on the **day of** graduation, no less! Somehow commencement just immediately SLAPS people back into reality, and they promptly no longer associate themselves with that deplorable lifestyle. What's funny is not only do alumni view themselves as instantaneously detached, but those underclassmen who remain in college acknowledge the adjustment as well. Have you ever been at a party where someone that has already graduated walks in? It doesn't matter if that person is two days out of college or two decades, the music skips, the lights turn on, and everyone stares awkwardly at him until he leaves. Seeing an alumnus at an undergrad party is as weird as hearing someone laugh in a bathroom stall.

If it weren't for the bubble of college, most college students would be raging, unabashed alcoholics needing serious and expensive counseling; yet in the bubble, they're par for the course. Waking up with that vague sensation of shame becomes the standard feeling for the average weekend. And no one wonders why. Well, every other college student in America is doing it so *not* doing it would be weird, right? And because students think this, they develop a strong institutional and intuitional pressure to conform to the norms of college.

Solomon Asch conducted a famous experiment that focused on people's adherence to "the norm." What he did was show subjects three lines of obviously different length, then surrounded the subjects with a group of people who insisted the lines were of the same length. When placed in this environment of group pressure, a staggering 70 percent of research subjects went along with the group stating the lines were the same length. Ultimately, only 20 percent refused to conform at all.[247]

These findings are scary, as this is just in relation to something as stupid and arbitrary, not to mention *obvious*, as the length of a line. Only 20 percent said no? Imagine how small this number must be when we're talking about something not obvious, like how many nights per week students should drink, or how much they should consume each night, or how about the fact the people persuading them are not strangers, they're close friends! Conformity is a survival instinct, and it doesn't take much more than social pressure to get you to obey.[248] The environment of college is a destructive place for an athlete to succeed, especially because the people in it refuse to admit they are a part of normal society. Students may *think* they're detached from our culture and our society, but they're already here; they're part of this society whether they believe it or not.

If we know that college students drink mainly because it is perceived as the social norm, then what needs to be changed is the perception of the norm. One set of researchers, H. Wesley Perkins and David Craig, set out to do just that. Through a three-year long, comprehensive set of interventions targeted at student-athletes in regard to social drinking norms, those exposed to the program experienced a 30 percent decline in frequent personal consumption, high-quantity consumption, high estimated peak blood alcohol concentrations during social drinking, and negative consequences after alcohol has been consumed. By intensively and accurately delivering data-based messages about actual peer norms, student-athletes with the highest level of program exposure reported a 50 percent drop of personal alcohol misuse.[249] These findings are incredible as they suggest when students learn that college drinking is not nearly as prevalent as they initial perceive it to be, they will drink less.

With this in mind, it's clear the object should not be forcing staunch, unwavering teetotaling onto athletes; rather, it's simply educating them on what alcohol does in the body. Perhaps with a better understanding of alcohol's relationship to exercise and recovery, an athlete will be more prone to moderate drinking, as opposed to the incontinent behavior of most undergraduates.

How the Body *Should* Feel

JUST A FEW DRINKS CAN affect the body in quite a dramatic way. Because the body perceives alcohol as poison, it doesn't get digested normally; instead, it's absorbed and metabolized *ahead of* most nutrients, thus receiving prioritization to any real food you eat, especially protein.[250] As soon as alcohol makes its way into your stomach, your body does everything it can to eradicate it as quickly as possible, literally treating the booze as a toxin. Regardless if you ate something nutrient-rich or nutrient-poor, your body will first deal with this substance that is nutrient-*empty.* On top of that, testosterone levels in both men and women, which are most affected during training, can be disrupted if alcohol is consumed too early post-workout.[251]

What's even more germane than that is the fact that consuming five or more drinks in one night can affect brain and body activities for up to three days. This means, cognitively speaking, if you party hard on a Saturday night, you will not be back to "normal" until Tuesday. Taking this one step further: two consecutive nights of drinking five-plus drinks can affect brain and body activities for up to *five* days. Therefore, if you go on a bender over the weekend, your body will not be recovered until close to Thursday.[252]

Given a hangover may only last the following morning, the body itself is still not 100% for another day or two; therefore, the competitions or training bouts that fall on those subsequent days will be hindered. Most people that drink have learned *im*plicitly how much they can tolerate without feeling awful the next day, but now they need to learn *ex*plicitly that although they may feel "meh, okay," they are nowhere near 100%.

With this information, it's clear that a large proportion of the student body does not know how good the body *can* feel. If only they could avoid alcohol for a few weeks, they would notice what they've been missing. I make a habit of telling this to college students all the time, and in turn, I routinely get e-mails and phone calls from alumni telling me, "You're right. I can't believe how good I feel now that I stopped drinking so much." Like most undergraduate students, when I was in the environment of college, I didn't think I drank that much. Only once I left school did I cut down and was able to feel *so noticeably different.* I have a memory burn of that epiphany, the same way I remember the street on which I learned to ride a bike and the classroom in which I watched the second plane hit the World Trade Center. The change was profound: it was like I woke up in a different body, as a different person. This feedback is exactly the same I continue to receive from people that lay off alcohol for any prolonged period of time. So many college students don't know that being alive can actually feel good; the lot of them are so sleep-deprived, stress-engulfed, vodka-infested, and vegetable-exempt they don't know how the body is *supposed* to feel. You *should* be invigorated in the morning, energized after each meal, sick very rarely, and physically prepared for any workout. You're in the prime of your life god dammit, and you should be *feeling* it. Instead of just existing in the world, the human body should feel as though it's *thriving!* Without this feeling, college athletes aren't only missing out on a better sporting career, they're missing out on life!

Have you ever thought about how long its been since you were more than a couple days sober? Awhile back, three days after a notoriously alcoholic celebrity died, one of my athletes told me a sick joke:

> Athlete: "Did you hear about [celebrity] dying?"
> *Me: "Yes."*
> "Well, guess what we're celebrating today?"
> *"What?"*
> "She's three days sober!"
> *"Hmm, when was the last time you were three days sober?"*
> "................whoa. I guess a year ago."

For some readers of this book, drinking every three days sounds crazy, but what about every week, or even every two weeks. A very serious question needs to be posed to you, and once you read it, truly stop and consider how you would genuinely respond. Most people that actually take the time to answer this truthfully are mortified at their own response:

When was the last time you were more than two weeks sober?

Historically speaking, most athletes that answer this have responses ranging from a few months to a few years. Plainly, when people drink this much, they have no idea how the body is *supposed* to feel. Just experiencing a day without a hangover is a miracle in itself for some college students, and you don't need to be a scientist to know it's going to be hard to become a great athlete under such circumstances.

There are just too many opportunities for people to go out! Think about it: how many nights a week are there big parties one could attend? Of course there's Saturday, that has always been *the* party night. But don't exclude Friday though, as that is the end of the week and thus the appropriate time to let off some steam. Only recently have college students been able to rid their Fridays of classes, giving them a convenient Thursday night on which to party. And while most people out of the loop think that is the extent of college drinking, Thursday through Saturday, they are forgetting Tuesday Bar Night obviously! So, taking Tuesday, Thursday, Friday, and Saturday into consideration, giving each of them a minimum three-day window of recovery, what are we left with for an optimum training time? Maybe Tuesday afternoon ... right before pub night of course.

By now, maybe you're thinking, "Not me, I only drink once a week," "I never get that drunk," or "I handle my liquor," but what if every member of your team is saying the same thing? One teammate is consistently getting plastered on Tuesday, while another is casually drinking every Thursday. With a schedule like this, the team is never meeting with everyone at 100% strictly because of alcohol, so even the ones that abstain have to get pulled down to an alcohol-dependent's level. When you look at it this way, it seems group workouts could prove to be counterproductive. The players who abstain will be at 100% and be forced to loaf, the inveterate drinkers will tear themselves down, and maybe one or two people in the middle will get an optimum workout. This is just a shame.

While it would be really lovely to end the chapter there, move on, and put some faith in athletes to tone down their drinking, we should probably delve into this a little deeper. At the risk of attempting to manage a problem that we should all be striving to end, we cannot ignore the fact people are going to drink in college. For some, it is extremely hard to avoid. Accepting this as fact forces advocates of teetotaling to get off their high horses and find ways to help people without asking them to completely abstain. So, if you must drink, there are a few rules you should follow, but this in no way is meant to promote athlete alcoholism with the connivance of a strength coach.

If You Must

1. *DO NOT DRINK WITHIN TWO hours post-workout.* As was discussed before, exercise is quite literally a breakdown of muscle tissue — it is catabolic. As soon as you walk out of the gym or off the field, your anabolic phase kicks in, but not for long, as your anabolic system is most active immediately post-workout. You want to do everything you can to assist it during this time, and alcohol is to anabolism as Statler and Waldorf are to optimism. Consuming alcohol after a workout can actually cancel out any physiological gains you might have achieved during the workout.[253] Your body takes care of the poison in your system before it draws any attention toward the healthy stuff in there. Take the time to get your proper post-workout nutrition into your body and fully digested before you get bombed.

2. *Keep caloric intake from booze as low as possible, and avoid congeners.* All the alcohol you imbibe is going to be empty calories: they are not going to make you any better as an athlete. That much is probably obvious. What may not be obvious is that alcohol can provide as much as 20 percent of calories in the diet of some heavy drinkers. There are typically between 100 and 150 calories in each drink, none of which carry any nutritional value.[254] So do what you can to ensure you're consuming the least amount of calories possible: drink only light beers, take shots, order mixed drinks with only club soda or seltzer; avoid soda and juice chasers/mixers like the plague. Also, alcohol stimulates the appetite, so be cognizant of that and perhaps plan ahead by keeping healthier snacks at your house, thereby avoiding the inevitable late-night pizza order. Finally, drinks that contain congeners — minor chemical constituents that add color, odor, and taste — tend to cause worse hangovers than

beverages without them. In a very general sense, darker-colored alcohols like whiskey, rum, cognac and red wine have more congeners than uncolored alcohols like vodka and gin.[255]

    3. *Drink as much water as often as you can while you're out.* You have probably heard this over and over again and have totally disregarded it, but drinking water during a night out is dramatically beneficial. Some athletes that receive the advice to drink water when they're getting hammered complain they won't get as drunk, or they'll look foolish. Oh what adorable little tawpies! First of all, the body still needs to metabolize everything that gets put into it, so it's not like you're going to trick your body into thinking all that liquor is only water. Therefore these people need not fret, they'll still get as drunk as ever. What must be realized though, is that booze dehydrates you. When you drink alcohol, even one beer, your body ends up getting rid of more water than is contained in the drink.[256] Second, if you're worried about what people will think when you get a glass of water at a bar or have a bottle of water with you at a party, chances are, they're not going to think anything. In fact, there have been studies conducted where test subjects blatantly commit faux pas, and the data showed most people don't notice anything at all. Even those that do disregard and forget the imperfections within a few seconds.[257] If you can get over that aspect of it, you will certainly have the last laugh as consuming water during your night out will not only lend you a decreased hangover, but your night will probably go better. Some side effects of dehydration include nausea, fatigue, and changes in body temperature — exactly the side effects of a bad night out.[258] Stay hydrated and you will most likely have a more pleasurable evening, and the potential to have a better workout the following day.

    4. *Track how much money you spend on booze for a month.* One surefire way to open your eyes to how much you're drinking is to focus on how much you're spending. If you're old enough for cab rides to pubs, include that in the cost of drinking as well, considering you likely wouldn't be taking the cab ride if you weren't going somewhere to drink in the first place. And a note to all the women out there that say they'll just let the guys pay for all their drinks: research suggests if a woman allows a man to buy her drinks, she is immediately judged, by both surrounding men and women, as more sexually available to him.[259] Be careful with that.

    5. *Try, just once, a stint of abstinence from booze.* Try, just once, to see what life is like without hangovers. A lot of teams have made pacts to have "dry" post-seasons when they make it into their conference or NCAA

championship brackets, which gives one hope. This shows that not only do most athletes understand how poorly drinking will affect their performance, they're willing to cut it out when the stakes are high enough. But we need to take this a step further. Instead of only having dry *post*-seasons, let's have dry *seasons*. By competing above the pack the whole regular season, your team will be that much better when the post-season arrives.

As it turns out, among the relatively small proportion of athletes who do not use alcohol, health- and performance-related concerns were among the most endorsed reasons for not drinking. One study indicated a total of 65 percent of athletes actually say they drink less in-season than out of season. To go along with that, there are at least five studies confirming alcohol consumption is lower during athletes' competitive seasons.[260] After all, because athletes are mainly only hanging out with their teammates during their season anyway, if everyone else is abstaining too, others won't feel like they're missing out on anything.

This is a great start, and an excellent way to begin to ameliorate the problem with college athletes and drinking. Abstinence is likely not a real world fix; instead, we should be focusing on responsibility and consequences. Depressingly, some teams are incapable of even attempting to back off, but it doesn't have to be that way. All it takes is one person to speak up, one person to suggest this intelligent idea to create a powerful change in his or her team. You can believe every person that has completed a short spell of alcohol abstinence has supplied the same feedback: *incredible*. Most of them admitted they had no idea they could feel *that* good.

Athletes need to start asking themselves what is more important to them, their love of alcohol or their love of winning, because they are undoubtedly mutually exclusive. You're not an idiot; you know that getting wasted is not good for you. Maybe the benefits of fitting in with your friends outweigh the risks of your goals as an athlete, and if that is the case, you may need new friends. So large an aspect is alcohol in some athletes' lives that if they *don't* drink, they may actually create *more* stress for themselves; if they were to give it up, their worlds would come crashing down. As pathetic as that is, it is true of some readers of this book. Be an individual and make the decision that suits you best, but know that the **only real advice in terms of alcohol is to completely avoid it**. Or, at the very least, don't drink during your season. In college you are going to learn socialization techniques you will use the rest of your life; if alcohol is your crutch, you will unfortunately be looking forward to an adulthood of chronic alcoholism. And if you're one of those people that plans to curb your drinking *after* graduation, what's holding you back from starting now? Take some time to evaluate your connection with alcohol and see if there is anything you can do to start making some changes.

Remember that your goals are performance-based, and if you truly want to succeed, there are some sacrifices you have to make for this short athletic career you have in front of you. You have got the rest of your life to get hamboned, but your sport's duration is pretty short. Just take a couple weeks off and see if it makes you feel as good as it has everyone else who ventures a try.

Five Major Points

- The "bubble" is not a good enough excuse to drink in excess. An alcoholic is an alcoholic.
- More athletes report experiencing alcohol-related "harms" than nonathletes.
- If you drink more than once every two weeks, you don't know how good the body *can* feel.
- Avoid alcohol as often as you can, especially during your competitive season.
- If you must drink, follow the rules:
    1. Don't drink within two hours post-workout.
    2. Keep caloric intake low, avoid congeners.
    3. Drink water as frequently as possible.
    4. Track your alcohol-related expenses.
    5. *Try*, just once, a short period (minimum two weeks) without one sip. See how good you can feel!

Part III

Training

Chapter Eight

Energy Systems

Why Learn Them?

IF THERE IS ONE THING an athlete or coach needs to know about exercise, it's energy systems. Why are they important? Without the capability of pinpointing the energy system your sport requires, you will be unable to train optimally for it. Sure, coaches and athletes can make educated guesses at the types of exercise styles and training techniques they think work best — already they clearly do — but unless they possess even a brief, elementary understanding of the body's three energy systems, their potential for success is greatly diminished.

Your body manages the physical stress of training in one of three systems, and applying that same energy system to your training is a vital part of becoming a successful athlete. Moreover, knowing which energy system is yours will allow you to avoid the other systems that have little or nothing to do with your sport. We don't need science to tell us football lineman shouldn't be running 10K's or that cross country runners shouldn't be bench pressing 350 ... With such extreme examples, it's easy to laugh, but there are scenarios much like these playing out at your school right now that are less extreme, nevertheless ridiculous.

Where you'll find the most severe cases of athletes training outside their energy systems is in the way certain coaches "test" their athletes before their competitive seasons. Just thinking logically, it sounds reasonable that volleyball players should be tested on their vertical jumps, baseball/softball players on their time to run to first base, and basketball players on their ability to dribble and run with the ball. But again, high emotions tend to overshadow intellect; therefore, it's inexcusably *commonplace* to see these aforementioned athletes tested on their ability to run a fast mile, to sprint their stadium steps, or even to do push-ups to failure. While it is completely agreeable that those capable of running a mile in five and a half minutes are "in shape," one could challenge if the shape in question has anything to do with their sport. Sure, a fast mile run is hard and may be a good gut-check for athletes, but as we'll learn, that gut-check may be costly, and could be doing a lot more harm than good. While it's obvious that each sport demands very specific and distinguishable traits from its athletes, what is not obvious is the fact that when athletes do not train specifically for their sport, they could be hindering their skills. As it turns out, that mile-long gut-check is the death-knell of these athletes' strength and speed.

The goal of this chapter is to teach you how to make informative decisions about the type of training you do, and avoid activities that may take away from your athletic prowess. By the end of this section, you should be able to answer the question: is my training consistent with my sport's needs by mainly adhering to my sport's energy system? Your coaches, whether it be team coaches or strength coaches, will most likely put you through all types of different training, demanding your body to endure all three energy systems. A *short* exposure to each is part of being a well-balanced athlete, and with one exception, you should not completely avoid any energy system. No matter who you are, though, the vast majority of your training should be done within the confines of your specific energy system.

Finally, before we delve into the specifics, there must be an issuance of a warning clause: information about these energy systems can get extremely, overwhelmingly scientific when studied in textbooks, but what you'll find in here is fairly simple. Also, understand that all three energy systems are at play at any given time, but the extent to which one is *dominant* depends on the intensity and duration of the activity. We will go through these three energy systems one at a time, with the objective being to introduce the basic structure of each of the three energy systems and open your eyes to the important differing characteristics.

Creatine Phosphate System: *Strength*

A GOOD WAY TO START is to point out something relatively obvious: the intensity of muscle contractions is directly related to the intensity of the activity, and exercise intensity is also directly related to exercise duration. When you think about it, any athlete working at their highest intensity can only do so for a few seconds, whereas if one were to exercise at a low intensity, he or she could go for hours.[261]   This inverse relationship between intensity and duration is basically the way all these energy systems are defined. When we start any exercise, say running, we are able to exert our maximum capacity. The first approximate 40 to 60 yards of a drill could be run at 100% of our possible speed, but if we continue to run past there, we will no longer be running at 100% speed. As any exercise prolongs, we must yield intensity in order to endure the duration.

What we'll discuss first is the energy system that is used for the very beginning of exercise, but one final thing must be made clear: when we're talking about intensity, we are *not* talking about effort. Yes, you can run as hard as you possibly can for five miles and die at the end of it due to your effort, like Pheidippides, but only the first few seconds could be run at your fastest *possible* speed — anything after that, undoubtedly you're slower.

So, this first energy system, the one that allows us to yield our maximum capacity, is known as the Creatine Phosphate System (CP), and is the primary energy system for anything lasting zero to six seconds, especially if the intensity is extreme. At such high intensity levels, the exclusive source of energy is muscle glycogen, a form of glucose, which is a form of sugar, which is a form of carbohydrate.[262]   Take notice that you can't be a CP athlete if you're on one of these anti-carbohydrate diets, and as we'll discover in the next sections, you can't be any kind of athlete without carbohydrates. For now though, what's important is that in order to exert maximal effort, athletes *must* use their CP system, which *must* use carbohydrate as its energy source (a table can be found in a few pages that compares intensity to macronutrient usage).

Creatine Phosphate provides the energy for any initial muscular contraction and without it, there would be no human movement.[263] Right now, as you sit still and occasionally raise your arm to turn the page, *that's* the CP system at work.   More relevant to us though is CP's involvement in sport, which is basically any moment you are operating near or at 100% of your potential.   In essence, any sport that has very short, extreme bursts of action followed by relatively longer rest intervals primarily depends on the CP system. Consider the sports involved here: short sprints, heavy weight training, football, diving, volleyball, throwing sports, high jump, long jump, etc.   True exposure to the CP system, meaning an extremely short, yet intense activity followed by a lengthy rest period, allows one to exert near-maximal muscle contractions.[264] For this reason, **CP provides the most capacity for strength**.

Your CP system can only last you about six seconds, which is the very reason you cannot maintain your maximal strength for very long. This is an important fact to keep in mind, as you are only capable of being at your strongest or your fastest for a few seconds. As you push past the six-second barrier, you must inevitably relinquish your intensity and move onto the next energy system. And before we move onto that next system, one other thing to remember is that in order to get to the second or third energy system, we must always begin with CP. Why does this matter? Well, because every athlete starts their sport in CP, every athlete could benefit from some exposure to training the CP system specifically. This would roughly translate to heavier weight lifting, short sprints, or jumping drills, depending on your sport.

After learning about Creatine Phosphate, many athletes begin considering the supplementation of creatine due to the name of this important energy system. While creatine is certainly vital for athletes, it is not necessary to supplement. Creatine aids this system dramatically and without it, the system could not function, but athletes consume plenty of creatine already. The sources of creatine are almost exclusively limited to animal products (red meat and fish, yet the cooking process destroys most creatine stores in foods — enter sushi), but that does not mean you have to be a carnivore to maintain a healthy amount of creatine in the body. Creatine can be "synthetically produced" in the body using amino acids found in many plants, and even vegetarians often do not suffer from creatine deficiency. So, if you are a full omnivore, eating a wide-ranging diet of meat and fish and plants, you're more than likely fine.   If you're a pescatarian eating sushi on occasion, you are also probably good. If you're a vegetarian and are smart about the way you eat, still you'd be silly to supplement creatine. But finally, if you are a vegan or a really bad vegetarian (eating french fries and mashed potatoes all day), then maybe you'd have a leg to stand on in regard to a reason for creatine supplementation.

Glycolytic System: *Speed*

BECAUSE NO ATHLETE CAN HOLD their maximum intensity for very long, due to the short duration of the CP phase, the Glycolytic System must take over as the duration endures past six seconds, and intensity lessens. At the 30-second mark of exercise duration, glycolysis reaches its peak then gradually loses steam as the third energy system ramps up to endure longer exercise bouts.[265] The Glycolytic System is responsible for activities lasting between six seconds and roughly two minutes. Given these time parameters, we could deem this the energy system most closely related to speed. While speed has many subcategories — such as detection and reaction to a stimulus, agility, acceleration, maximum velocity, and speed endurance — one would still identify most speed training as glycolytic-dominant.[266]

Because the exercise intensity can't be at 100% due to the duration, the typical intensity of the Glycolytic System is probably somewhere between 70 and 90 percent. As it happens, the reliance on carbohydrate as an energy source in this system is roughly the same: 70 to 90 percent carb usage. In short, during low-intensity exercise, fats predominate as the primary energy source, and the reliance on carbohydrates increases as exercise intensity increases.[267] As we saw with CP, when the intensity is 100%, so is the carbohydrate usage; similarly, with the Glycolytic System, the carbohydrate usage matches the intensity.

To pinpoint the sports occurring in this system, we have to think of ones that float around this intensity level. The activity has to last between six seconds and two minutes, thus the sport has to be marked by bursts of action followed by short periods of rest. Given that description, it would be safe to say most ball sports occur predominantly in the Glycolytic System, including, but not limited to, basketball, soccer, tennis, hockey, lacrosse, rugby, and middle-distance races in track and field.

Several athletes from these sports have a hard time believing this is their energy system, especially if they play the whole game. They reasonably think that because a half lasts roughly thirty minutes, and they're moving the whole time, how could they possibly be a Glycolytic-athlete? The truth is athletes from these sports aren't running the entire time, rather their motion could be better characterized by bursts of energy followed by short rest intervals. Very few sports, in fact, incorporate constant motion, as those sports are set aside for those truly willing to tolerate agony.

Oxidative System: *Endurance*

FOR THOSE OF YOU ENDURING pain the longest, the final energy system is your kingdom. Distance runners, swimmers, rowers, and cyclists endure straight through the first two systems and utilize an energy store that is nearly limitless: the Oxidative System. The oxidative energy system yields the least amount of intensity, but if trained properly, this system can allow athletes to endure almost indefinitely.

Due to the nature of the Oxidative System, in the sense that it is used when the activity endures past two minutes, there is no opportunity for high intensity work. To put it more scientifically, intensity and volume are inversely related.[268] Athletes cannot hold their maximum speed or strength for more than a few seconds, and as the duration prolongs, their maximum potential *must* diminish. As the intensity lessens, carbohydrates are used less and less, as well. At very low intensity levels, say 25 percent of max, most of the energy your body uses is derived from fat, and as the intensity increases to 50 percent of max, fats and carbohydrates split the energy usage about 50/50.[269] Yet again, we see how important carbohydrates are for athletic endeavors.

Intensity	Energy System	Carbs as Energy Source	Fats as Energy Source
25%	Oxidative	~ 25%	~ 75%
50%	Oxidative	50%	50%
70%	Glycolytic	70%	30% or less
90%	Glycolytic	90%	10% or less
100%	CP	100%	0%

Williams (2005:124) & Carmichael (2004:22)

On top of the importance of carbohydrates, we must also recognize the importance of rest for non-oxidative athletes (meaning CP or Glycolytic athletes). Think of it this way: if your body, chemically-speaking, cannot maintain its potential to be at 100% speed or 100% strength without short rests, it is vital athletes make short breaks for themselves during games, practices, or training in general. Whether this means calling time-out or pulling yourself out — even for 30 to 60 seconds — brief rests like these will save you for the fourth quarter. Oxidative athletes need not be concerned about this due to the nature of their energy system; they only need to be concerned with learning how to tolerate pain.

Below you'll see a rudimentary graph that expresses how the three energy systems balance themselves out over the duration of any given activity. Creatine Phosphate starts off booming at 100% right off the bat and has an extreme fall-off almost instantaneously. The Glycolytic System ramps up until around 30 seconds, where it then steadily loses steam as the Oxidative System works to take over. Somewhere between 90 seconds and two minutes, the two energy systems switch places, and finally the Oxidative System endures for any duration thereafter.

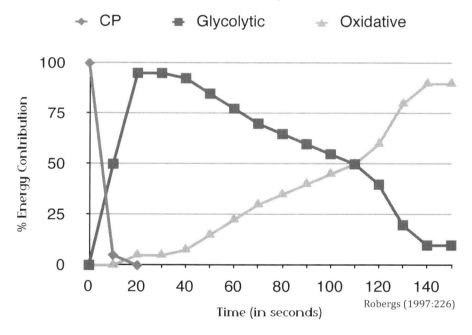

Robergs (1997:226)

Comparing and Contrasting

TAKE THE TIME TO DETERMINE the physical demands of your sport, and attempt to apply them to one of these three energy systems. Once that is accomplished, you have a very basic model of how your training should be structured. Whatever energy system your sport utilizes, that is the energy system where you should be spending most of your training time. That said, all athletes can benefit from a short exposure to the other types of energy systems, but the subjection to them should be fairly minimal and far away from their competitive seasons.

Knowing the relationship between these three energy systems is *critical* if one is to truly excel in his or her sport. The next step in understanding energy systems is learning that while strength, speed and endurance don't *exactly* correspond to the energy systems of Creatine Phosphate, Glycolytic and Oxidative respectively, their relationship is strong. So now we beg the question: which energy system helps you the most?

Duration	Intensity	Primary System
0-6 seconds	Very Intense	Creatine Phosphate
6 sec. to 2 min.	Moderate	Glycolytic
2+ minutes	Light	Oxidative

Baechle (2000:83)

First, let's consider strength's impact on speed and endurance. Without using any science, just mull over this concept: over the course of the next month, nothing changes about your current workout regimen, except for the fact that you get stronger. Will this extra strength help or hurt your speed? Will it help or hurt your endurance? For both, the answer would be help, and it's not a hard sell. Remember that in order to get to the Glycolytic and Oxidative systems, athletes must go through their CP system first. In addition to that, consider this: if Jim can squat 500-lbs and Ryan can only squat 200-lbs, which one of them can squat 50-lbs more times? Because it's such a light weight, both of them will endure longer than a few seconds, thus entering their other energy systems, but who wouldn't put their money on Jim? With this logical rationale, it is safe to say that most, if not all, athletes can benefit from an exposure to at least *some* CP training.

Moving on, we must now appraise the value of speed in regard to strength and endurance. Again, consider that month of training: this time, nothing has changed about your workout program except for the fact you have become much quicker/faster. Will this extra speed help or hurt your strength? What about your endurance? These are tougher questions, as speed's effect on strength and endurance is highly objectionable and would vary considerably depending on the type of speed training. With that in mind, it would be hard to argue that speed work would *impede* strength or endurance. Therefore, while speed's positive effects are not as great as strength's, it's reasonable to say all athletes should be exposed to speed training at some point during their training year.

Finally, we come to the main purpose of this chapter, which is to discuss the repercussions of the oxidative system. **Endurance work, i.e. training in the Oxidative System, not only fails to assist other physical qualities, it actually *hinders* them.** While resistance training adaptations can help everyone, even improving the "kick" of endurance athletes, aerobic endurance training, in fact, may actually compromise resistance training. Studies have shown that oxidative stress may actually promote a decrease in muscle fiber size, and in the process take away from athletes' strength and speed.[270] Prolonged exercise is also accompanied by decreases in the body's skeletal muscle and liver glycogen stores[271] — the exact mechanisms that separate elite athletes from the rest. To put it simply, endurance training ruins athletic ability.

Stop the LSD

THERE ARE THOUSANDS OF PEOPLE out there that love or *"need"* to go for runs, or elliptical, or bike, or whatever it is. They believe so strongly in the benefits of distance training and have become so emotionally attached to it, it has become like a religion to them. The hard truth, however, is that while religions are deeply-rooted and perpetuated through beliefs, training is supposed to be the opposite. All training techniques should have a lot of clout and reasoning behind them, and most importantly, they should be science-based, not emotion-based. And the science is very clear: distance training hinders strength and speed.

Everyone is born with a mixture of fast-twitch muscle fibers and slow-twitch muscle fibers, and they are rarely distributed evenly. The fast-twitch muscles respond to short, intense bouts of training, while the slow-twitch are built to endure lower intensity training for longer periods of time. While it is certainly true that some people are more biologically built for certain types of training, athletes can *promote* one muscle type over the other through deliberate training, and can, in effect, out-train their own biology.[272] If, however, they are consistently training the *wrong* fiber type, at least in relation to their sport, or they are training each one evenly, there can be no distinct change in their chemistry. In short, you cannot train two different disciplines at the same time.

Most people do not know this, however, and they've established many emotional counter-arguments. Most notably, athletes do not believe these results apply to them because they correspond to nothing in *their* experience. *They've* gone for runs their whole athletic vocation, and *they've* been successful, so who the hell is to tell them what they're doing doesn't work? A typical response to this is that while these athletes may have been successful doing things their way, the science is still very clear, and if they were to cut out this detrimental element of their training, they could be vastly *more* successful! Sure, it's possible to go for long runs and still be *somewhat* fast at quick sprints, but the point is there is more to gain by cutting the long runs out.

And if the science isn't enough to convince nay-sayers, we can resort to anecdotal evidence. One of the best real-life, anecdotal indicators of how poorly long, slow distance (LSD) training relates to sport can be found when you look at two-sport athletes at the collegiate level, or even the high school level. Take a moment to think about the two sports in which these athletes perform: typically, it's football/baseball, field hockey/lacrosse, or something of the like. *Rarely, if ever,* is a two-sport athlete coming from cross country or track and participating in a fast-paced ball game. This is not saying that cross country athletes are incapable of playing other sports, but their energy system promotes no other, therefore they are forced to always compete in distance events.

Another germane nugget of anecdotal evidence comes from simply looking at your playing field or court. Consider this: how far can you actually run in your sport without having to cut, change directions, or stop? Most people can't answer more than 100 yards. So why ever train for it then? Getting even more specific, how many times during play of your sport do you actually reach your all-out, maximum speed? First, remember to get to your maximum speed you're going to need a straight runway to accelerate, then you're going to need to be able to run with no cuts, no distractions, and in a perfectly straight line. Athletes attain their top speed maybe, *maybe* once every game. So what starts to become more and more apparent is that **acceleration and agility are the two defining characteristics of a good athlete, not max speed and endurance**. Not to mention training for endurance takes away from your speed and strength. Consider the table on the next page: with all other variables remaining constant, a positive three being great and a negative three being miserable, the basic relationship between strength, speed, and endurance demonstrates that if all other variables remain constant, adding strength and speed training to any athlete's regiment is a good idea, whereas adding endurance training to non-endurance athletes is a very bad idea.

	Strength	Speed	Endurance
Strength	+3	+2	+1
Speed	+1	+3	+1
Endurance	-3	-2	+3

Now, of course, there is no Archimedean point outside of ourselves from which we can view the absolute truth, but *science* does offer itself as the best tool for fashioning provisional truths. Everyone's reality does not deserve respect, and anecdotal associations that form faulty conclusions are all too common. Just because you heard someone's long distance running made them a better field athlete, how can you tell for sure? The only surefire method of proper pattern recognition is science. Only when a test group is compared to a control group can we draw valid conclusions, and sometimes not even then. Luckily for us, the question of endurance training has been tested, and there is no room for debate here; the science is clear. Long, slow distance impedes strength and speed. No athlete that plays a ball sport should be caught in flagrante delicto LSD running, biking, or ellipticalling. Plain and simple.

This is mainly for the girls out there, the ones that run and elliptical every other day so they don't get "chubby" or "bulky:" you're killing your athletic ability. For starters, there's no way you are getting fat. While you participate in the intense training of a sport, it's going to be tough, if not impossible to put on additional fat. If, however, this is happening beyond a shadow of a doubt, first take a look at your diet, as that will be the largest contributor to weight loss or gain. Cut out the sweets, soda, and caffeine, and start eating less, more frequently. Better health is often the result of small, frequent meals.[273]

Most people attempt to counter science's anti-LSD policy by stating that going for long runs or bike rides keeps them "in shape," or better yet, it keeps them "healthy." While it's true these modes of LSD are great ways to stay heart-healthy in the future, your goals are not health-based at the moment, they are *performance*-based. Moreover, that extra long running is highly likely to make you overtrained, thus putting you out of shape and closer to injury than to health.

And if you haven't been completely swayed yet, remember this undeniable point: your field is small. Think about the longest you could *possibly* run in one continuous straight line without having to stop, or cut, or change direction at all. Even if you consider the full length of your field, corner-to-corner, is there *ever* really an opportunity for you to run that distance without decelerating, accelerating, cutting, or stopping? Of course, the answer is no. Respectfully, why you would ever train for it then?

If however you think the answer is yes, yes you are running all over your field or court constantly, then let's pause and consider what you actually mean. While it's true you may be running all over all the time, more specifically you are probably running back and forth and back and forth and back and forth across the center line with bursts of speed here and short rest intervals there. This is undeniable; look closely. The absolute best way to see this is to watch game film of only one player. Don't just watch how much running is happening during the game in general, be specific. Keep your eye on only one member of the team and within a few minutes the evidence will be before your own eyes.

In fact, if you want to see this right now, there was a documentary made about one of the greatest soccer players in history, Zinedine Zidane, called *A 21st Century Portrait* that displays this rather well. Seventeen cameras follow Zidane for every minute of a 2005 match between Real Madrid, for which he was playing, and Villarreal. Throughout the entire documentary, the camera barely pans off of him to view the rest of the game and you just get to see Zidane and his actions, which eventually lead to one epic assist and one comical red card. Most importantly, though, you get to watch a highly skilled athlete *move*. And even though Zidane is one of the greatest players of all time, even though he is without a doubt a play-maker and integral to the game, it cannot be argued that he's walking or moderately jogging the *vast* majority of the game. What one *can* see watching this film is a player sprinting only so many yards then stopping, cutting hard, trying to make a play, walking, jogging, walking, accelerating, sprinting, then stopping, cutting, and walking again. What one can *not* see is a guy running at a constant speed the whole game, or even for more than a few seconds. Find your sport's version of the Zidane film and base your training on that evidence. You want to become a good mid-fielder? Running LSD is not the answer; instead, it's doing drills that get you to stop, cut, and accelerate as you would in a game.

Alternatives

LONG, SLOW DISTANCE TRAINING IS actually rarely done because people think they *need* it for their sport. Most of the time, it's done in an effort to be healthier, or to look better — a very emotional type of training indeed. A lot of athletes gauge their entire self-confidence based on how fast they can run one or two miles. Once you can run any distance fast, you become anchored to that idea and it will be difficult to accept any regression.   Furthermore, if anecdotal evidence isn't enough, many psychological studies have proven that once we do become anchored to a high standard, we fail to accept lower ones in the future.[274]   So perhaps we cannot completely kick the bad habit; instead, we should replace it.

To do that, let's start with the ideal: true speed work. If you need to run more and accept you cannot be doing LSD, then the best things to do are quick sprints with quick cuts and sharp executions: awkward starts (e.g. starting a sprint lying on your stomach or on your back), ladder drills, cone drills, hurdle drills, plyometrics, etc.   This type of training is very sport-specific, and thus, would be the best type of additional running one could add to his or her routine.

If this isn't a proper replacement of your LSD habit, however, and you still feel the urge to run distance, then your only other choice is interval training. Get on the treadmill, the bike, the elliptical or whatever for as long as you want, but never allow yourself to go the same pace for more than 30 consecutive seconds (because of the confines of the Glycolytic System). If you're running outside, sprint from one telephone pole to the next, then jog for the next two. If you're on a stationary bike, go 30 seconds heavy resisted, then 30 seconds fast-paced with no resistance, then ride easy for 60 seconds before repeating. Mix it up any way you want, but LSD can no longer be a part of your training; **interval work could be the best alternative**.[275]

Interval training has been researched since the 1930s, after being meticulously studied by German track coach Woldemar Gerschler and physiologist Hans Reindell.   What these two discovered is that after dozens of repeated sprints (typically 200 meters or less), with increasingly regimented rest intervals, the pumping power of the heart had improved better than it did with any other exercise.   Gerschler entitled this method "interval training" because he and Reindell noticed the cardiovascular improvement typically occurred during the rest interval between the sprints. This new idea would assist Gerschler's 1938 athlete Rudolph Harbig run a 1:46.6 800-meter dash, a world record that would stand for 16 years.[276]

What's important to take from this is how the rest interval is what allowed runners to improve. Gerschler and Reindell would watch the runners go all out, then not allow them to sprint again until their pulse had returned to 120 beats per minute or less.[277] Although we may not want to get that specific with our own training, we must learn from their research (and certainly what has come after theirs) and replace any LSD training with intervals. This is no longer a debated idea among strength and conditioning professionals, and the hope is that more athletes and coaches will subscribe to this soon.

Although after all this, perhaps some still disagree. There is undoubtedly a core group of people who will read all that and will refuse to believe it. To those people, I'll offer this: you're wrong.

This is not a theory or a fad or the next big thing; this is science. Science is an empirical endeavor that is elitist dominated by Ph.D. researchers, kinesiologists, and athletic trainers — not a bunch of non-credentialed amateurs.   Scientists assume the null hypothesis that oxidative training does not aid in development of strength and speed *until proven otherwise*; fad starters reject the null hypothesis and base their arguments on emotion and the potential to make money. Science is grounded in induction, the process of drawing generalized conclusions from specific findings, from data to theory; DVD sellers work with deduction, making specific statements from a generalized source, or from theory to data. People like this perform studies to show how their predictions are right, whereas the scientific method consists of procedures designed to show that their hypotheses might be wrong. The physicist Richard Feynman echoed this principle of science well when he said:

> If it disagrees with experiment, it's wrong. In that simple statement is the key to science.   It doesn't make any difference how beautiful your guess is, how smart you are, who made the guess, or what his name is. If it disagrees with experiment, it's wrong. That's all there is to it.[278]

After all, you cannot know with undoubted certainty that a proposition is true; all you can really *ever* know is if it is untrue. As David Hume wrote, "No amount of observations of white swans can allow the inference that all swans are white, but the observation of a single black swan is sufficient to refute that conclusion."[279] So while you certainly can find successful speed/strength athletes that persistently train long distance, that is not enough to prove the theory.

Understanding the confirmation bias and how the mind yearns for consonance — often rejecting information that questions our beliefs — should teach us to be open.[280]   Despite what we have been told to believe, we must accept we live in the Age of Science, where beliefs are supposed to come from empirical data and rock-solid evidence. The best part is that anyone can come up with alternative theories, provided they have empirical ways to test their theories and back them up. What's most important here is that you do not allow yourself to be swayed when you hear about how great LSD is.   Stick to your guns and proclaim the significance of science over opinion!

Perhaps the most powerful example of someone choosing science over tradition is when Galileo was forced to recant his belief that the earth moves around the sun. After publicly apologizing and taking back everything he had observed about heliocentricity in order to appease the Church and its traditional belief that our planet was immobile, he ultimately showed commitment to observation over authority when he muttered about the Earth, "Eppur si muove" — *and yet it moves*.[281]

We all must take a page out of Galileo's book, and find the power we can attain through knowledge. What cannot be stressed enough is the importance of understanding *your* particular position in *your* particular sport. Watch game film more often, and determine the specific characteristics of your role in the game, then apply them to your training. Your intensity, your amount of rest, and your total time spent training should all be relevant to your sport.   To most, this is very sound, reasonable advice that is fairly easy to follow. Yet there are some that will remain skeptical. When information like this comes around and contradicts one's firmly entrenched views, it is easy to turn a blind eye. After all, evolution has wired us to care more about what we already have than what we might possess in the future;[282] the longer we hold onto a belief and the more we have invested in it, the more we endow it with value and the less likely we are to give it up. We are all guilty of this to some extent, especially when it comes to training, but do not let your skepticism become an excuse for your continuation of unwise training methods. Abstain from all things not relevant to you as a one-of-a-kind athlete, because the best way to be successful in your sport is to train as closely pertinent to that sport as possible, and the best way to do that is to remain in your specified energy system.

Five Major Points

- Identify your sport's energy system, then train within the confines of it as often as possible.
- Nearly every athlete could benefit from a short exposure to the CP and Glycolytic systems (roughly translating to lifting and running sprints).
- Endurance work not only fails to assist other physical qualities, it actually *hinders* them.
- Never perform long, slow distance unless you are that type of an athlete. Intervals may be the best alternative.
- Carbohydrates provide most of the energy for the majority of sports, so do not avoid them.

Chapter Nine

The Imbalance of Sport

Sports are Dangerous

ULTRA-SUCCESSFUL ATHLETES ARE ALL alike; every unsuccessful athlete is unsuccessful in his or her own way. To some of you, this might sound a little familiar, as it is an amended version of Leo Tolstoy's first line in *Anna Karenina,* "Happy families are all alike; every unhappy family is unhappy in its own way." What Tolstoy was getting at is that to be happy and successful at any great endeavor, whether it be cultivating a strong family or in our case, a strong body, it takes an exorbitant amount of effort and requires us to simultaneously succeed at several different disciplines. Tolstoy thought that all happy families have a couple at the head of it that are sexually attracted to one another, they share the same values and methods of parenting, they enjoy spending time together, etc. In contrast, he argued, all unhappy families are different in the ways that they've failed. Some share the values system, but lack the sexual attraction, others just the opposite. Why they are unhappy is always a case-by-case scenario. The "Anna Karenina Principle" attests to the broad idea that in nearly all situations in life it is possible to fail in many ways, but to succeed in only one: by means of avoiding each possible route to failure.

This principle is a little discouraging when applied broadly as it invokes the idea only one of our threats to success needs to be present to bring us down. Ultra-successful athletes are mostly cookie-cutter models of the same defining qualities: they work really hard, they have sacrificed what could have stood in their way, they constantly focus on winning at the expense of everything else, and they believe every facet of their lifestyle to be driving toward their ultimate success. This is a deplorable, yet ultimately truthful conclusion to be made, but let's quickly remember one thing: most people reading this book do not aspire to be medal-finalists in the Olympics, merely just successful in college. This is a much easier goal where mistakes can be afforded; we just need to know which ones.

Training just happens to be one of those fields with some gray area. Provided athletes are working out "balls-to-the-wall," they almost can't go wrong! That said, we should recognize the important differences between training for sport and training for health or vanity. There are considerable differences in regard to difficulty, stress on the body, and safety. And while exercising for health is the easiest, least stressful, and most invulnerable to injury, training for athletic performance is certainly the opposite.

Sports are dangerous. Contact sports are unsafe for obvious reasons, but even those with little or no contact yield opportunities for injury all the same. Think about this: when people expend all of their energy into one motion repetitively, inevitably that motion becomes stronger, more accurate, and arguably safer. So the more baseball players swing their bats, the more volleyball players spike volleyballs, and the more hockey players crush slapshots, the better off that motion will become. *However,* while the muscles responsible for those motions become stronger, the ones acting in direct opposition to those muscles inevitably become weaker by comparison. The imbalance of these opposing muscle groups is what makes all sports eventually dangerous.

To understand this, let's use the example of the baseball pitcher, one of the more commonly injured athletes one may encounter over the course of a year. When a pitcher becomes injured, do you know what muscles are usually hurt? Rotator cuff. Think about where the rotator cuff is (on one's back, identical on both sides, right around the scapulae bones). Does this muscle have anything to do with a baseball pitch? No, except that it is acting in direct opposition to the muscles actually performing the throwing motion (primarily the pectoral muscles of the chest). This is exactly why a good baseball lifting program does not include a lot of bench press, but rather incorporates a surplus of rotator cuff exercises in an attempt to even out an imbalanced body.

Every sport out there has similar qualities that create discrepancies in the body, thus making the sport dangerous. Consider the sport you play, and what disparities it creates in your body. Does it have a positional stance (e.g. football linemen, hockey players)? Does it have a predominant motion (e.g. all stick/racquet sports, volleyball, basketball)? Do you use your dominant side more often than not (e.g. almost all sports)? The more often you train specifically for your sport, the more often these imbalances get promoted, and the more likely you are to become injured due to that imbalance.

The body craves symmetry, and yet most sports promote asymmetry — whether right to left, or front to back, or commonly both. Thus, **the number one reason to lift weights should be in an attempt to rebalance the body.** Failing to realize this can easily exacerbate the problem(s) your sport is creating. Athletes or coaches that do not recognize this fact often overtrain the exercises they should be limiting (predominantly bench press as most chests overpower most backs as it is), which is why it is so important to be educated about this stuff.

A seemingly reasonable, verisimilar counterargument to this is that if the sport requires a lot of pushing (e.g. checking in stick sports, football linemen, etc.), why wouldn't an athlete of that sport want to be good at the bench press? A strong bench, they argue, would translate to a powerful push on the field. No one could disagree with this, and those making that argument would be right to assume a strong bench press can and will aid in a push-dominant sport. But we mustn't forget most athletes in these types of positions are already exposed to a lot of pushing, which has in turn placed their shoulders in an unhealthy position. If a season of a sport lasts four to five months, that means a third to almost a half of an athlete's year is spent pushing and pushing and pushing. Thus, when they finally reach their off-season, they're going to need to do a lot of pulling just to get close to a healthy equilibrium. Although they certainly need to train the bench press, pull-dominant exercises need to be *prioritized* in an attempt to rebalance their shoulders.

In the end, however, lifting will never be able to keep up with sport. No matter how much people train in the gym, they will never match how much they train for their sport — nor probably should they. What this means is athletes, as long as they're training for their competition, will always be flirting with disaster. Sports create imbalances in everyone, and one's likelihood of injury simply comes down to how their body copes with the disparities.

For many sports, the imbalances are easy to see, and the more you look, the more you'll notice. Baseball and softball players have disproportionate shoulders, hockey players stand with bowed knees, swimmers develop intensely arched low backs ... the list is endless. Once athletes get into their respective seasons, their sport will start to take its toll on their bodies. Because each position requires a very unique skill set, it will naturally build strengths and weaknesses in the body. Stick and racquet sports, in particular, develop outrageous disparities between left and right sides. Unbidden though they might be, these imbalances develop in every position of every sport.

One could easily have first-hand experience of this simply stealing a glance at nearly any athlete at his or her school. Take Brittany here for example. Just looking at her at a glance, you won't notice much, except a healthy 20-something female ... but at closer inspection, there is a lot happening here.

As a practiced, national championship-winning field hockey player, Brittany spends copious hours of her year, whether passing with  friends or ripping shots in games, holding her field hockey stick, haunched over. Over time, this position becomes such second-nature to her, her body eventually develops its muscle tissue to mimic this posture.

Although holding a field hockey stick may feel very natural to Brittany, this position is extremely unnatural for the human body. Just looking at that picture of her with her stick, it is apparent how disproportionate her body must behave while she practices or plays her sport. Over time, without any doubt, her body will surely adapt.

To hold her stick appropriately, Brittany's left shoulder must be higher than her right, and her right hand be more externally rotated than her left. Looking at this picture of her standing without a stick, one can easily see how much lower her right shoulder lies, and how much more internally rotated her left hand rests. No surprise. She can't spend two hours a day, six months a year in the same position without her body molding itself into that posture permanently!   While her hands and shoulders show obvious discrepancies between left and right, these same imbalances can be viewed in her feet, knees, hips and back. Full disclosure: I specifically chose an athlete with *minimal* imbalances so it would require readers to focus intently to see the discrepancies.

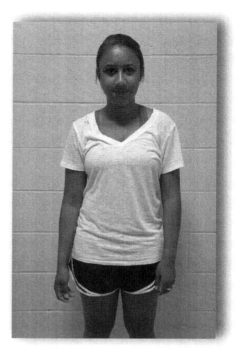

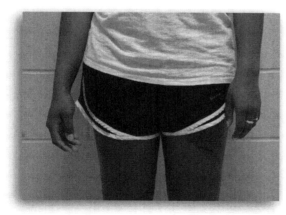

Many athletes have far greater disparities than Brittany here, and if you look in the mirror, you'll probably see it.   These problems in athletes' postures must be coped with frequently and should not be overlooked, as any inequality in the body yields susceptibility to injury.

Sport's Effect on Posture

WITHOUT QUESTION, SOLVING SOME MINOR imperfections in your posture could result in huge benefits. A good posture aligns your bones properly and allows for muscles, joints, and ligaments to work unfettered. Your internal organs are also assisted into the right position, and can therefore be more effective when standing and sitting properly.[283]   On top of all that, new research suggests our posture could have dramatic effects on our self-esteem and hormones.

Amy Cuddy, a social psychologist at Harvard Business School, gave a TEDTalk in 2012 about her enlightening research in the realm of posture and body language.   Cuddy, in her talk, demonstrates how our body language not only communicates feelings outwardly, but also has a surprisingly potent influence on our own feelings, behaviors, and even hormone levels.   According to her research, holding a "power pose" — a posture that is very open and domineering like standing arms akimbo or reclining in a chair with your hands on the back of your head, elbows wide — for two minutes effectively generated a 20 percent increase in testosterone, and a 25 percent decrease in cortisol (the hormone linked to stress).   Meanwhile, holding a "lower power pose," or a posture that is very small and reserved, produced a 10 percent decrease in testosterone, and a 15 percent increase in cortisol.[284]   Powerful findings for a simple, two-minute action. Just think what could happen if we taught ourselves to stand and sit "powerfully" every minute of every day.

Even as you are playing your sport, or waiting around after a time-out, your body language is speaking volumes about you.   Imagine the psychological difference in the fourth quarter between seeing your opponents hunched over, hands on their knees sucking wind, or standing up straight, unflinchingly rigid.   A superior posture commands respect, and of the 168 hours in a week, the only time your posture is *not* being judged are the 63 hours you're asleep — or supposed to be asleep. Even correcting just a few simple things will not only make you look more athletic and powerful, but you will be healthier as well. Focusing on your posture when you sit, stand, walk, and exercise is not the easiest task, but simply being aware of it is the hardest step to manage.

As you've learned, every sport generates imbalances, and every training program, no matter who wrote it, creates a discrepancy in your body. Earlier, we discussed how most sports contain a larger element of pushing than pulling, and how the muscles in the front of your body overpower those in the back. The more imbalanced the sport or program, and the longer it goes untreated, the greater the disparity in your body. Eventually those shoulders roll so far forward your palms face behind you; this is especially noticeable in meatheads that bench press five times a week. Although it may not seem like a huge deal, these inconsistencies within your muscles leave the door wide open for injury.

Another way that your posture creates itself is by minute experiments with your gait and stance. Say, for instance, that due to your flexibility imbalances it feels better to stand with almost all your weight on your left leg while you turn your right knee out. Because it feels good to stand that way, because that "experiment" of posture worked, your body remembers it and henceforth it becomes a habit. These sort of "experiments," if you will, are happening at all times with your gait, stance, and even skills during sport. If something works for you, your body will remember it. Sometimes they are really noticeable and innocuous like MJ's tongue sticking out while he drives the lane, while others can be much deeper under the surface and may be throwing things off-kilter. This is why we must develop a keen understanding of what a posture should look like.

Now, in order to exhibit this to you thoroughly, we have to get specific. Creating a perfect posture is an exceptionally meticulous activity, but understanding which imbalances create each discordance in your body helps you to tackle them effectively. Taking the upper body chest-to-back example from before, the two major dilemmas we see are that your chest is too tight from overuse, and your back is too weak to compensate. To fix this, there are four major strategies we can employ:

1. *Stretch the tight muscle.* In the chest-to-back example, your chest has literally lost length. Because it has been overworked — at least in comparison to your back — the muscle has become shorter, thus pulling your shoulder forward with it. By spending some time in a static pectoral stretch, you will slowly give length back to that muscle.

2. *Strengthen the weak muscle.* Again, using this same example, your back has not been given a sufficient amount of exercise exposure to counteract the strength of its opposing muscle. By allotting some energy to prioritize pulling exercises over pushing, you will, in time, offset your chest.

3. *Consciously compose yourself in the proper posture.* While the prior two strategies are certain to assist you, they require time set aside to perform. We can relate this back to the 168-hour concept by pointing out no matter how much time you spend stretching the tight muscle or strengthening the weak muscle, what you do outside the gym is going to matter more. There is no doubt that you need to stretch your chest and strengthen your back, but the easiest way to accomplish this simultaneously is to always stand and sit with your shoulder blades pinched together, especially when you're not in the gym. Ideal posture, in your upper body, requires your scapulae, the chicken bones in your upper

back, to be drawn into one another first, then pulled down — we call it "scapulae retraction and depression." Typically, when that's said, people go way overboard and throw their chest up in the sky overconfidently like they just got a boob job, but there is no need to overdo it. Just consciously think about pulling them a little more together and a little farther down toward your bum. Slightly drawing your shoulder blades together has a two-pronged effect: one, it forces your back into muscular action, thus making it stronger; two, it compels your chest to open up, thus making the muscles longer. Jokingly, let's call it "back cleavage." If you're walking around and your back is one smooth surface, something is wrong. You

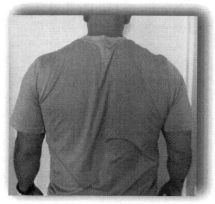

always want to be drawing the muscles together to ensure you've got some ridges and bumps in your back. Not only will you look like a Greek god or goddess doing it, but you will be creating an environment in which your body is less prone to injury.

4. *Turn trivial tasks into exercises.* On top of stretching, strengthening, and standing correctly, you can change the way you do some of your every day tasks to help you progress even quicker! A great way to get some more external rotation work is to put your watch on the other side of your wrist, so the watch face points toward your hip. Now, every time you check the time, you have to rotate your hand out, thus giving you an additional rep of external rotation, or back exercise, for the day!

So far, these recommendations have been dealing with your upper body and the chest-to-back dilemma. Now that you have a grasp on how to deal with that, let's focus our attention to the lower body. Applying the same concepts as before, this time dealing with your hips and hamstrings overcoming your quad and hip flexor strength, you will learn how to stand properly.

We always work from the ground up, as quite often problems in the hip come from a complication in the knee that actually arose in the foot! Again, these recommendations are in no way exhaustive, they are just an attempt to fix some of the easier, commonplace hitches that plague most athletes:

Start by pointing your feet straight ahead. If you only resolve one issue with your posture, make it be this. The positive effects that centering your feet forward have on the rest of your body is pretty nuts. Sometimes simply directing your feet forward solves all the other problems! One way to direct your attention to this would be to buy a few memory-foam floor mats. Put one in front of your bathroom sink, another in front of your kitchen sink, or anywhere else you regularly stand. Not only will your feet and legs feel really good while you stand on them, you won't be able to stop yourself from checking your feet. What you'll notice is that when you're standing on the mat, you might not always be cognizant of where your feet are pointing, but if you briefly step away to return moments later — e.g. cooking at the stove then returning to the sink — you can't help but notice the floor mat's indentations of your feet.

Unlock your knees. Do not misinterpret this to mean "bend your knees." No, just put a little give into them. The stress relief this creates in your low back is monumental. To demonstrate this, jump up and land on locked knees. Doing that, you'll feel the jolt all the way up into your jaw. Conversely, jump and land on knees with a little give in them, and the stress is minimal. While you might deem this example extreme when compared to walking or simply standing, the affect of 20+ years of locked knees adds up.

Suck your stomach, tuck your tail. Just like your shoulders, this doesn't need to be overdone, slightly draw your stomach in a little while attempting to flex your bum underneath you. All athletes with which I work hear me bark at them "SUCK AND TUCK!" The goal here is to create a neutral low back — not arched, not rolled.

Scapulae retraction and depression. "PINCH!" The benefits and reasoning behind this one have hopefully been pounded home to you by now.

The first time you take a glimpse of yourself standing like this you might chuckle. To you, you look different, and change is a terrifying thing to most. The truth is, to others, you look prouder, healthier and able. These are easy fixes, things you can work on all day every day with minimal effort. Every time you stand up from a chair or come to a halt while walking, run through the checklist in your head, "Feet straight, knees unlocked, suck, tuck, pinch." Make that a habit and you will quickly begin to intimidate, even at first glance.

Of course, this may not be as easy as it sounds. For some, standing correctly is a lifelong battle, and for others, it comes very easily. You must realize the harder this is for you, the farther your body is from a safe, correct posture. Your sport will happily take over your body if you let it, and it is up to you, and you alone, to compensate for the discrepancies sports create.

This should be the reason strength coaches have their jobs, and is in fact one of the major reasons for this book. Coaches *should be* hired to keep people healthy, first and foremost, with strength and speed gains being simply byproducts of the health they aim to create. When you can truly rationalize how imbalanced a sport is — and it doesn't matter which sport is in question — you will be able to conceptualize how important your off-season becomes. That is, if you have an off-season.

The Purpose of the Off-Season

I CAN REMEMBER THIS TIME I was in college, eating at the dining hall, when I saw one of the best athletes at my school come in on crutches. She was a volleyball player, and she was damn good. Her specialty was spiking the ball so hard it famously gave girls bloody noses. We secretly called her "The Devastater" and after she would crush one of her spikes during a game, we'd all chant, *"It's not your fault! It's not your fault!"* at the other team because really, there was nothing they could do.

I couldn't believe I was seeing her on crutches, as her senior season was just about to start. She had been working her ass off all spring, and I specifically remember seeing her in the gym nearly every day practicing that devastating blow. Now, right before the season, she's supposed to be the healthiest she's ever been ... How could she be injured now?

The answer to this question is often the same answer to why high school players don't incur more injuries: the off-season. College athletes typically play one sport, and one sport only. Because of that, their entire year of training is devoted to that one, single activity, and the imbalance their sport creates never has an opportunity to be rebalanced. Without ever truly having time away from their sport, they have a hard time keeping their bodies healthy and ahead of the injurious curve.

High school athletes, on the other hand, *rarely* play one sport. They use their off-season time from one sport to play another, thus often correcting (without even them realizing) their respective imbalances. When you think about it, high school kids probably *should* be getting hurt more often than college athletes. After all, they're less experienced, they have less time to practice the right skills, they are basically in-season year round (with different sports), their coaches are (presumably) at an inferior level (with some exceptions) ... So, why aren't they injured all the time? While the body is extremely synergistic, and it would be erroneous to say it all came down to one variable, the fact that they do have months away from their favorite sport certainly plays a major role. On top of this, high school athletes live healthier day to day, and thus their non-injurious health is often taken for granted. As high school coaches, the object is to make the most out of athletes' effort, health being abundant. In college, these values reverse, and the goal is to make the most out of their health, effort being abundant.

The off-season is where this health needs to be regained for college athletes. See, even if high school athletes did want to play football in the spring, or softball in the fall, they'd have little or no options; they're forced to take time off. College players, on the other hand, have a lot more resources and much bigger teams to pull off "captain's practices" to ensure their players are never far from "game shape," despite their season being months away. This is a foolish pursuit. To put it simply, **athletes cannot be in peak performance all year round**. Attempting to maintain that level of athletic capacity will not only make athletes psychologically go nuts, their bodies will physically suffer from it. Although no sane person could recommend this, scientifically-speaking, all athletes need to do is practice their skills at least once a month in the off-season, as skill will evaporate if their circuits are kept from firing for 30 days.[285] Obviously, that would be a benchmark minimum, but you still should be nowhere near where you were during the season. Your goal then is to find a balance between maintaining/improving your skills while allowing your body to physically recover from your season.

Every athletic body needs rest and a reasonable amount of time spent away from their sport. Because of this, it is not all that rare for some athletes to say their personal bests were set in high school. Especially in track and field athletes, where their performances are very easily trackable, college's environment can depreciate athleticism. While the drinking and eating and stress all play major roles, the lack of an off-season is a huge factor as well. This should not be. Obviously, athletes should be getting faster and stronger in college, and most athletes are, but without proper rest and time spent away from their dangerous sports, they'll all eventually suffer.

An athlete by the name of Jack demonstrated this pretty well. Jack was kind of a meathead who used to squat twice a week in his college years and absolutely loved it. For whatever reason, *that* was his thing, and he wanted to do a lot of it. Because this was during college and therefore before he gave a damn about proper recovery or even proper warm-ups, not to mention it was probably during the most unhealthy time of his life, it didn't take long for him to develop some tightness in his quads. In time, he began to suffer from the sharpest, most uncomfortable knee pain. He would complain that he couldn't sit in a chair with his knees bent as that quad stretch, minute as it was, was too much for his tight thighs to handle. To fly on an airplane, he used to buy Exit Row seats only so he could sit straight-legged, and had to travel wearing knee sleeves under his pants. Eventually, it got to the point where he couldn't even do the thing he loved anymore: he got so tight in the quads, he couldn't perform a proper squat. But, being the stubborn type, as most athletic people are, he refused to give it up. Instead he got creative.

This is where most athletes make their errors: even when they *know* something is hurting them, they don't heed the warning. When these problems arise, as they did with Jack and his knees, there are typically three options on the table: 1) stop doing what hurts, at least for a short while, 2) stretch, foam roll, and massage the tight muscles, 3) ignore it, and/or figure out a way around it. Unfortunately, instead of listening to our bodies and abiding by their rules, most athletes choose option three, which is exactly what Jack did. Instead of easing off on squats for a few weeks or stretching more, he just warmed up longer and longer, sometimes up to a full hour before he could squat, to allow himself to keep doing what he wanted.

How did this end? Poorly, as you might imagine. Over time, even his long warm-ups didn't save him, and Jack became essentially crippled. He couldn't do any exercise that required any knee bend (e.g. squat, lunge, deadlift, leg press) and he had to perpetually wear his knee sleeves. Finally, he caved and began to foam roll and paid yours truly to stretch his quads almost every day. But his obstinate experiment cost him. How much? Two years of knee pain, without the ability to run, bike, or lift weights for his legs. Yeah. He couldn't squat for two full years after he finally gave it up. And to this day, Jack still foam rolls and stretches his quads every day so that he can keep doing what he loves. He's happy to report he's back on the squatting horse.

Allow this to be a cautionary tale. While Jack's story and the words before it are not promoting you to avoid the practice of your sport out of season, you just must understand what the off-season is supposed to be about. Correcting the imbalances of your sport will make you much less susceptible to injury, and will, in turn, make you better. You've got to find the right balance between honing your skills and correcting your imbalances, which should be the job description of all strength and conditioning coaches. Unfortunately, most of them instead want their athletes to have strong bench presses and squats at the expense of their overall health. This inadequacy to correct for imbalances is one of the major causes of athletic injury.

Injured Person ≠ Wuss

NOW, REMEMBER THE INJURED VOLLEYBALL player, the Devastater? The Devastater's problem wasn't that she was underprepared or lacked strength — quite the contrary. Her injury occurred because the muscles she needed to be competitive at volleyball became so overdeveloped, her joints and skeletal structure associated with those overpowering muscles were forced into unsafe positions and eventually had to succumb to the stress. This goes against the popular dogma of our little subculture. Typically, when people get injured, the consensus is, "Well they were pansies to begin with and most likely deserved it." The reality often stands in complete opposition to this. Most often, those that get injured are the ones that work the hardest and cross the line from being optimally prepared to overtrained. Chief among the forces affecting injury is work ethic.

The inconvenient truth (trademark Al Gore) is that everyone reading this book has a bit of the stubborn Devastater within them. Everyone trains hard for their sport, becoming stronger and more skilled in the process, yet simultaneously they creep closer and closer to that injury few athletes see coming: the injury of the overtrained. The athletes that maintain their health throughout their college vocation of sport are typically the ones that acknowledge the purpose of their off-season: to rebalance. Whether it be psychologically by taking a few weeks off, physically by stretching more and training their weak muscles, or both, successful athletes recognize their sports are dangerous and take the necessary precautions.

And one final thing should be made clear: your body is your responsibility. If you get injured, at least if you incur a non-contact injury, the blame is all yours. Of course a coach can push you to overtrain, but it is solely on you to keep up with your recovery. Your body doesn't care what you used to be able to do, or what you can normally keep up with, the only thing that matters is how you feel day by day. History is irrelevant in relation to your body, and all that matters are your options <u>now</u>, and their likely consequences. Doesn't it make a lot more sense for you to react to how your body is *genuinely* feeling, instead of how you or your coach think it *should* feel? While it's nice to assume a best-case scenario, there are too many different ways for our plans to fail, and we cannot possibly foresee them all. Every single day there needs to be a reset button pushed that allows us to assess our actual well-being, not just our hopeful vision of ourselves.

If you feel as though your body is no longer able to keep up with your training, or a specific muscle group is getting more and more painful, there is a very simple, eye-opening activity for you. Let's say that your knee is starting to bother you (and this works for any muscle group or joint), and as the days and weeks go by, you notice it is not getting any better — in fact, it's getting worse. What you do then is ask yourself two straightforward questions: what am I doing that's making it worse, and what am I doing that's making it better? Given that the vast majority of pains and injuries athletes incur are results of overtraining, all you need to do is measure out how much training you're doing and compare it to how much recovery you're receiving. Remember, while exercise is of course good for health and athletic abilities and so on, it is certainly bad for a muscle group or joint that is overworked and needs more rest! Use the table on the next page to see some excellent active recovery methods (the best recovery method being passive: sleep).

Active Recovery Methods	Description
Sauna + Cold Shower or Contrast Shower	Sauna for 10-15 minutes, then immediately hurry into a freezing cold shower for 1-2 minutes. After which, you can turn the water onto hot to get more comfortable again. A "contrast shower" is when you alternate hot and cold water in the shower, typically for 1-3 minutes each.
Foam Rolling	Self-massage tight muscles by placing a foam roller on the meat of the muscle and roll your body back and forth over it. Avoid rolling over joints or bones (e.g. knees or backs of knees). Focus on "trigger points," especially if rolling one spot causes pain to radiate to other areas of the body. The pain whilst rolling should definitely be uncomfortable, but not to the point where you have to wince in pain and tense up because of it. Quads and IT bands (front and outside areas of legs) are typically the most bothersome for hard-working athletes.
Stretching	Hold positions for a minimum of 30 seconds, but do not be afraid to expose yourself to durations you've never experienced: it's not unheard of to hold certain positions for 10 minutes or longer. Especially if you can find a way to be comfortable during the stretch, hold it for a long time!
Ice (baths)	Icing is not just for those that are injured. If all athletes lived in a utopia, they would finish all workouts with an ice bath and supplement it with icing sore joints later on throughout that day and into the next.
Hot Tub	While it would be inadvisable for athletes to use a hot tub immediately after a workout, it would be *very* advisable for them to use it at almost any other point during their day or week. Hot tubs are excellent means to relax both the body and the mind.
Floating or Light Swim	Do not swim laps or push yourself in the pool to recover. Find something on which to float or very slowly and very casually swim around for 10 or so minutes.

So, to go back to your hypothetical bothersome knee, all we need to do is count how many hours per week you are running and lifting versus how many hours you are performing one or more of the recovery methods on the previous page. What most people notice is that their "work-to-rest ratio" — the time they spend exercising (thereby exacerbating their problem) versus the time they spend actively recovering — is something like 10:1, and in extreme cases more like 30:1. The table below shows the weekly routine of a fairly average college athlete.

Examples of Weekly Activities	Duration	Work or Rest
Three days of lifting weights	4 hrs total	Work (4 hrs)
Three days of running	3 hrs total	Work (7 hrs)
Walking to class or elsewhere	3 hrs total	Work (10 hrs)
Stretching	45 minutes	Rest (0.75 hrs)
Foam rolling	15 minutes	Rest (1 hr)
WEEKLY TOTALS — WORK: 10 HRS, REST 1 HR, 10:1 RATIO		

Imbalances such as these, especially for injured or ailing bodies, are indefensible. If you are just starting to ache, that ratio needs to get closer to 3:1, if not 1:1. But if you're really hurting and it's beginning to affect your capabilities — like what was happening with Jack and his knees — you need to act fast and turn the priorities in the other direction. Don't wait two years like he did, because by the end of it, his work-to-rest ratio was something like 1:30, and you can trust that rankled. Had Jack acted faster with a ratio of 1:2, he likely still could've trained every week and wouldn't have had to endure the pain and difficulty while traveling or walking.

Every sport and every type of exercise carries with it a series of imbalances. Gone unchecked, this lopsidedness will eventually catch up to the athlete and cause either discomfort or injury. Whether we're talking about tennis or the bench press, this is true of all types of training, and we need to recognize that if we are going to stay healthy and successful. But most important is knowing if you fall behind in your attempt of balancing, you can't cram recovery in the eleventh hour. Just like if you're out of shape, where a 12-hour workout on one day isn't going to make up for your past month of laziness, nothing can immediately make up for a long imbalance of work-to-rest. Sometimes athletes treat this relationship like the metaphorical Bed of Procrustes from Greek mythology. Procrustes would make all his visitors "fit" into his bed by either stretching them to the appropriate length if they were too short, or severing their limbs if they were too tall. Athletes similarly will attempt to force quick bouts of stretching or foam rolling to recover from their training. Yet, without spending enough time actively recovering to stay healthy, it's as if athletes are trying to force something that won't fit to fit.

During one's competitive season, it's especially easy to let the thrill of the sport take precedence over adequate recovery. Truthfully, between the demands of coaches and professors alike, there is probably insufficient time for athletes to recover during their season even if they wanted to do so. When athletes get out of their seasons, if they can make it out without injuries in the first place, there *must* be a priority on rebalancing and recovering from the past season before anyone starts worrying about the next season(s) to come. Pre-season does not start nine months before your first game, and it's okay to not be in "game shape" while you work to recover from the end of your season. Be patient in your off-season and prioritize your health above all else. Do this, and you stand to gain a lot more when you do finally enter your next competitive season.

Five Major Points

- Sports are dangerous. Each one creates discrepancies in the body that can only be ameliorated by weight room training.
- The number one reason to lift weights should be in an attempt to rebalance the body between competitive seasons.
- A good posture aligns bones, muscles, and organs to work more effectively, and can even have dramatic effects on self-esteem and hormone levels.
- The four major ways to fix posture issues: stretch the tight muscle(s), strengthen the weak one(s), stand/sit/walk correctly, and find ways to exercise better posture throughout the day.
- The off-season is in place so you can recover from the season. Do not attempt to be in game-ready shape 12 months out of the year (no pro would even dream of that).

Chapter Ten

Exercise Specifics

Fads

NOT LONG AGO, I WAS having a conversation with my friend and mentor Mike Pimentel. He, being a bit older than I, was able to reminisce about the "good old days of training." As he put it, "It used to be that training was simple: training was training." Now we have cross training, balance training, high intensity training, MMA training, boxing training, kickboxing training, suspension training, functional training, sandbag training, tire training, sled training, waterbag training, stability ball training, medicine ball training, rope training, core training, bootcamp training, kettlebell training, barefoot training, etc. etc. etc. etc. ad nauseam. Each one has its own website with all sorts of sciencey-sounding words scattered all over it to attempt to sell us on how vital their training method is. What we've learned is that people will buy into phony explanations if they are dressed up with a few technical words from the world of science.[286] Each "training method" has its ephemeral moment in the spotlight where people treat it like it's some empyrean concept handed down to us from Zeus himself. Shortly thereafter, it's expeditiously replaced and forgotten like a dirty bread plate at a fancy restaurant.

What's most interesting is that almost all of the aforementioned "training methods" each has its own certification program associated with it. Hmm ... On top of that, Mike noticed how the dominant method of implementation for nearly all of these forms of training is circuit training. As Mike said, "Get the most people through a class in the shortest time possible and get them out. Takes very little skill to teach, implement and execute on everyone's part — trainer, trainee and administration!" What a great business model! What better way to promote your product than to create a whole new training genre around it?!? Ballyhoo as loud as possible and see who you can get to stumble through the door.

The scary thing is people are being lured into these groups not out of weakness in character or reason, but truly through the desire to excel and be athletically successful. If these people find something that makes sense to them or appeals to their preferences, they will probably go for it. Once they try it and create an affinity for it, their positive attitude yields to a sense of ownership and responsibility to remain a part of that group. With this comes the danger: a feeling of power that breeds the certainty they are doing the right thing. This is how these movements build from the ground up and how these incorrigible businesses have been picking up steam as of late. At least for now, they're here to stay. Evidently, the good old days of training are long gone and the simplicity of practice is welcomingly being replaced by these new waves of exercise.

This isn't meant to be neophobic, but training is not nearly as complicated as these new "programs" would suggest. While college athletes would be silly subscribing to one of the aforementioned training models, it will be hard not to hear about them. And while it'd be easy for an educator to say, "Do this, not that," that method leaves you powerless against future exercise fads. Not to mention that given explicit instructions like that often quells your curiosity, and leaves you less likely to explore information on your own.[287]

Three Reasons to Train

TAKE A MOMENT TO REALLY ask yourself why you are training. Is it to win? Or is it to look good in a bikini? A banana hammock perhaps? This thought matters more than anything else, because to truly excel in sport, you will get pretty banged up, and your body may not look the way you would like. Can you handle that?

Pragmatically speaking, there are three reasons to work out: for sport, for health, or for vanity. Sure, there will always be some overlap, but each one of these ambitions compel contrasting ideologies. If your goals are *performance*-based, then you are all set, as there is truly nothing glamorous about training for competition. People outside athletics believe athletes get to enjoy playing their sport, bask in the public recognition that comes from winning, then be afforded a position of social privilege higher than their nonathletic counterparts. In reality, the sporty life is not as glamorous. The time constraints of a full course load with games, practices, lifts, runs, physical therapy and film study; the sweat; the smell; the trouble breathing; that flinty feeling in your throat; the soreness in your quads; the parties to be skipped; the quality food to be eaten; the sleep to be forced; all the additional laundry ... Who would ask for all that? Anyone who'd play a varsity sport for pleasure'd sure go to hell for a pastime!

College athletes train so hard and are willing to sacrifice so much, it's such a shame when some aren't willing to sacrifice their good looks and an element of their health. Even some of the most successful athletes are not comfortable in their own skin. As the French essayist Michel de Montaigne wrote in the 1500s, "Even on the highest throne in the world, we are still sitting on our ass." Make an effort to be more comfortable with your body and understand the training you endure may create one you're not expecting. Take a look at the best athletes out there, and compare them to fitness models on the cover of magazines. Many world-class athletes do not have impeccable bodies. Sure, sprinters typically look great, but most sports do not yield specimens like that. New York-based photographer Howard Schatz produced a phenomenal series of photographs of Olympic athletes that revealed the wide array of body shapes that different sports create. Look up his work and you will immediately understand that training for sport is nothing like training for health or vanity.

Understanding Exercise

WHAT IS ESSENTIAL TO UNDERSTAND is that unlike nutrition, where there are very clear cut rights and wrongs, everything in the realm of training is much more up in the air. All that really matters is effort. Training's effect on one's body is a little like the manufacturing of tape: you've got to make it by the mile to sell it by the inch! In order to make the smallest gains, you really have to work hard and long at it, and the specific exercises you do in that metaphorical "mile" to gain the "inch" don't matter a whole lot. This is why exercise books, magazines, and fads sell so well, because everyone can benefit from almost anything (to a certain degree) as long as they're working as hard as possible.

Much like the "placebo effect" in medicine — where some patients show signs of improvement just because they *thought* they were on the real drug — people on these fad training regimens experience results, too. By working hard, even on a "placebo program," people are bound to see some pleasing results; after all, "placebo" is Latin for "I shall please" (used in the 14th Century to refer to sham mourners who were hired to sob loudly for the deceased at funerals).[288]   The possibility of placebo programs being successful is why you will not read anything about specific training practices here.   You could ask 500 strength coaches for a training regiment and easily receive 500 extremely varied programs, all of them carrying with them potential for success.   So it's clear that the program itself matters little when compared to the work ethic behind it; the harder people bust their humps, the less important the quality of the program becomes.

For this reason, this book spends almost no time discussing specific training regimens, as there is a lot more for you to gain with an education of how to treat your body after these hard workouts are complete. The truth is, as long as you are working as hard as you possibly can, and your coach isn't a total fool, you're likely to be alright. Well, in terms of training at least. You may not be able to survive the training because of your lifestyle, but fact is most coaches, even bad ones, have a plan. While it may not be a progressively more intense escalation of exercises and skills to peak you as you enter the post-season, it will, nevertheless, be a plan in his or her mind. What would be uneconomical, stressful, and stupid would be to jump from one training style to another, or from one coach's plan to another, as every coach's style is different, despite the possibility of them all being successful.   Of course some coaches are simply better than others, but what makes good coaches great is not found in their mastery of the sport or their playbooks, it is in their ability to motivate their athletes to work their hardest. A brilliantly intelligent coach that knows everything about the game but is unable to motivate his athletes will lose every time to the ignorant coach that can get his athletes to train like savage beasts.

The only common denominator among world-class athletes is the *manner* in which they train: like their lives are depending on it. They live by the Chinese proverb, "No food without blood and sweat."[289]   If you were to compare one person's training methods with another's, you would not find them doing the same activities, techniques, or styles of training.   Nevertheless, even though athletes all over the world are training using different styles, when they show up at international events, such as the Olympics, they are all finishing within hundredths of seconds from each other.   There are an infinite number of ways to train to be a sprinter, or to be a shot-putter, or to be a bobsledder, which makes effort the most important variable when it comes to training.   But because subjective experience can't be shared, it's very hard to put down into writing the feeling a workout should give you.   In the same vain, no one can explain what the color purple looks like, or what coffee smells like. These are all called "qualia," and they are the deepest we can go into our explanations of experience before hitting the bottom.[290]

The existence of qualia is the reason world-class athletes describe their training so vastly differently, and they all have different experiences to which they try to relate it.   Some say their training is as painful as having a child, others say it's like walking into a room *hoping* you get the crap beat out of you by someone.   A personal favorite would be to relate the feeling one should have after a workout to the sentiments an enervated captain famously proclaimed to his crew after a harrowing race.   In this true story, the men of a badly leaking American yawl were finishing a week-long siege plagued with some of the most formidable and fatal weather in history.   As they crossed the finish line, all of them completely dejected and utterly exhausted, the owner turned to his crew and said loud enough for everyone in the harbor to hear, "All right boys, we're over now.   Let her sink."[291]   This expression has become gospel among those few true masochists who enjoy sailing in dangerous conditions, and it perfectly encapsulates the similarly masochistic mindset athletes must have in regard to their training.   If, by the end of your workout, you're muttering to yourself, "That's it.   I'm over now.   Let me die," it almost doesn't matter what type of exercise you're doing.

If, however, you are not in the mood to workout or you're low on energy, you might as well just go home, if you have the choice (more on this in a second).   Daniel Coyle observed this type of behavior amongst the most talented people and trustworthy coaches in the world.   He noticed that when they departed what he termed "the deep-practice zone," they might as well have just quit for the day.[292]   Anything else is just setting one up to be burnt out, as you can't have that "Let her sink" end-of-the-workout feeling if you've already sunk at the beginning.   One must always put life in perspective, balancing kith and kin and work and stress and whatever else.   Training should be an extension of that, focusing on balance and efficiency.   If you're keeping yourself mentally and physically healthy, you should always *want* to train! If not, what are you going to get out of the workout?   A perfunctory, tired workout is probably not going to add to your potential, right?   That seems obvious, as we can only get better when we are training at 100% of our capacity. So, waiting until the afternoon or the next day when you have wind in your sails again makes a little more sense than plodding along through a disconcerted, nonplussed effort.

Of course, most of the time college athletes don't get much of a choice as to when they can work out, which brings us back to the thesis of this book and the reason it was all written in the first place:

College is an unhealthy place and athletes need to take care of their bodies outside of the gym in order to be successful inside of the gym and on their respective playing fields.

If you do find yourself tired and not wanting to work out, think about why you're tired in the first place, and it'll most likely be one of three reasons. One, you didn't get enough sleep.   Two, you haven't eaten enough or enough of the right stuff to have energy.   Or three, you haven't recovered from yesterday's workout yet and need the additional rest anyway. IF — and that is a big if during college — IF an athlete is eating right, stretching, foam rolling, and sleeping enough, there is no reason why he or she shouldn't be able to train six days a week and not become overtrained.   The general guideline to follow is to allow at least one rest day between sessions that stress the same muscle groups.[293]   This means people should not be doing the same *type* of training two days in a row. In regard to running, this means athletes shouldn't do the *same* running on consecutive days.   Make one day intervals, the next day straight-forward speed work, the next day agility, etc. In reference to lifting, this means people should not train chest two days in a row, no matter if one day is dumbbell fly and the next is barbell bench; your body needs the 48-hour window of rest.

The soreness that is typically felt in that 24-48 hour window is a product of tissue breakdown, which means the only thing that's going to help it is rest.   I remember putting a soccer team through such an excruciating leg lift once that everyone I saw the next day was limping and crawling around. One girl that was particularly sore, and was openly complaining about it, decided on her own that the best way to heal herself was to go and do some box jumps ... oh boy. If you do anything at all when you're painfully sore it cannot be more work, it must instead be some form of active recovery — examples of which can be found on the table in the previous chapter. So, for all of you meat sticks out there crushing your biceps every day, you're just killing yourself slowly. Remember, what builds the muscle is proper nutrition and *recovery*, not more lifting; the only thing exercise does is *stimulate* the body to produce change, not actually create the change itself.

Also relevant here is what kind of movements create the most tissue breakdown. Eccentric movements — in other words, the lowering phase of an exercise (e.g. downward motion of a bench or squat) — induce the most muscle soreness.[294]   Just for your information, the eccentric motion is stronger compared to its counterpart, the concentric, or upward, motion. You are typically 120 to 160 percent stronger going with gravity in a movement as opposed to against it.[295] This is the reason why athletes never fail in a bench press on their way down, it is always on the way up when the failure occurs. Because of the painful, and in the short-term harmful, effects of the eccentric phase, athletes are implored to have a *full day of rest* between working the same muscle groups. Never train the same exercise nor muscle group two days in a row, as your body needs time to repair the damage you created on the previous bout.

For those of you extreme workaholics that are heartbroken by this fact, there is one muscle group that marks an exception: your abs. Your trunk's range of motion is nothing compared to that of your elbow or knee, therefore the abdominals mainly work in an isometric way. Because of this discrepancy, they can be trained every day.[296] So if you need to get into that weight room every day, go ahead and do crunches 'til you puke!

In essence, these two big principles — training hard and minimum recovery time — comprise most of what you need to know about exercise in order to be successful in college. Of course there's *more* to know, but without these fundamental concepts, you might as well be rowing a boat with a broomstick. Remember, training is only one of a surplus of variables contributing toward your success or demise.

Gambling

WHEN THINKING ABOUT EXERCISE, ESPECIALLY in relation to sport, one can get easily caught up in the little intricacies of his or her workouts.

When strength coaches discuss weight room programs with athletes, they notice athletes tend to put their emphasis on exercise selection, ways to do said exercises, and number of sets and/or reps, which one could consider the small nuts and bolts of training. Every exercise out there could be tweaked hundreds of different ways, and too many athletes are concerning themselves with it. Take the bench press, for example. One could take this simple exercise and apply hundreds of variations: barbells vs. dumbbells, free weights vs. machines, grips (wide, middle, narrow, underhand, hammer), bar placement (high to neck, low to stomach), feet placement (tucked under you on floor, on bench, in the air), bench angle (decline, incline, flat), blah blah blah. The question is why would any athlete need to know about any of this in order to be successful?

Of course exercise selection is important, and without question, the number of repetitions you perform matters, but these are not concerns that need to take up space in a college athlete's head. The knowledge of which style of benching to do or how many bench reps to perform is so insignificant compared to the intellect it would take to understand *why* you are exercising the bench press in the first place. Your strength and conditioning specialists will take care of these nuts and bolts of training, while you are responsible for the lumber: personal athletic intelligence, like knowing how to take care of your body after the bench pressing is complete.

Try not to get bogged down with the inconsequential notion of how many sprints are best, because there is no right answer. Conversely, there is a huge right or wrong when it comes to the ineffables. The point is simple, if you are one of these athletes that likes to rationalize why certain exercises are better than others, why six reps are better than eight, or why five sets are better than three, your valuable time could be spent doing something else that will yield you much more results: **the ineffables.** For everything you do in regard to training, there will be a ratio of effort-to-result, and focusing on sets and reps is not a cost-effective way to spend your time.

In addition to sets and reps, there are other little details that are bogging athletes down. They'll ask how soon after they wake up should they eat (within an hour, but not a huge deal), when is the right time to stretch (there's no wrong time, except with the possible exception of 30 seconds before a one rep max attempt), or how often they should eat fish (certain deep-water fish have more mercury than others, but you are still unlikely to eat yourself into a problem). There *are* answers to questions like these, clearly, but it's this sort of stuff that shows our focus is too narrow. Allow yourself ample time to conquer the big issues before you home in on the nuts and bolts. To reuse the examples from above, before you worry about when to sleep, when to eat breakfast, when to stretch, or when to eat fish, first ensure you are sleeping enough, eating breakfast at all, stretching every day, and eating different varieties of fish every week in the first place.

Once you do reach the level of nuts and bolts, more often than not, only *you* can determine the answers you seek by first trying them out in practice. The best possible advice one could give you is to always try something first in training before you test it out in a game-time situation. Test then retest to see if it works. Too often, athletes who heard about some fresh fad folly, whether it be a futuristic supplement to energize or a cutting-edge technique for warming up, try it for the first time immediately before an important game. Why would anyone ever do that? This is a plain-and-simple gamble, something George Washington would call, "a vice which is productive of every possible evil."[297] If you attempt something new, guess what, there are only two outcomes: either you progress or you regress. There ain't no third direction. Whenever you add something new to your life as an athlete, you will either get better from it or you will get worse. Don't leave this up to chance before a big event. Doing something this foolish would have been grounds for dismissal from the ultra-successful Oregon Track Team of the Bowerman Era. So adamant was legendary head coach Bill Bowerman to control his callow runners, he made it a team rule, on pain of termination, to never try anything untested before/during a big race.[298] Athletes need to learn about their bodies in training, then adhere to what they've learned as they head into important games/events, *even if what they're doing is wrong*.

When our men's lacrosse team was heading into the national championship game for the first time in school history, they were invited to practice at the New England Patriots' Gillette Stadium and the owner, Robert Kraft, came down to speak to them for a few minutes. In one quick sentence, he encapsulated everything I'm trying to say, and although I'm going to paraphrase, it was poetic: "Remember that tomorrow's game (the national championship) is just another game on the schedule. Treat it any differently and you lose." We all must recognize that if we make it to a big event, the reason we got there is because of the way we've been conducting ourselves.

Don't worry about what else is out there, just do what you know works! Life would be so much easier if there weren't so many choices to be made. The more options there are, the less likelihood one will make the right choice; this is why exceptional coaches run tight ships. In fact, there are few examples in history of success coming to a divergent group of individuals, whether it be in war, in politics, or in sport. Barry Schwartz wrote an entire book, *The Paradox of Choice*, about how people actually prefer *less* choice, albeit subconsciously. His research concluded that, contrary to popular belief, people are actually happier when fewer items are on the menu, or in general, when there are fewer items from which to choose.[299] Imagine how healthy you would be if the only thing you were allowed to eat were vegetables, quinoa, fish, and chicken!

Form

ONE OF THE MOST BASIC principles of athletic intelligence, though, is understanding how to execute exercises in the correct form. There are a billion different techniques a coach can unleash on one exercise, or one drill, and the disparity from coach to coach can be vast. The truth is, there is no right or wrong, as every technique of each lift or basketball shot or lacrosse rip or what have you is going to create different strengths and weaknesses. But a "law of least effort" does apply here, which means if there are several ways to do one motion, people will eventually gravitate toward the one with the least demanding course of action.[300] In other words, laziness is ingrained in each of us, and if you're not careful, you will start exercising in a manner that causes less muscle tissue breakdown. Understand this is not to say *you* are going to be lazier, because your workouts may actually be getting more challenging as time goes on; instead, your body will learn how to work less as you exercise.

As an example, it's physically less strenuous to perform a squat without flexing your bum; therefore, even if you have learned to do it while flexing your bum, in time you will likely squat the easier way: unflexed. That said, no matter what the goal you or your coach choose for each exercise, when you are in the gym, there are a few rules to which you must adhere in regard to form.

Execute a full range of motion. First and foremost, touch the bar to your chest every rep of bench, sit down to parallel every rep of squat, and lower all the way down every rep of pull-ups. Training muscles in their entirety develops them fuller. Breaking down the muscle in its totality forces your body to rebuild it all the way through, not just in half of its scope.[301] Also, extending your muscles past their parameters and strengthening them in the fullest way possible is safer in the long run.

Ultimately, lifting is just a means to an end. Having your strength developed in those real stretched positions will prepare you for game-time situations when you get lodged into an awkward orientation either running or coming into contact with a competitor.

Understand when to cheat. Yes, there is a time when you could and maybe even *should* cheat up a rep any way you know how. Comprehending when to do this requires you to recognize the goal of the exercise you are performing. If you are in a phase with slow movements or lots of reps, perhaps your focus should be on utilizing the correct form and attempting to recruit the right muscle groups. Conversely, if you are in a maximum strength phase, where your rep counts are really low, hell, do whatever you can (safely) to move that weight. The reason form is so important is because when you utilize the correct form — although it may feel awkward at first — you are allowing your body to fire the strongest muscle groups to move the weight. For example, teaching yourself to fire your glutes in a squat or deadlift, by consciously flexing your bum as you drive the movement up from its lowest position, will make that pattern of motion second nature to you. By the time you get to your max strength sets, you hopefully won't have to cognitively focus on correct form. You'll just perform!

This is particularly true when studying professional athletes playing their sport. They have practiced perfect form for so long, they can now do it without thinking at all. We'll get into this much more when we discuss habits, but for now just understand that when a beginner attempts to perform a specific skill, there is an explosion of brain activity. Conversely, when a pro does the same activity, there is very little cognitive effort being expended.[302]

Executing a full range of motion and knowing when to cheat are the two most important things to understand about form. No matter who your coach is, these two things should be apparent in his or her instructions. Whether you have the hell-bent coach focused only on your strength increasing, the sensitive one that never allows weights to be increased past a point of total control, or the other that has no dogma and just mimics whatever the most successful college teams are doing, the two rules should still apply. Finally, thinking outside the parameters of form, there's one other thing that is vital to understand about training, warming up.

Warm-Up

"WARMING UP BEFORE WORKING OUT" has become a kind of a trite, cliché aphorism that doesn't pack a whole lot of potency anymore; notwithstanding, warming up is one of the most important components of injury prevention. By literally raising the temperature within your body, your muscles are able to move more freely through their respective ranges of motion.[303] A fine example of this is attempting to stretch first thing in the morning as opposed to in the afternoon. You will notice that because your body is more warmed up from your daily activities, you can reach much farther within stretches in the afternoon as opposed to the morning. Apply this same idea to your sport: **the warmer you are, the safer your workout becomes**.

The manner in which you warm-up can range dramatically day to day, but it is an absolute *must* before training or competition. Scientists agree that one effective way to safely prepare for a workout is with five to six minutes of general warm-up followed by eight to twelve minutes of sport-specific stretching.[304] This general warm-up can be done actively, such as jogging, biking or easy drills, or passively, such as in a sauna. Either way, the goal is to raise the temperature within your muscles, as they will respond better to the stretching performed thereafter.

People always ask when is the best time to stretch, before a workout or after, and with a better understanding of what stretching exactly does to your body, you'll be able to decipher the best answer for yourself. Stretching muscles basically strives for one major goal: attempting to increase the length of the muscle. A longer muscle can move through its scope of motion more readily while also being able to be forced into elongated positions more safely. Especially if you are in a contact or semi-contact sport, where you are not entirely sure of how your body will be forced to be juxtaposed, muscle length is extremely important. A long muscle of good quality has the potential for more strength, speed, and injury protection than one of a short, poor quality.[305]

Finally, you might be asking what type of stretching is best. Dynamic stretching, much like a specific warm-up, uses motion — such as high knees, butt kicks, single leg swinging kicks, etc. — to warm the body up, whereas static stretching is comprised of slow, constant stretches with the end position held for a minimum of 30 seconds. While intelligent strength coaches adhere to static stretching the most, deeming dynamic not as effective due to its inability to mark improvements over time, consult the table on the next page to see some pros and cons of both types. A score of five on the table below denotes the high end of the scale, i.e. a good score, whereas a one indicates the low end. As you'll see, static stretching is excellent in regard to the ability to be relaxed during the stretch, to be able to show improvement over any prolonged stint, and to stretch one muscle at a time, while dynamic stretching is not. Conversely, dynamic stretching is great at raising one's body temperature, mimicking specific movements, and training several muscles at once, while static stretching pales in comparison.

	Static	Dynamic
Able to be relaxed during	5	1
Able to show improvement or lack thereof	5	2
Can devote time to one specific muscle group at a time	5	3
Able to perform while injured	3	2
Able to perform quickly	2	4
Can work several muscles at once	2	5
Effective for raising body temperature	2	5
Can mimic specific movements	1	5

Regardless of which one you choose, remember that a proper warm-up will include both general and specific elements to appropriately prepare you for your upcoming tasks. You can be your own judge, but everyone should get some static stretching exposure every day. Static stretching is an excellent way to recover from a heavy workout, a relaxing event with which to start or end your day, and just about nothing feels better than a long, devoted stretch, especially if spent solely on one muscle group. Try stretching your hamstrings ten or more minutes each side and you will immediately know which way is best.

That campaign for static stretching should not negate the benefits of dynamic stretching, however. Dynamic flexibility does have its place. Immediately before a workout, dynamic flexibility is a great way to prepare for specific exercises, especially if the movements mimic the upcoming events. Either way, something is better than nothing!

And when you're done working out, a cool-down would be nice too. When athletes hear the phrase "cool-down," most of them picture a slow jog to bring them back off of their high from working out, but a jog does not cool anybody down. A proper cool-down does what the phrase implies: cools the muscles down, literally. No matter if you are hurt or not, you should be trying to ice after every workout as the post-workout icing of joints may aid in prevention of injury as well as in recuperation.[306]   As a matter of fact, cooling down reduces muscle cramping and allows the heart rate to slow gradually.[307]   Remember, while you are working out, you are breaking down muscle tissue and are consistently overheating to boot, so right after a workout, you need to bring your body back to its equilibrium as quickly as possible to aid in the removal of those damaging, catabolic hormones. Especially if you experience joint pain during your workout, do not hesitate to ice the moment your workout is complete. If your college has the resources, an ice bath is potentially the greatest way to recover immediately post-workout.

However you choose to cool down, realize it is just as important as warming-up. While a proper warm-up aides with injury prevention, a good cool down can lead to better and faster recovery! Simple yet potent concepts like these point to the reason why athletes do not need to know very much about lifting, running, or training in general — that's what coaches are for. The commercial variables certainly are titillating, but it's the ineffables like long static stretches and immediate ice baths that can really mold impressive athletes. Avoid the fads, and focus on these very easy goals so many young athletes overlook.

Five Major Points

- Be skeptical of new training methods. Remember why you're training.
- Hard work and minimum recovery time (48 hours for same type of training) are the only real concepts athletes need to grasp about training. Recovery builds muscle, exercise only stimulates the change.
- Because college athletes do not have the luxury of choosing when to work out, lifestyle becomes ever more important to ensure they can keep up with their training.
- Try everything, *everything*, in practice before applying it to a competition.
- "Warm-ups" and "cool-downs" are not trite aphorisms, they are scientifically-proven mechanisms that prevent injury and aid recovery.

Chapter Eleven

Sleep

Sine Qua Non

IN A BOOK ABOUT ATHLETIC performance, one might languish about where to insert a chapter about sleep, or if to write a chapter about it at all. Come on, what person does not know sleep is vital for performance or happiness or mood? Sleep is located at the end of Part III of this book, about training, because training cannot happen without sleep. Sleep is the sine qua non of training, where one cannot progress athletically without ample attention paid to sleep habits. We've been saying that training simply *implores* change, and recovery is what *creates* it, but now we need to be more specific and recognize that *sleep* is what creates it. As Mike Colgan writes in *Optimum Sports Nutrition*, "bodily growth and repair occur *only* during rest or sleep, never during training."[308] Remember, training is actually pretty horrible for you if you're not getting adequate rest. In the extreme short-term, meaning the course of a few minutes, exercise is one of the worst things you can do to your body. Lifting and running and all other exercise quite literally cause micro-tears in muscle fibers, and deplete most muscle glycogen stores, rendering you weaker than before your workout.[309] The more intense the training session, the more muscle gets broken down. While your mind may be able to interpret what you're doing, your body just takes the beating and does what it can to protect itself from getting hurt like that again. Essentially, after a muscle experiences the break down, it builds itself back up to be able to withstand another battering, should it ever happen again. This rebuilding in question can only properly occur during sleep.

Most people think that relaxing is the same as sleep, in terms of recovery, but this is not the case. During sleep, your body is going to repair injuries, build new physical structures, and dispose of wastes.[310] Anything else that you do makes it harder to properly and rapidly recover. Relaxing is not the same. Consider if an athlete is just sitting and snacking while watching TV. Suddenly he drops one of his cheese balls on the floor and it rolls under the couch. Now he's got to get down on his hands and knees, move the heavy couch aside, find his floury ball of cheese and cram it back in his mouth. Although that may have seemed like nothing, he just broke some muscle tissue down — performing a partial push-up and squat — and inhibited his recovery just a fraction. Joking aside, it's true that every step that you take outside of your workout is breaking down your muscles just a little bit more than they already have been, each stride acting like a miniature lunge. While the tissue damage from a few steps isn't debilitating, it is still noteworthy. To wit, bodybuilders have developed a particular method of walking that allows them to burn the least amount of calories possible. This enables them to save energy for the gym and to not use up calories that could be making them bigger![311]

Concepts like these point to the importance of sleep over just "rest." Inattentiveness to sleep will ultimately lead to an under-recovered body, which will lead to a decrease in performance, then eventually to a plateau or injury. Maximal strength outputs decrease after only three hours of sleep loss in one night. Go two days in a row of losing three hours each night, as many do during midterm and final exam periods, and the drop offs will be extreme.[312] Incur rapid sleep loss, meaning a loss of eight hours of sleep in one night, and you will have even more impairment of your alertness, memory, and performance compared to the loss of only a few hours.[313] In general, sleep loss represents an important risk factor for weight gain, insulin resistance, type 2 diabetes and dyslipidaemia.[314]

By now, perhaps you're saying this is all common sense; it's obvious sleep loss yields negative performance. What is not obvious nor common sense is the effect of *more* sleep. One researcher studied basketball players that raised their sleep from around seven or eight hours in bed to a minimum goal of ten hours in bed per night. Before long, these subjects demonstrated a faster timed sprint, their shooting accuracy improved by about nine percent, and they reported overall ratings of better physical and mental well-being.[315]   Businesses around the world are trying to increase performance by one percent here and two percent there ... imagine the difference in as much as *nine percent* being as easy as sleeping more.

Everyone loves to sleep, and especially loves when they can sleep in late. Haven't we all noticed the difference sleeping in can have on our mood and how good our bodies feel?   Realize that this is how life is supposed to be all day every day, and only recently could people actually start controlling when they got up in the morning.   Personal, bedside alarm clocks are a fairly recent invention, yet it is hard to imagine a time society could function without them. Before them, all humans had to rely on was a clock tower, the sun in their face, or their body's natural ability to arise itself after it was fully rested — an art most of us only experience on the weekends, if at all. Nevertheless, that is the way we are supposed to be living, according to nature. This natural human clock is called the "circadian clock" or the "circadian rhythm" and more and more research has been pointing to the importance of adhering to our inherent body clock.

Circadian Clock

THIS MAY COME AS NO surprise, but your body enjoys adhering to its inner clock. Anecdotally speaking, we don't like eating mashed potatoes for breakfast, going to bed at six o'clock at night, or working out at two in the morning. On top of all this anecdotal evidence of circadian rhythms, scientists at sleep laboratories have been studying the physiological responses to the sleep-wake cycle, and have found some data extremely relevant to aspiring athletes.

Turns out that most physiological actions and behaviors are affected by the circadian rhythm, and eating practices are an especially big part of it.[316]   Missing a meal during the day is associated with sleep quality and snacking after dinner is associated with trouble falling asleep.[317]   To add to that, college students' sleep and eating habits were studied recently, and researchers found that students who went to bed the latest reported the greatest intake of empty calories compared to those going to bed earliest.[318] So what does all this research mean? The common denominator between all these studies seems to be that regularity drives a healthy sleep cycle. Fall out of your own circadian rhythm, and you set yourself up for failure in other facets of your life, most notably nutrition.

While in college, finding the time to sleep can be a challenge, but it is a worthy one. You must develop habits, such as bed times, that allow you to prioritize sleep in your lifestyle. If you were to make a dot graph of your weekly times to bed and weekly times to rise, you should discover two straight lines, indicating you are falling asleep and waking up at the same respective times every day.

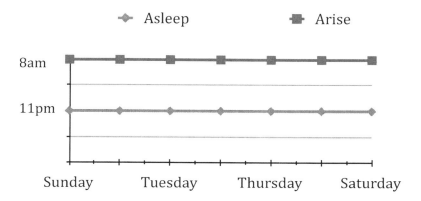

Establishing a pattern like this allows for one's body to become accustomed to eating at the same time, exercising at the same time, sleeping at the same time, and so on, thereby releasing the appropriate hormones when necessary. For example, research has shown that people have a five percent higher aerobic and anaerobic capacity in the afternoon.[319] Get out of rhythm and that five percent of consequences can matter. One group of scientists found that West coast teams win more Monday Night Football games than East coast teams, simply because the games' kick-off times typically fall into their circadian rhythm better than the later time-zoned East coast teams. Surprisingly, West coasters perform better than Las Vegas odds.[320] Results like this support the presence of an enhancement of athletic performance at certain circadian times of day.

Your body wants to be in a rhythm where it's active during the day and passive at night. There have been many studies showing how nurses or security guards that work the graveyard shifts — starting their work day after dark, then trying to get their sleep during the next day — suffer from countless sleeping disorders. One would think that if a body got eight hours of sleep each day it wouldn't matter if it was from 11pm to 7am or if it was from 11am to 7pm, but there's a large body of evidence that says there is a significant difference. The sun has a powerful effect on how awake we feel. One study demonstrated how brief indoor exposure to natural bright light improved physiologic arousal in the afternoon, the effects of which lasted for more than an hour.[321]

All this research demonstrates if your sleep-wake cycle is out of rhythm, and represents more of a sporadic configuration resembling the Himalayan mountain range, you'll have no consistency with your hormones, or eating habits, or alertness. No matter how perfect your workouts and nutrition may be, without a sufficient amount or consistent schedule of sleep, you will fail to progress.

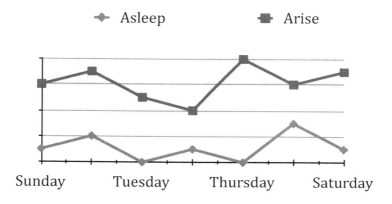

If the chart above represents your sleep pattern, you can be sure you have no circadian rhythm, and you are certainly losing out on all the benefits of regularity. By now, you might be thinking to yourself that you're in college and you never know when a term paper is going to sprout up or a big party is going to summon your attendance. If you do find yourself occasionally having to sacrifice some sleep, please refer to a recent 2013 study in the Journal of Strength and Conditioning Research that found early rising is more detrimental than a late bedtime in relation to muscle strength and power, at least when the athlete is training in the afternoon.[322] If you know you're going to need to lose some sleep, lose it at night as opposed to the morning.

To train your sleep effectively only requires a touch of cognitive foresight: if you are aware you're going to have a late night, arrange a late morning accordingly. Although no one could condone staying up late *any* day of the week, if you must do it during the weekdays, plan ahead. You know that Tuesday night is your big night out? Well then don't have any Wednesday morning classes. On the flip side, if you do find yourself with Wednesday morning responsibilities, perhaps you're not going out Tuesday nights this semester. These are the types of simple sacrifices omnitects must make in order to be successful athletes in college.

Strategies

BY NOW THE IMPORTANCE OF sleep is abundantly apparent, and the only thing left to discuss is how much to get and how to go about it. While you have probably heard the normal advice of obtaining eight hours of sleep each night, those recommendations are not based on people destroying their bodies like you are. As it turns out, fit people sleep significantly longer than unfit people — and this actually has nothing to do with how hard one's workout was that day. People in good shape sleep longer than the sedentary.[323] Data like this suggests that the requirements for athletic people are greater than the nonathletic. Fittingly, scientists working specifically with high-trained athletes counsel them to sleep *nine* hours a night, with an additional nap in the afternoon.[324]

While the nine hours per night may seem a little chimerical — easy to wish for but harder to achieve — the daily nap may be more attainable. Naps even as short as *ten* minutes have been shown to improve alertness and performance. And when determining how long to nap, keep this ten minute nap in mind. With regard to subjective alertness, naps of five minutes and twenty minutes showed no benefits compared to not napping, whereas a ten-minute nap gave subjects improved subjective alertness immediately after napping and were able to maintain that for the following two and a half hours. Longer naps, such as thirty-minute naps, typically resulted in a period of reduced alertness immediately after napping, but then allowed for a longer period of alertness — 95 to 155 minutes — thereafter.[325]

Results from this study, and others like it, make it clear there is no better way to improve one's alertness than to sleep. Caffeine can cause a clear spike in performance and alertness, much the same as a nap can, but the difference is in how the time-course affects the body. The positive effects of napping can be felt for hours afterward and do not sharply drop off after that; more succinctly, naps show relatively little decay effect. Of course both caffeine and sleep have dose-related effects, whereby if you sleep for a few hours or drink several cups of coffee, there will be different results compared to napping for ten minutes and having a sip of coffee. As a rough generalization, a nap lasting between two and four hours is similar to the effects of consuming 150-300mg of caffeine, roughly 1.5 to 3 cups of coffee.[326] More practically for us, an hour-long nap would seem to be as effective at increasing alertness and performance as a small cup of coffee, but naps still have a clear advantage of a long-lasting effect and one does not have to worry about developing a dependency, tolerance, withdrawal or side effects. Based on the aforementioned studies, below there is a table with some some comparable statistics between sleep, caffeine, and alertness.

Amount of Sleep	Comparable Cups of Coffee	Immediate Alertness	Duration of Alertness
5 minutes	n/a	n/a	n/a
10 minutes	n/a	Improved	90m - 2.5h
30 minutes	1/2 Cup	Reduced	90m - 2.5h
1 hour	1 Cup	Reduced	1.5 hours +
2 hours	2 Cups	Unknown	3 hours +
4+ hours	4 Cups	Unknown	6 hours +

Regardless of how you choose to remain alert during the day, all athletes must be recusants about obtaining their nine hours of sleep at night; no matter who or what is standing in the way, athletes are obligated to push it aside and get in bed. One NCAA Player of the Year said sleep was her most valued asset. She wrote, "I would make sure to sleep a minimum of probably nine hours a night for most nights out of the week. I would do any work that I had until maybe 10pm then go to bed no matter where I was with the assignment." She would go on to say that she didn't feel like she focused too much on what she ate and could have been much healthier in regard to nutrition and alcohol, but sleep was something she refused to squander. Because her sleep graph was two straight lines (see previous charts), she had a perfect circadian rhythm that allowed her to train hard and recover well.

College is like New York City, it never sleeps. There will always be *something* to do every night, no matter what, the only question is if you'll be involved or not. However, being an athlete requires sacrifices, and we all know how willing college athletes are to sacrifice their bodies, now we need a similar sacrifice in their lifestyles.

Sleep is not something with which you can negotiate, because sleep will always win. You don't need scientific studies to tell you how abysmal you feel those days you don't get enough sleep, because you've experienced them enough on your own. By the same token, you don't need science to tell you how good you feel those days you get a full night's rest. Make sleep one of your priorities, and the positive side effects will surmount rapidly — your training will flourish because of it, and perhaps most importantly, you'll simply be happier.

Five Major Points

- Fit people need more sleep than the sedentary — scientists recommend 9 hours a night plus a nap.
- One should attempt to fall asleep at the same time every night and rise at the same time every morning, thus creating a healthy circadian rhythm.
- Eating practices, mood, and performance can all be directly related to- and affected by one's circadian rhythm.
- Increased sleep could improve performance overnight, and if one is required to be deprived of some sleep, it is preferable to lose it at night compared to forfeiting the auspicious morning hours.
- In relation to feelings of alertness, one hour of napping is roughly equivalent to one cup of coffee, but of course sleep is always preferable to drugs.

Part IV

Progress

Chapter Twelve

100% of Capacity

Horizontal Dependency

IN JARED DIAMOND'S BOOK *COLLAPSE,* he studies the rise and fall of powerful societies, and what he discovers is true of the Maya, Anastazi, Eastern Islanders, and other past great societies is, in his words:

> Societies' steep decline may begin only a decade or two after the society reaches its peak numbers, wealth, and power ... on reflection, it's no surprise that declines of societies tend to follow swiftly on their peaks.[327]

Whether it be in the lust for power, or the simple disregard for the environment in which they live, past societies that have fallen are reminiscent of athletes that have been injured. Everything will seem perfect, and athletes will think they are invincible, until a quick peripeteia — or reversal of fortune — suddenly, and unmercifully tears them down.

For a society to stand the test of time, *every* variable must be in check, for as the society becomes grandiose, wealthy, and heavily populated, what used to be easy to sustain, such as providing basic needs, becomes more challenging. Policies need to be in place to ensure the society, as a whole, does not overextend its resources, thus leaving the society vulnerable to collapse. This is a perfect metaphor for college athletes in regard to training and lifestyle.

As you get better at your sport and more athletically impressive, what used to be non-issues, such as your food choices or your recovery methods, need to become the center of your attention. The more intense you train, the more you need to eat and the more you need to sleep. Great societies have dropped from their pinnacle to their nadir due to the fact they kept the same policies in place despite becoming larger, wealthier, and more productive. You must learn from them and adapt your lifestyle to meet the needs of your current training regiment. Perhaps even more so than the Maya or Anastazi, you are walking the finest line of being at your highest peak and tumbling to your lowest gully.

In order to be optimally prepared for competition, you will inevitably be just a shade away from being overtrained, thus on the verge of injury. This becomes such an issue when we think about group workouts, because invariably there will be a large range of athletes in the mix, some more in shape than others. If they all train as a group, those near the bottom of the spectrum will be near death while those at the top will just be starting to break a sweat — only a few in the middle will receive optimal training. In an ideal world, each individual would be training as hard and as much as possible without exceeding the critical point from which he or she cannot fully recover, otherwise known as becoming overtrained. In a group, this is very hard for multiple people to attain simultaneously.

■ Undertrained   Optimal   ■ Overtrained

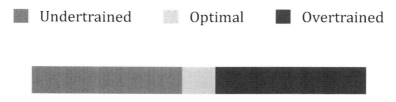

As you can see, there's a big scale where the window of optimization is tiny by comparison; with all the variables out there, it's nearly impossible to find an "optimally trained" athlete, one that is neither under- nor overtrained. Becoming optimally prepared at all is pretty tough, and hitting it at the appropriate time in your season is incredibly rare. And if you were to guess on which side of this scale most college athletes land themselves in their quest for optimization ... it's undoubtedly on the overtrained side. Trying to find an *under*trained athlete in college is like trying to find a Sasquatch. This is why rational coaches should promote the idea of active recovery, day in and day out, to anyone and everyone that is willing to listen.

You might think that as a strength and conditioning coach for a university, I would be promoting exercise as much as I could. Well, the truth of the matter is that most strength coaches out there do. In fact, I've visited many other schools only to find the stereotypical, steakheaded strength coaches vituperating their athletes to work through the pain while yelling trite lines like "pain is weakness leaving the body," "no pain no gain," "you can rest when you're dead," or the fan favorite, "you can feel sore tomorrow or you can feel sorry tomorrow. Choose now." Unfortunately, this is what players and administrators alike aim to find in their coaches: an unwavering, steadfast dedication to hard workouts. In reality, this monolithic system is dangerous and disregards the fact most college athletes are overtrained. Far too many talented athletes get ruined by a zealous coaching staff that finds recovery methods and days off to be blasphemous; they believe a little too strongly there is no limit to hard work.

I, on the other hand, have looked at the evidence and recognize how much athletes train. Given the data, I actually *beg* them to train *less*. The fundamental problem with our psyche as a culture is that there is some sort of natural tendency to believe that if something is good, then more must be better. We are in universal agreement that in order to improve, an athlete must train, and the more they train, the better they will become. However, there is a major asterisk on the latter part of that sentence. There is a point where too much training becomes a major issue. Because of this, college-aged athletes, in a struggle for glory, consistently train themselves past a level appropriate for optimal performance. In other words, **nearly all athletes playing a varsity sport are overtrained**. The fear of being underprepared for competition is so prevalent in coaches' and players' minds alike that most athletes train so much they become unknowingly drained, forcing themselves to constantly train and compete below their 100% potential. This nervousness is especially endemic in new coaches and rookie players that have such a drive in them to succeed, it blinds all other emotions and rational thought. If we are ever going to progress as athletes and coaches, we need to quash this dangerous mindset that inevitably leads to overtraining.

The biggest challenge is to convince athletes, coaches, and administrators alike that exercise is only *one* of a nearly infinite amount of variables that factor into an athlete's success. While it is no secret that training may be the most powerful variable, few contemplate how impotent it is without an equal emphasis on other factors — the ineffables. Unwisely, exercise gets placed on a pedestal above all else, thus creating a vertical dependency in people's minds. So, instead of contextualizing the relationship of all variables working synergistically together, athletes tend to prioritize training to a point where they incorrectly believe it can overcome all others (including, but not limited to, nutrition, sleep, stress, and alcohol habits).

Vertical Dependency
An Incorrect, Destructive Concept

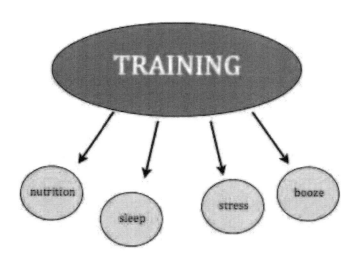

Instead, people need to consider their training working in unison with everything else, thus creating the idea of a horizontal dependency where nothing can improve unless it all improves together! Therefore, the more you want to train, the more you need to sleep, the better food you need to eat, the less you can stress, and the better your management of alcohol must be. This pari passu model is a simple, universally accepted idea, but few people actually care to do anything about it, thereby remaining overtrained. They move from high school, a place where their time and training is very regimented, their bodies are extremely resilient, and their training comparatively less intense, to college where their schedules are all over the place, their sleep levels drop, stress levels rise, and training intensity doubles on bodies less durable. Inevitably, performance will suffer.

Horizontal Dependency
Nothing Can Improve Unless it All Improves

Because college is the last platform for competitive sport, athletes perceive their brief four year window as a ticking clock and routinely overtrain the hell out of themselves. Yet, they are not to blame. We live in America. Our whole culture is built upon the premise that if you work hard enough for something, you're sure enough to get it. The problem with this inspirational concept is that it ignores natural human limitations. We all completely buy into the idea of hard work, but we must find more meaning in *smart* work. Learning to understand your body, your training, and your lifestyle within the context of reality and your innate limitations allows you to succeed indefinitely. And perhaps the most important thing to learn about your training is the General Adaptation Syndrome.

General Adaptation Syndrome

NO MATTER WHAT TYPE OF training you are doing — regardless of the intensity, duration, timing, or volume — you will experience a three-stage response to the stress. The response is known as the General Adaptation Syndrome (GAS), and the three stages are termed alarm, resistance, and exhaustion, respectively.[328]

Exercise leaves one weaker, slower, and more fatigued than before he or she started the workout. Because of this tissue breakdown and general shock to the system, the time period immediately following a workout is known as the "alarm phase" of the GAS. From here, there are two roads an athlete can take: one is to recover properly (by focusing on the ineffables), and two is to squander the recovery. Should you take the high road and meet the alarm with proper recovery, the body will positively adapt to withstand the stress, and will eventually build itself back up to where it started. Given quality food and quality sleep, it will actually experience a "supercompensation," becoming stronger than it was prior to the workout.[329]   In this "resistance phase" of the GAS, the body makes all the right changes structurally, biochemically, and mechanically to increase its capabilities. At this point, the body is in a better place than it was, and is ready to endure another alarm phase — read: workout — so it can be met with another supercompensation, and continue to progress nearly indefinitely.

General Adaptation Syndrome

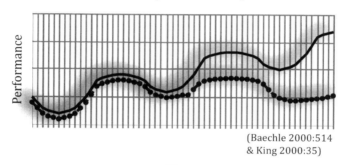

(Baechle 2000:514 & King 2000:35)

Time

— Alarm & Resistance Processes Creating a Better-Performing Athlete
● Not Enough Rest Creating Plateaus and Poor Performance

Fail to meet the intensity of your alarm phase with an equally intense recovery, and you will miss the resistance phase, spinning you out of control into the dreaded third phase of the GAS: the "exhaustion phase." One might correctly expect the exhaustion phase to be met with feelings of exhaustion, but there are other telltale signs as well. One major indication of the beginning of the exhaustion phase is experiencing a plateau, meaning your maximum effort decreases or levels off. You may start to feel tired without a plausible reason, and soreness could set in again without change to your program. **As soon as a plateau is hinted upon by the body, you need to rest. No questions asked.** When this rest takes place, a new resistance phase will occur progressing you forward.   Omnitects need to recognize these principles, which will not only allow them to grasp what is happening within their bodies during new workouts, but will help them to adapt positively when they see a plateau forming.

With an elementary understanding of the GAS, one can appreciate his or her 100% capacity.   Unfortunately, most athletes get themselves into the mindset of a "good workout" being one that leaves them completely gassed at the end, but this is a total miscue.   Any athletic person can conjure up a running or lifting program that will leave people drained, but think of the kind of a mindset in which these athletes become embedded.   Instead of focusing on *quality* and exerting their *full potential*, they simply aim to "get through it."

Bill Bowerman, legendary track coach of Oregon in the '60s and '70s, was nearly histrionic in his plead for athletes to take more rest. He was the first and quintessential advocate of recovery days during a period when every other coach was seeing how far an athlete could be pushed. Bowerman literally created the idea of an "easy day" of training, and the way he planted the seed was delivering a speech to his team at the start of every season. The address was so passionate, so filled with charisma and certainly not lacking an element of fear, it resonated with athletes for years to come.   One runner, Kenny Moore, wrote in his book *Men of Oregon* what he remembered Bill saying:

> Take any primitive organism, any weak, pitiful organism.
> Say a freshman. Make it lift, or jump or run. Let it rest.
> What happens? A little miracle. It gets a little better. It
> gets a little stronger or faster or more enduring. That's all
> training is. Stress. Recover. Improve. You'd think any
> damn fool could do it ... but you don't. You work too hard
> and rest too little and get hurt ... But I regret to inform
> you, you cannot just tell somebody what's good for him.
> He won't listen. He will not listen. First you have to get
> his attention.[330]

Sadly, sometimes the only thing that can get athletes' attention is blowing out an ACL, the same way sometimes the only way to get the attention of unhealthy adults is for them to have heart attacks.

Bowerman understood this about athletes, but refused to accept it. He knew that all athletes needed to possess an abandoned work ethic with an ironclad control over themselves, and he forced it down all of their throats. For those that didn't commit to the concept, Bowerman offered them the opportunity to quit the team. This absolute and unwavering dedication to adequate rest, thus allowing his athletes to perpetually train at 100%, allowed Bowerman to coach NCAA champions in fifteen of college track's seventeen individual events.[331] The man knew what worked.

This concept is not applied nearly enough. There are way too many overtrained athletes in college and the far majority of them have been so for so long, they don't even know what being at 100% feels like. And to be clear, being at 100% of your potential is not synonymous with "giving 100%." Coaches ask athletes to give 100% of themselves all the time, but that just means to work hard. The fact you're reading this book demonstrates you are someone who is *giving* 100% as often as is humanly possible. *Being* at 100% is vastly different though: it means that you are consistently training at your absolute fullest potential. You're not just working hard, you are working in a biological environment that could not be better prepped for exercise. You are optimally hydrated, you are adequately stretched out and warmed up, you are properly recovered from previous workouts, your hunger is satiated, you are not distracted from any external forces, you are not even a little tired, you're happy and your body feels strong and fast. Because of this, every sprint that you run is the fastest you can possibly run, and every weight that you lift is the most you can possibly lift. *Being* at 100% does not mean you're just working hard, it means you could not be better. When athletes train with 100% of their capabilities at all times, the benefits are immense:

Six Benefits

1. *MUCH LESS SUSCEPTIBLE TO INJURY.* All injuries to your body are due to an overload of some kind, either from harsh contact with an object or simply overdoing some sort of exercise past a healthy point of fatigue.[332] The people that injure themselves during practice or in training are almost solely those people that drain themselves to the point of running on fumes. From what I have witnessed, rarely do people injure themselves in the first few minutes of a game or practice, it almost solely happens at the end. That "last sprint" that gets people injured is the last straw for a fatigued muscle that finally lets go. Understanding that a fatigued muscle is an unstable muscle is the first step in protecting yourself from an avoidable injury.

This may be hard for you to initially accept, but it's true: **if your injury did not come from blunt, contact trauma, *you* have faulted.** One hundred percent of the blame of a non-contact injury is on its host body. And when we're talking about "injuries" here, we're not only in reference to ACL tears and broken bones ... Let it be known that anything short of feeling invincible is considered an injury. This includes all "tweaks," "twinges," "pulls," "strains," "popping of joints," and anything else that makes you have to baby it, nurse it, or overly think about it. If you are unable to run at 100% because you're afraid of your hamstring, or you're unable to do the bench press because of a "shoulder twinge," these are exactly the non-contact injuries in question.   These are absolutely, without question, *fully* avoidable, and if you are experiencing them, the responsibility of recovering from them rests solely on your shoulders.

	Cause	Avoidable?	Who's to Blame?	What to Do
Contact Injuries	Direct, blunt force trauma, e.g. player running into your knee or stepping on someone's foot and rolling ankle	Rarely, if ever. Short answer: No. This is one of the main reasons why sports are dangerous.	No one.	Build up muscles around joints, increase flexibility, then ... cross your fingers.
Non-Contact Injuries	Two possibilities: overtrained or undertrained, e.g. running and hamstring tweaks/pulls	Absolutely YES! These injuries should never happen to optimally-trained athletes.	YOU Know your body, rest when you need it, take recovery seriously	Take days off. Stretch. Foam roll. Drink water. Eat protein. Listen to your body.

These types of injuries might have been a long time coming, because you never stretched or slept well, or it could have just been because you *way* overdid it on that one particular day. Remember the whole point of exercise is to make you better, but if you're hurt on one day and feel like it's possible the bench press could do more harm than good, then skip it! Every athlete will encounter something like this eventually. They'll go to their coach and say something along the lines of, "My shoulder is really bothering me and my warm-up set of bench felt a little off. What should I do?" Considering it's probable your shoulder is bothering you because it's overworked, taking the day off from any sort of shoulder training is likely going to benefit the shoulder more than a workout. Fail to heed your body's warning, and you'll end up being injured — a result for which you asked.

Regardless of what the specific injury is, if you incurred it on your own volition, you need to take responsibility for it. People, perhaps college athletes even more so than others, have an impressive record of blame shifting, buck passing, unaccountability, and refusal to admit guilt, but when your body fails on its own, there's nowhere else to look but inward. Non-contact injuries result from one of two scenarios: the muscle was undertrained, or it was overtrained. That's it. Make the call between the two and adjust, because you certainly didn't get injured because you were well prepared.

If you deem you were undertrained — as in you had taken a month off from running sprints and then you hurt your hamstring on the first one — then you know you need to ease into your training a little more and perhaps strengthen that hamstring. More likely, you've been training like a madman and your hamstring kind of starts to bother you, then it goes away, then comes back a little worse, then resides, etc. This is an overtraining injury and can be remedied by ample stretching, foam rolling, and time off — the ineffables.

Finally, some athletes end up blaming their coaches for their non-contact injuries saying the coaches pushed them too far. Recognize, however, there are no malicious coaches trying to hurt their athletes. If more athletes were able to drop the ego of trying to "tough it out" and could instead communicate with their coaches about the pain they are experiencing, the coaches will likely give them as much rest as they need. While their coach may have been the one telling them to run those last sprints in which they got injured, it was ultimately up to the athletes to make the final decision if they needed an additional moment's rest. Trust that if you're not lobbying for your body, no one else will.

2. *Training at 100% of Capacity Increases Your 100% Capacity.* Should you not take enough rest between sets or between workouts, you'll perpetually be training at your 90-95% capabilities, and therefore not be able to improve. To increase ability, you need to be training at the

absolute limit of it. If you are a power athlete, this could mean as much as 5 to 25 minutes between sets, so that your body can fully recover. Charlie Francis, Olympic-level track coach of Canada, would give his Olympic sprinters 25-minute breaks between high-intensity sprints; to boot, he'd allot them ten full days of rest before any competition. Coach Francis understood that the sheer power it took to run at one's highest capacity taxed their central nervous system more than anything else, thus the long rest intervals were necessary for a full recharge.[333] Not allowing lengthy-enough rest between maximum effort sets pushes athletes' capacity down to well below 100%. When normal athletes train in the 60 and 70 percents of full capacity on a consistent basis, all they're doing is making their 60 and 70 percent effort better. 100% of 70% is still 70%, right? If there are any coaches out there looking for an athlete with a great 70 percent effort, please speak up now ...

3. *Prepares You for Game-Like Situations.* If you are training correctly, and following the rules of your specified energy system, the work-to-rest ratio during your workouts should mimic that of your sport's. Football players will typically rest as much as two to four times as much as they'll work, but their work is much more intense than most. Field and court sports are conditional, being primarily based on the position, and range anywhere from a 1:1 ratio to a 3:1. The best part is, if you have been training correctly, the additional rest you'll need during games will be minimal.

Should you need extra rest, however, do not view that as a sign of weakness. Intelligent athletes, omnitects, will take rest when they need rest during a game, and not allow their egos to get in the way of it. Because they have been training smart, their bodies will recover faster, and they'll be able to get back into the game sooner. Athletes that refuse the rest they need will run themselves into the ground by the second quarter and be more harm than good come true game time in the fourth. While it's trite to say there is no "I" in team, especially because there is a "me," omnitects will unselfishly give up game time to ensure they are giving their team the most of themselves they can. All coaches would likely agree they would much rather have 100% of their best athletes for 80% of the game than 80% of their best athletes for 100% of the game.

4. *Reduces, If Not Eliminates Plateaus.* One of the most damning and consistent problems with athletes is that when they notice themselves starting to plateau, they think they need to work harder. Way, way, **WAY** more often than not, these athletes are experiencing the beginning symptoms of overtraining and will gain substantial benefit

from more rest, not more work. If you do not allow yourself to work in the 70 and 80 percents, breaking down far enough to be overtrained is rare. If your recovery rates match the length and intensity of your training sessions, overtraining plateaus are nearly impossible to encounter!

5. *Keeps Interest Piqued.* Face it, when you feel tired, you train tired. Keeping your workouts limited to what your body can handle keeps you interested in what you're doing, and keeps you away from the dreaded burn out. If you know that you are too sore or too stressed or too whatever to get a good workout in, save it for the next day. In the short run, you might think that missing that one day is totally detrimental and appalling, but zoom out to the big picture, and that one day of extra recovery is probably more beneficial than an added day of work sub-100 percent. So, if you don't feel like training today, train tomorrow, and if you don't feel like training tomorrow or the next day, well then maybe you need to reevaluate your interest in this sport! And, most important to recognize, if you have no control over when you train, this makes the ineffables all the more important.

6. *Spotlights Poor Nutritional Habits.* Taking unnecessary fatigue out of the picture as a training variable, one can mark a decrease in performance as perhaps an outcome of insufficient nutrition. Your nutrition is one of the largest factors in guaranteeing your survival toward the end of your workout, and if you are eating correctly, you should have sufficient energy to last. Again, our goal is to train as closely relevant to game-like situations as possible, and if you are consistently unable to finish your training sessions, you'll similarly be unable to finish the final crucial minutes of competition. As you now know, it's impossible to be at 100% if your nutrition isn't allowing you to be. Dedicate time to scrutinize your diet as your success is quite determinant on what you are putting into your body.

Listening to Your Body

WHEN MOST ATHLETES INJURE THEMSELVES, their first inclination is to consider it a freak accident — a random, unlucky occurrence that will never happen again. This is a dangerous situation. The reason athletes get injured (without contact) is because of an inconsistency in their training that has driven them into an unsafe position. As mentioned earlier, the predicament is not in their physical readiness, but rather in their lack of recovery from the extreme stress they are enduring nearly every day. Athletes *must* abide by the warning signs their body provides, and recover when necessary. When this fails, injury occurs.

Without understanding the rationale of these non-contact injuries, after recuperating from their tweaked or torn muscles, athletes throw themselves right back into the environment that got them injured in the first place.

This cannot be.

You cannot heal selectively.

Attempting to solve a problem in a busted knee requires attention to be placed on many more sources than just that knee. Yet instead of injured athletes taking a long, hard look at their lifestyle to perhaps pinpoint where this affliction surmounted, they head to athletic trainers, massage therapists, and doctors alike to find their "mono-cure." Many injured athletes just want to hear a person with a degree tell them what the misfortune is, then give them their one, expeditious cure. But, *there is no mono-cure to an injury.* Athletes go to these specialists because it does not mandate them to take responsibility for their imperfections that led to their injuries. They'll blame coaches, the weather, their shoes, and their teammates, when all along, it is their fault.

More time spent with specialists does not solve problems nor lessen the probability of injuries, only intelligence does. Most specialists treat symptoms; it is their job to do so, and there is absolutely nothing wrong with it. Rolled ankles? Wrap 'em up and send 'em on their way. This becomes an issue when athletes don't learn anything from the experience. Of course, responsible specialists exist that attempt to educate athletes on how to avoid similar injuries in the future, but these specialists are not as commonplace as they need to be. Every athlete needs an education of how to avoid their mundane injuries, because they are altogether preventable. Treating symptoms instead of root causes (e.g. lifestyle choices which led to an athlete being overtrained and/or underrecovered) is like teaching calculus to the elderly ... it doesn't make any sense.

If you injure yourself, stop and look at what's going on in your training and lifestyle that led to such an event. *Non-contact injuries are not unlucky, random acts.* They happened for a reason. There was something wrong with your training that led to this problem, so don't just head to the trainers for your quick fix. Of course you'll need to head to the training room no matter what, but treat that encounter as a mechanic putting a piece of gum over a hole in your tire. Their job is to deal with the immediate trauma, *you* are responsible for the larger, more impactful solution in regard to the future. Especially for those of you who have hurt yourselves before, you need to be aware of how you felt right before it happened, never allowing yourself to experience that sensation again.

Listening to your body takes time and practice, but only because we have been conditioned not to do it. When you were born, all you did was do exactly what your body asked. Babies sleep when they're tired and eat when they're hungry — just about nothing gets in their way. We need to take a page out of the baby's book. Because so few athletes listen to their bodies, so many run themselves into the ground, developing muscles with high tension issues that inevitably get injured.

Where many athletes typically overtrain themselves is in the middle of their competitive seasons. If, by the middle of your sport's season, you are getting tired in the 4th quarter, it is not because you are out of shape; in fact, it is just the opposite. Halfway through any athlete's competitive season, one would be hard pressed to find an athlete out of shape on the *under*prepared side. So if, out of the blue, you are suddenly feeling tired at a point in the game unnatural to you, you need more rest.

Perhaps the most important time to trust this concept is as you head into the post season. For some inexplicable reason, as athletes head into their conference or national tournaments, they feel the need to do more. Again, they feel tired as these final games approach, not because they're out of shape, but because they're underrecovered, and they panic. They fail to recognize they made it to the post season because they were healthy and clearly in better shape than most of their opponents, evidenced by their winning record. Therefore, when the post-season arrives, trust your training. The absolute worst time to add to your regiment is in the post season. You're already successful!

A perfect example of this happened to a freshman swimmer with which I was working. She was in the middle of a great season where she was winning a lot of races, and suddenly started to experience some low back pain. Instead of interpreting this as a warning that she was being overexerted, she construed it as a sign of weakness in the muscles of her low back. When she asked me what exercises she could do to strengthen her back, *in the middle of her season,* I was shocked! What she should have realized, first of all, was that if she wasn't strong enough by the middle of her season, she had already missed the boat. *No one* is going to get any stronger during the end of their competitive season. More importantly, however, she needed to understand that in-season pains are rarely, if ever, signs of weaknesses; rather, they are indications that you lack sufficient recovery for all the hard work you are accomplishing during competition. Fatigue will mask one's true level of athleticism. For this particular swimmer, I forced her to schedule stretching appointments with me twice a week for the rest of the season. Not surprisingly, after stretching her hamstrings for 20 minutes each side our first session, she was relieved of pain.

If you are under the supervision of a coaching staff, they should never allow you to reach this point, or to make a poor decision like that. However, due to the scope of talent on any given team — not to mention just the sheer number of athletes on some teams — no coach can keep up with everybody. You will need to pay close attention to yourself, as you are the only one that knows how you are feeling. You will need to be the "monarch of all you survey," as the poet William Cowper wrote of Alexander Selkirk — a man who was marooned on a deserted island for four years in the early 1700s. By becoming the monarch of all you survey, you'll be able to see your body's signs of overtraining early and change your lifestyle accordingly.

After all, you can't fight the body: that is a battle you simply will not win. Listen for symptoms of fatigue and make the necessary adjustments to keep yourself healthy. The road to injury is mostly unconscious and unintentional; sometimes it takes that injury to open up some eyes. Of course, after the injury occurs, the attempt to get well becomes a *very* conscious and *very* intentional state of awareness. The question is, why do people have to get injured before they start listening to their bodies? This goes for adults later in life too. Most people aren't cognitively aware of their health until they discover they have diabetes or suffer a heart attack. We need to be better about being proactive. You must be vigilant with your body's signs of fatigue/plateaus if you plan to make it out of this training environment unscathed.

Five Major Points

- In the scale of undertrained, optimally prepared, and overtrained, nearly all athletes playing a varsity sport are overtrained.
- Plateaus are almost always the first signs of overtraining. Rest when you experience them.
- Training at 100% of your capacity makes you much less susceptible to injury, is the only way to increase your 100% capacity, prepares you for game-like situations, reduces plateaus, keeps interests piqued, and can spotlight poor nutritional habits.
- If you are experiencing aches and pains, you cannot heal selectively. Focus on your lifestyle in aggregate.
- Non-contact injuries are not unlucky, random acts. They result from either over- or undertraining.

Chapter Thirteen

Healthy Habits
How To

Svengali

As FALLIBLE HUMANS, WE ALL share a common flaw: we possess the power to justify ourselves as reasonable, logical beings, even when our actions can sometimes be irrational and only a product of habit. We like to think what we ate this morning, or what we are currently wearing was the result of a calculated weighing of benefits and risks performed by our super-logical, utility-maximizing brain ... when, in actuality, we are hardly as in control as we like to think. One paper published by a Duke University researcher in 2006 found that more than 40 percent of the actions we perform daily aren't decisions, but habits.[334]

We might not remember the experiences that created our habits, but once they are lodged within our subconscious minds, they will influence the way we act, often without our comprehension.[335] This fact is why the human habit patternicity could be referred to as a svengali. This word comes from George du Maurier's 1894 novel *Trilby*, and has come to be used as a noun for a person or a thing that controls another, often with a malevolent intent. Charles Duhigg, the leading expert on habits, would agree with this assessment, as he wrote in his book *The Power of Habit*:

> Habits are powerful … they can emerge outside our consciousness, or can be deliberately designed. They often occur without our permission, but can be reshaped by fiddling with their parts. They shape our lives far more than we realize — they are so strong, in fact, that they cause our brains to cling to them at the exclusion of all else, including common sense.[336]

A fine example of this can be found when we head to the grocery store with a list in hand. Despite having clearly designated, written objectives, 50 percent of purchasing decisions occur at the moment customers see a product on the shelf. Consumers often act surprisingly habitually, automatically repeating past behavior with little regard to current goals. People, in general, act against their better judgment with disturbing regularity. Habits are stronger than our best intentions, and live up to the name svengali.[337]

Despite your best efforts to be a healthy athlete, you currently have habits in place that are probably working against you. You are likely aware of many of these habits, it's just that you have some emotional tie to them. Whether it be an affinity for chocolate chip cookies after dinner or a fifth of spiced rum after classes on Friday, a lot of people are guilty of what Jonathan Haidt would call allowing the emotional tail to wag the rational dog.[338] We are not rational creatures: we are extremely emotional and often behave in ways that allow us to enjoy something now over something we *may* be able to enjoy later, even if the latter reward is far greater.[339] This supremacy of emotion over reason has been handed down to us through our genetics, and scientists have proven the emotional brain has been exquisitely refined by evolution over the last several hundred million years. We weren't even designed to be rational, evidenced by the mind's composition of a messy network of different areas mainly involved with the production of emotion.[340]

Emotion was particularly important when our ancestors were out on the plains hunting big game, which is why our emotional brain remains lightning-fast and our rational brain remains quite slow by comparison. Think about it: if our ancestors heard a rustling in the bushes, they could've pontificated about how loud the rustling was and analyzed the probability of it being a large animal about to eat them, *or* they could let their emotion take over and just assume it was a lion and run away!

To this day, we remain an emotional species, even when reason stands in opposition of our decisions. We are more apt to eat and do what we want, instead of what we probably know is best. Or, even worse, we'll be good for awhile, then use that brief bout of healthfulness as leverage to be destructive. "I had a salad for lunch then worked out really hard, so I deserve this sundae tonight!" Sometimes, when we're not careful, being healthy allows us to justify unhealthy behavior in the future. This mindset was seen when anti-lock brake systems (ABS) first came into automobiles. Drivers immediately used the additional element of safety found in this new system to drive more recklessly and rely more heavily on their trustworthy brakes.[341] So, in effect, the risk reduction offered by ABS was *consumed* by motorists, instead of saved, and the rate of accidents did not decrease as it should have.

Ths is the same way people act when their noble actions are not habitual: they take their one healthy act and employ it as a bargaining chip to do stupid things later on. This is what makes habits so much more impactful than simple actions: **a habit is so mundane to the beholder that it will entice no future response**. An action, on the other hand, often promotes a false state of confidence where people can over-compensate down the road. One single action, of course, does nothing to define who we are, but nevertheless we interpret it as evidence of our benevolence and believe we are entitled to something special in return. So where an action can be a noteworthy event seemingly worthy of making a day distinctively unique, a habit is simply a mundanity, part of an average day.

Examples of this type of behavior can be seen daily with college athletes. When athletes don't make it a regular habit of working out as hard as they can every day, on those days when they are pushed hard, they'll reward themselves with dessert later on that night.   When students aren't accustomed to skipping nights of drinking, they'll reward themselves with extra alcohol the next time they drink. When people with poor eating habits eat well at lunch, they'll reward themselves with something heavy and nutrient-poor for dinner. When the good actions become more regular and habitual, however, they will elicit no future response.

And thus the source of habits' power. They are so unexceptional to the person doing them, they require, and receive, no brain power. Unless you deliberately fight a habit from forming, it's going to happen automatically.[342] The automaticity happens so naturally and subcon-sciously, it's nearly impossible to perceive the habit growing. And when it gets pushed into the subconscious like that, it becomes infinitely more potent as the unconscious mind is able to process 11 million pieces of information per second, while the conscious mind can handle only 40.[343] For this reason, it's vital to turn those healthy actions you do every so often into habits that are ritualistically performed daily.   As we'll see, doing this not only gives you a healthy habit but also allows you to conserve your willpower for other areas.   So then, how do we turn an action into a habit?

How Habits Form

WHAT IS PERHAPS MOST INTERESTING about habits, is that the more we practice a particular habit, the less we need to think in order to make it happen.   Scientific research on rats has shown that as rats learn how to navigate a maze, their mental activity decreases.   As they get faster and faster through the maze, their brains work less and less, and as almost all other brain activity shuts down, one tiny, ancient, neurological structure seems to take over: the basal ganglia.[344]   In effect, when a habit emerges, the brain stops fully participating in decision making.   The basal ganglia will store habits so the rest of the brain can focus its attention elsewhere.

Scientists have determined this is the way elite athletes function. When the most skilled players are performing at their peak, there is very little brain activity; they truly perform better by thinking less.   Super Bowl-winning coach Tony Dungy wanted to tap into this idea by getting players to stop making decisions during games.   He wanted them to be automated to do the right things.   As he explained, "Champions don't do extraordinary things, they do ordinary things, but they do them without thinking."[345]   He knew that experts did not need to concentrate on their skills.   Beginners, on the other hand, need to think a lot to be operative, and unlike veterans, newcomers have a barrage of brain activity while attempting to perform new skills.[346] The better they get, the less they will think.   Essentially, with enough training, the automatic centers of the brain will control movements unconsciously.

This automaticity is responsible for all habits, whether good or bad.   So while it'd be good to learn how to wrangle this concept and train yourself to automatically make your bed when you wake up, this same mechanism explains why some people can't walk through a grocery store without buying an onslaught of junk they don't actually want.   Their routines have become so habitual, their loyalty to brands so automatic, they don't even recognize when it's happening anymore.   Unless we truly stop and think about these habits, to turn the invisible into the visible, our habits will occur outside of our consciousness, where our brain activity won't be occurring in the center of the mind devoted to cognitive reason and thought. Businesses discovered this well before psychologists did (e.g. studies show most people buy the same deodorant week after week almost no matter what[347]), but once psychology started looking for examples of automaticity, a deluge of cases were uncovered. Even today, it isn't clear how much of our behavior is under our conscious control.[348]

Before this miraculous transformation of action to habit can occur, however, we first must get deeply ingrained into the action. The only way to do that is to cultivate a neurological craving by putting together a cue to trigger the habit, a routine that carries it out, and a clear reward to make it all worth while. For example, if you want to start eating fruit with breakfast, it's essential that you choose a simple cue (such as putting a bowl of apples and oranges out on your kitchen table) and a distinct reward (which could be a sense of accomplishment by checking it off your "impelling habits" list provided in the appendix).

This simple habit loop — cue, routine, reward — can be used to define all habits. Over time, this loop becomes so hardwired, it essentially becomes part of who we are, and attempting to deviate from it becomes nearly impossible. Even if we accidentally alter our habit, the mind can immediately pinpoint the error as it's happening. Patric Rabbitt of the University of Manchester found that typing mistakes are made with slightly less pressure than correct strokes. The brain recognizes deviations from the norm as we make them, and can even force us to unknowingly hold back at the last second.[349] Just another eerie example of how powerful habits are once they have formed.

The dangerous thing is habits don't need much out of us to become part of us. Once our body impersonates an attitude or a behavior long enough, the mind simply adopts it. But since we often don't recognize habit loops as they grow, however, we can't always pinpoint them; thus, we have a problem controlling our habit loops. As was mentioned, habits are so powerful they create neurological cravings, but other habits, like smoking, create biological cravings.[350] Most of the time, these cravings emerge so gradually, we are blind to their influence. This sway over us only becomes apparent when we try to say no and change the habit. The problem is, by the time we're trying to say no, the svengali is in full effect, and it takes incredible willpower to alter the cycle.

Where willpower is necessary, most humans are fraught with the likelihood of failure. Historically, we've been pretty bad at containing ourselves, but new research is helping us to understand how to better tap into our willpower stores. There have been more than 200 studies that all yield the same results: willpower isn't just a skill, it behaves like a muscle.[351]   So not only can we train it to become stronger, but it also fatigues when we use it over and over again.[352]   Like your luscious quads or bulging biceps, willpower too gets tired as it works harder (e.g. a long day of saying "no" to temptations), and has less power to give at the end of the day. This is why so many dieters can survive the day but backslide at dinner; why stressful days typically lead to comfort food at night; why we find ourselves taking shortcuts in the afternoon but strangely never in the morning.   Generally speaking, wearing down your willpower will make you considerably less capable of regulating your desires and can even make you less honest as well.[353]   Simply put, the more battles you wage against yourself throughout the day, the more likely you are to be mentally bushed come nightfall, creating a tug-of-war between impulse and reason.   Even being somewhat aware of this propensity for dishonesty can move us in the right direction and help us to avoid temptations altogether.

The key is to find ways to decide less. Recognizing we only have a finite capacity to make wise decisions and exercise willpower is an important stage in understanding habits. If we know going into it that more decision-making will result in less willpower, then we need to remove some of our choices; it's much easier to avoid temptation altogether than to attempt to overcome it.[354]   So instead of having a bowl of fruit and a bowl of candy on your table, just get rid of the obvious. Instead of wrestling with the thought of making your bed every morning, just make a deal with yourself that you are going to make it the moment you get up, no matter what. If there's a choice between french fries or a side salad, you're not thinking about which one you want more, you're just diving into the salad. No thinking, just *boom! Action!*

Baked or fried? *Boom:* baked.

Escalator or stairs? *Boom:* stairs.

Water or soda? *Boom:* water.

Shoulder pads or cowboy ties? *Boom:* neither.

Eliminating choices is a great first step toward willpower development.   Eradicating the willpower component of seemingly mundane decisions will leave you with more capacity to exercise better willpower throughout the day.   By cultivating these mini-habits and accumulating small wins throughout the day, your confidence and willpower will meet the night with a newfound resilience, and you'll finally be able to turn down the late night pizza order!

Continue this routine, and you'll be well on your way to a healthy lifestyle and a huge reserve of willpower, which has more benefits than you might imagine. Dozens of studies show that willpower is the single most important habit linked to individual success. Remember the marshmallow study? Self-discipline is better than IQ and intellectual talent at predicting every single academic-performance variable,[355] *twice* as accurate in predicting students' grade-point average.[356] To boot, the correlation between IQ and occupational success is between 0.2 and 0.3 — negligible at best (your height, for example, has a 0.7 correlation with your parents' height).[357] Willpower, then, is the most important trait an athlete can possess. And as your willpower gets stronger, it positively affects what you eat and how hard you are willing to work. Willpower touches everything.

Even if you don't initially *want* to make your bed or get the side salad, faking it goes a long way. Remember, habits form simply by a recurring loop of cue, routine, and reward, regardless if that loop is genuine or forced. Then that little habit, no matter how inconsequential it may seem at first, can spread to other aspects of your life and before long, you've changed into the person you wanted to be. With a little training, and a little foresight, you can easily create some seriously potent and beneficial habits.

Impelling Habits

SOME HABITS ARE SO POTENT, in fact, they create a spillover effect into other areas of your life. Countless studies have shown that exercise is the single most important habit to possess, as those that regularly exercise seem to have an easier time creating additional healthy habits that complement the exercise. In a lot of ways, it's just a self-fulfilling prophecy. When we work out, we view ourselves in a more positive light, thereby believing we are healthy people that *should* have other healthy habits to boot.

In social psychology, there is a version of the self-fulfilling prophecy called "labeling theory," which works off the premise when someone believes you are a certain kind of person, you tend to live up to those expectations.[358] For example, if a teacher thinks you're smart, he'll treat you as such — more attention, more respect, more expectation. In return, you're likely to react with more effort, put in more time, and yield him a better grade; thus, perpetuating an endless positive feedback loop leading to the fulfillment of your label. Once we believe something about our character, we have no desire to be hypocrites.

A great experiment conducted in 1980 by Steven Sherman illuminates this point pretty well. Sherman wanted to test people's adherence to their label, so he asked two sets of people over the phone, in two distinct manners, to donate three hours of their time for a cancer drive. In the first group, Sherman simply asked if they would do it, to which most responded yes ... later, only four percent showed up. The second group was asked if they *thought* they would show up *if* they were asked. To this question, most said of course they would, because they viewed themselves as generous people. Once they were in fact asked, almost all of them showed up.[359] How could this be? Well, the first group didn't have to compare their decisions to their values, they simply had to decide if they wanted to give up three hours of their life or not. The second group, however, first had to make an assessment of their own personalities; they needed to publicly declare what type of people they were, then act. Once they had painted themselves as kind-hearted, giving people, they needed to conform to that idea or risk cognitive dissonance.

Another study conducted at Arizona State asked people if they would be willing to take part in an experiment for a good cause, and about half said they would. After they agreed, the experimenters dropped the bomb by saying the experiment would begin at 7:00 am. Shockingly, ninety-five percent of the respondents still showed up. Later, the researchers administered the same exact experiment, but told the people up front about the early wake-up call. To this, only 24 percent agreed to take part.[360] Of course, the people in the first study weren't seren-dipitously morning people, they were inclined to make their behaviors consistent with their views of themselves. No one desires to be a hypocrite.

These studies are important to understand, as they can be used to harness a healthy lifestyle. If we can pinpoint a few habits that routinely make us *feel* healthier, research leads us to believe that we will then start leading better lives and making healthier choices. This tendency to be consistent strongly compels us to do things we might not ordinarily do. As Sheena Iyengar writes, "When we experience a conflict between our beliefs and our actions, we can't rewind time and take back what we've already done, so we adjust our beliefs to bring them in line with our actions."[361] And herein lies the key to changing our lifestyles: all we've got to do is perform a few actions that make us seem like healthy people.

In turn, we'll start to believe that we are healthy, and change aspects of our lifestyles accordingly!

These habits in question, the ones that can change other aspects of our lives, could be called "**impelling habits**." Impelling habits are not only quality habits in themselves, but research has also proven each one catalyzes better decision-making throughout your day, even if the better judgment is subconscious. Psychological studies show that we quickly and easily start believing in the things we say and do, even when the original reason for saying or doing them is no longer relevant.[362] So if you just force yourself to complete these impelling habits every day, it won't be long until you're doing them on your *own* volition, instead of some book's.

Below is a list of the top eight impelling routines in conjunction with possible cues and rewards. None of these habits are particularly challenging, yet they still encourage widespread change by creating cultures where new and improved values become ingrained. As was said earlier, exercise is the most important and powerful impelling habit we know, and since this book is written for college athletes, it's probably a fair assumption to believe we've got that one down pat. In addition to training, however, there are many other impelling habits that promote personal growth and buoy health. The cues and rewards you utilize to complete these eight habits are completely up to you, but the hope is once you read the research behind each habit, you will recognize there is a strong need to complete each one of these routines. To supplement the list below, a checklist has been provided for you in the appendix to track your efforts with these habits. The checklist will ideally shift this abstract lesson in health, one you no doubt have heard countless other times, to a practical and personal challenge you are willing to accept.

1. *Record your hours of sleep from the night prior.* (Possible Cue: Moment you wake up; Reward: Awareness that yields a more diligent pursuit of adequate sleep) Countless studies have proven the most successful dieters do one thing very well: keep a food journal. Although it may sound excruciatingly elementary, often getting people to simply *look* at their diets, lifestyles, or habits on paper can be enough to promote the necessary changes. The simple *awareness* is more than half the battle of creating change; thus, putting a magnifying glass up to your sleeping pattern will make you notice whether you're getting enough sleep or not, and typically, just seeing the lagging written on paper is enough to get you to pursue more!

2. *Make your bed.* (<u>Possible Cue</u>: As soon as you get out of it; <u>Reward</u>: Better productivity and well-being) At the risk of sounding like your mother, you really should make your bed. Studies have shown that making your bed every morning is correlated with better productivity, a greater sense of well-being, and stronger skills at sticking with a budget.[363] Again, it's not that this tidy bed *causes* good grades and good moods, but rather the habit initializes a chain reaction that helps other good habits take form.

3. *Eat plants.* (<u>Possible Cue</u>: Fruit with breakfast, a salad at lunch; <u>Reward</u>: Incalculable health benefits, less need for supplementation) This one shouldn't need to be justified all too fervently. There are literally hundreds, if not thousands of studies demonstrating how diets rich in plants reduce the risk of dying from all Western diseases.[364] Between the vitamins, minerals, antioxidants, phytochemicals, and everything in between, no sane person could argue against eating more fruits and vegetables. The trouble, then, is establishing habit loops that promote the consumption of plants. One good cue is to eat fruit with breakfast, or a salad with dinner, or to prepare several snacks to eat over the course of the day consisting mainly of fruits and/or veggies (e.g. carrots with hummus, bananas with peanut butter, apples with cinnamon). Don't just say to yourself, "I'm going to eat more fruits and vegetables." How many people declare that every other day, only to backslide?   What is mandatory to create change is to develop a habit loop — cue, routine, reward — that is easy to follow and impossible to mess up. Find your cue.

4. *Carry a water bottle at all times.* (<u>Possible Cue</u>: Leave it by the front door or in your bag; <u>Reward</u>: Perpetual hydration, and less likely to drink junk) There has already been a full chapter devoted to the clear and untainted benefits of water consumption, but it's worth mentioning again: *nothing substitutes for water*. Water is the life force, and because there is no storage system for water in the body, it is a daily necessity to drink it often and gratuitously.   Carrying a water bottle with you everywhere, like the way you carry your wallet, allows you to sip frequently, save the money you would spend on bottled water or sodas, and prevent the disposal of potentially the largest scourge of the earth: plastic bottles. And in addition to all this quantifiable data, carrying a water bottle also has a qualitative aspect: the aura of health (i.e. the feeling you're being healthy). This mindset, as we discussed, can go a long way toward benefitting your lifestyle, especially in terms of

impacting other habits. When you view yourself as healthy, you tend to want to be healthier.

5. *Leave places (or things) better than you found them.* (Possible Cue: Whenever you see something out of order, such as trash on the street; Reward: Potent feeling of control and responsibility) What this means, in essence, is that *you* take responsibility for yourself, and your environment. For example, if you see a mess on a table in the dining hall, *you* do something to clean it up. If your section in the gym is plagued with misplaced weights, *you* spend your rest intervals rearranging them. If you see trash blowing down the street, *you* pick it up and put it in a garbage bin. Ameliorate your surroundings. This may seem like an abstract thought, or that you're being forced into public service, but the intentions here are much more about personal service. This idea is essentially control and responsibility in a nutshell, and several studies have examined the importance of these qualities. One such study followed senior citizens in a home, and compared those who were in charge of watering plants and had autonomous control over their daily lives with those who were given plants that were watered by the staff and whose decisions were essentially made for them. The researchers concluded those with the extra responsibilities lived longer, happier, and healthier lives than the other residents. Apparently these tasks (although seemingly menial) imbued in them a feeling of control that affected their health and mood.[365]   What we can take from this is how the feeling of control, even in small, trivial doses, can make one measurably happier and healthier.   What better way to feel in control than to take responsibility for your surroundings?

6. *Eat something immediately post-workout.* (Cue: The moment your workout ends; Reward: Faster recovery and higher levels of muscle glycogen) As you learned in the *Macronutrients* section earlier, what exercise does is literally break muscle tissue down and deplete your stores of muscle glycogen, which is the source of almost all your athletic energy. Immediately following your workout, your body works hard to restore and grow those stores. Anything you can do to help will greatly supplement your potential. Remember, elite athletes have been shown to have unusually high stores of muscle glycogen, and you can too if you train yourself to eat within thirty minutes post-workout.

7. *Stretch for at least five minutes.* (Possible Cue: Before you get in bed; Reward: Longer muscles less susceptible to injury)   As we've discussed in previous chapters, most athletes need more exposure to flexibility yet few claim they have the time to do it. Sitting down for a

quick stretch before bed has many advantages: the obvious being longer muscles that have more capacity for strength and speed while also being less susceptible to injury. In addition to that, however, a stretch before bed could help calm you and better prepare you for sleep. Finally, why five minutes you might ask? While a half-hour to hour-long stretch would be ideal, everyone can find five minutes before bed to get this done, and something is better than nothing. Perhaps after a few weeks of allotting the minimum five minutes, you might notice you're feeling better and you'll start to add time to that on your own volition.

      8. *Pleasure read for at least five minutes.* (<u>Possible Cue</u>: When you get into bed; <u>Reward</u>: Feeling of control, higher probability of achievement, as well as the obvious benefit of more intelligence) College is a time when nearly everything one learns is out of obligation. Take a few minutes every day to learn something voluntarily, and you will be instilled with a feeling of control. In addition to the aforementioned study with the elderly plant waterers, there are others that show the relationship of control and health quite well. For example, when people are given details about what is going to happen during surgery, they have less anxiety and can actually recover faster after the surgery is finished.[366]   Also, when people think they are doing something for personal reasons instead of obligations — if they feel it's a choice — they find it more enjoyable. If, by contrast, they feel as though they have no autonomy in the decision, their willpower gets tired much faster, and they will inevitably lose their interest or self-control.[367] My father used to sail almost every day of his life because he enjoyed it, and by the time he was in college, he had gotten pretty good. With the increased free time and surmounting skill, he sailed even more often and looked for opportunities to get out on the water with competitive sailors. Eventually, he got so good he was invited to sail in the ISAF World Championships, something you'd think would excite him beyond control. Instead, he remembers the immediate switch in his brain that turned his voluntary joy rides into obligatory training sessions. Nothing had really changed in his life — he was still sailing the same amount, hanging out with the same people, racing the same boats — but the feeling of *requirement* made him almost resent an activity he otherwise loved. Take something away from this and apply it to reading. You're forced to do a lot of reading you probably would rather live without, so take a few minutes every day to read something you enjoy.

And there you have it, the full eight impelling habits! While most of these habits might seem so inconsequentially small to you, that's kind of the point.   There is a huge body of research that shows these tiny victories influence disproportionate power to the victories themselves. Yes, eating a salad at lunch is a pretty trivial thing when done once or twice, but these little wins fuel big changes by convincing us that our bigger goals are within reach.[368]   Piling on too much at once has never been the answer, but with these impelling habits being so small yet capable of producing big changes throughout the day, people can dive right into them without feeling overwhelmed.   Of course, in order to change our habits for the better, we must believe that change is feasible!

Below you'll see the Impelling Habits Checklist. Appendix B has several more copies for continued usage, and there is a "Beneath the College Jersey Healthy Habits Workbook" available online as well that includes a 12-week food journal as well as a 12-week Impelling Habits Checklist.

Week:	M	T	W	R	F	S	N
Record My Hours of Sleep from Last Night Here							
Make My Bed							
Eat Plants (fruit w/ bfast, salad w/lunch)							
Carry a Water Bottle Everywhere I Go							
Leave at Least One Thing Better							
Eat Something Immediately Post-Workout							
Stretch for 5 Minutes (before bed?)							
Pleasure Read for 5 Minutes (before bed?)							

Changing Habits for the Better

ONCE WE DEVELOP A ROUTINE of two hours of TV every day or dessert with every dinner, those patterns will always remain inside our heads. Sometimes the decisions we make are limited by the decisions we've made in the past, even though prior circumstances are no longer relevant or necessary to consider. This is called "path dependency," and can negatively affect us if we are not careful. A very interesting example of this lies with the history of the QWERTY keyboard. Jared Diamond, in his book *Guns, Germs, and Steel* describes how the initial design of the keyboard layout, in 1873, was made as a feat of anti-engineering. The creators knew that if adjacent keys were struck in quick succession, the typewriters of 1873 would easily become jammed; therefore, they manufactured a keyboard scattering the most common letters all over the board and put the most used ones on our left hand in an effort to slow down typists.[369] Later on, with the development of less-jammable keys, came the creation of a much more efficient board that could double our typing speed and reduce our effort by 95 percent.[370] Did we adopt that board and junk the QWERTY one designed to slow us down? The answer lies attached to your laptop.

Our habits become so entrenched in us that even when given obvious reasons to change, it can still be difficult to do so. By the same rule, however, if we can create new neurological patterns that overpower old behaviors — a new cue, a new routine, or a new reward — we can force those bad tendencies out of our habitual lives.[371] The first step in this process of habit change was made famous by Alcoholics Anonymous (AA): admitting you have a problem.

Alcoholics Anonymous actually has a lot to teach us about kicking bad habits. For instance, AA insists alcoholics recognize their cues for drinking. Getting people to describe what triggers their habitual behavior is a form of awareness training, and is the most effective first step in habit reversals.[372] So now start thinking. What is a bad habit you possess? Carousing every Saturday night? Eating pizza with late night studying? Whatever it may be, start the process of reversing it by discovering *why* you do it.

Allow me to give you my personal, embarrassing example. In high school, I was a cross-country stud. Weighing in at 135 pounds, I left for college with three school records: the fastest 5,000-meter run, the fastest 3,200-meter run, and the most turnovers in a career of basketball. Once I got to college, however, I was psychologically burnt out from running, couldn't play basketball (for the aforementioned reason) and decided to turn to the weights instead. My sole goal was strength, and by junior year, I had increased my squat from 135 to 450, my bench from 95 to 335, and my body weight from 135 to 220. And a *disgusting* 220, I might add. I justified my weight and fat stomach the same way smokers justify their dirty habit: reducing dissonance by creating self-deluding, ingenious excuses. Smokers convince themselves smoking isn't so harmful since it helps them relax or prevents them from gaining weight, and so on. I justified my fat ass in essentially the same way. I admitted I was fat, but immediately followed that up by commenting on how I was the strongest I'd ever been. I told people I *needed* the extra weight to ensure I'd remain strong.

As you can imagine, this fat boy in my past had some pretty bad habits. Like most people, my diet was not quite a series of conscious decisions, but rather a history of habits. The one that really sticks out in my mind was how I started every morning, *every morning,* with a sausage, egg and cheese on an english muffin at the local diner. I had done it so often, and skipped it so rarely, that repugnant sandwich became part of my very being. The habit was firmly entrenched to say the least. In order to analyze this habit properly, let's start with AA's advice and find the cue. Why did I do it?   Charles Duhigg writes that experiments have shown almost all cues fit neatly into one of five categories: location, time, emotional state, other people, or the immediately preceding action.[373] So did I eat the sandwich just because it was morning?

Was it plain old hunger?

Did I need a break from the dining halls?

Maybe I wanted to see the employees that seemed to like me?

Did I think this was the breakfast of champions?   After all, I thought, how else could I get this much protein?

And while these may have been the initial triggers to get me over there, I also needed to continue the teachings of AA and search for the rewards … What was I getting out of this habit? Was it the deliciousness of the sandwich itself?

Knowing I just had 30-plus grams of protein?

Maybe it was the chance to get in my car and drive off campus every day?

The satiation I felt so early in the morning?

I can tell you the reward certainly wasn't the guilt I experienced after dominating a sausage sandwich at six in the morning. Thinking back on it now is honestly making me queasy, but it comes as no surprise. I even knew at the time how gross the habit was, but I had so many ways to justify it to myself, and besides, what else was I supposed to eat to ensure fullness in the morning, while also obtaining all the obligatory protein my body needed?

This thought process was so asinine and naïve, I'm embarrassed to admit it is a part of my history; nevertheless, it's true. Anyway, when I finally got my act together and held my body, habits, and lifestyle up to the mirror, I was *not* pleased with what I saw. I knew I needed to start changing my habits, and first on the hit list was that sandwich. After great deliberation, I determined my greatest driving force behind the sandwich was the protein. I realized I didn't even like the taste or the diner that much. In fact, I'm pretty sure everyone who worked or ate there despised the chubby college kid who routinely came in to disrupt their ineffectual morning grumblings. After more than 350 fat-boy-specials, I had finally come to the conclusion it was not the food itself I was after, just the nutrients; therefore, the cue was the psychological necessity of protein in the morning.

As for the reward, I knew from the onset it was the feeling of fullness that would last hours and the mind-easing awareness I had consumed a couple dozen grams of protein. Although it took me over a year to realize it, I finally understood the motivations behind my deplorable little habit. And while I hadn't *really* done anything to change it yet, pinpointing the cue and reward associated with it made me feel like I had already moved mountains. "It seems ridiculously simple, but once you're aware of how your habit works, once you recognize the cues and rewards, you're halfway to changing it," Nathan Azrin, one of the developers of habit reversal training said. "It seems like it should be more complex. The truth is, the brain can be reprogrammed. You just have to be deliberate about it."[374] Once I took responsibility of my problem and a.) admitted I had a terrible habit, b.) knew why I had it, i.e. pinpointed the cue, c.) took the blame for it, and d.) was committed to changing it, I felt free! There didn't seem like there was really anything else to do, as the hardest thing was the initial ownership of the problem.

I found my cue was nutrients, and my reward was satiation, so I moved onto the next step, which is replacing the bad routine with a good one. What research has shown us is that habits are most malleable when the "Golden Rule" of habit change is employed: if the cue and the reward are the same, a new routine can be inserted.[375] By dressing something new in old clothes, nothing will seem amiss about the change in behavior; the familiarity of the habit loop will drive the new pattern seamlessly into fruition. To change people's diets, then, we have to camouflage atypical health food as commonplace. This is how we get from burgers, potato chips and soda to veggie burgers, veggie chips, and kombucha — we're doing our best to disguise the good stuff. Few people in America would order an explicitly healthy option like a plate of raw vegetables, but when we veil the exotic and make it familiar, there is a chance. Even the Committee on Food Habits concluded the secret to changing the American diet was familiarity.[376]

So it seems pretty easy … in theory at least. Keep the cue, keep the reward, disguise the good, and you're off to the races. Of course, change will probably not be fast nor will it be easy. For me and the breakfast sandwich debacle, I needed to change more than just the sandwich in order to get over it. I knew I first needed to create a new habit of visiting the grocery store every week. By doing that, I could ensure I was setting myself up for success every morning instead of relying on what I could find open at 5:30am. Years later, I am still going to the grocery store (now almost daily), and thanks to this new habit, I get to enjoy far healthier breakfast options. Whether it be vegetable omelets, fruit smoothies with plant protein powder, oatmeal with fresh fruit, or the occasional plain greek yogurt with chia seeds and berries, at the end of these meals, I'm full, I know I got a bunch of nutrients and protein, and I believe in the health benefits of my selections.

The important thing to remember when attempting to change a habit is you must *believe* in your new routine's ability to yield you the same reward. Research has indicated belief was the variable that made a repeated habit loop into a permanent behavior.[377] So on the one hand, you have the rational, logical, and ultra-intelligent part of your brain telling you your habits are foolish and need change, and then you have the snap-judgment, emotional part of your brain feeding you with intuition about whether or not the change is worthwhile. Research pretty clearly suggests that intuition ignores statistics, which is a perfect rationale for why people smoke, or eat fast food, or drink 'til they pass out.[378] There are limits to pure reason, and understanding we are emotional creatures will help us go a long way when attempting to alter our behavioral patterns. With this knowledge, we can heed the words of William James when he wrote that the will to believe is the most important ingredient in creating belief in change.[379]

If you don't *believe* in the necessity or motive to change, even though the scientific evidence is clearly against you, the "now" you must dupe the "future" you into doing what is best for both parties. As David McRaney writes, "This is why food plans like Nutrisystem work for so many people. Now-you commits to spending a lot of money on a giant box of food that future-you will have to deal with."[380] When you get this concept, you realize **planning is the only way to succeed**. Given an opportunity to commit up front to your preferred path of action, you stand a good chance of succeeding in the future. The only caveat is you need to find a way to make your plan stick.

You want to eat better? Okay, well be specific and pinpoint your problem areas. If you know you typically order pizzas or seek out junk food when you study late at night, *plan ahead* and bring some healthier option with you in advance. If you want to drink less in season but predict avoiding it will be too difficult, socially or physically, *plan ahead* by focusing on how you will handle each specific moment of anticipated doubt. If you want to get more sleep at night, *plan ahead* by setting a bedtime and completing all necessary homework before that time.

Set definitive goals for yourself in relation to these things. "My goals for this week are _____. My goal in terms of eating healthier is _____. My bedtime is _____." Write down exactly what you are going to do so the planning is easier. If you're going to eat more vegetables, which ones? When? Think ahead to those times when you usually won't want vegetables; how will you handle that? Foresight is the only way to tackle the deeply ingrained habits you've unknowingly created after all these years. Without any preparation beforehand, you will inevitably pro-crastinate in the moment by taking the comfortable, sure thing in the present over the unfamiliar, caliginous prospect someday in the future. This is the number one reason healthy lifestyles are so illusive. The healthy decisions people make daily affect their lives so gradually, they are hard to appreciate. Eat the right stuff for a few days, and you're not likely to feel a whole lot better; instead, what you'll probably feel is upset you're missing out on your regular diet of cheesy puffs and mozzarella sticks. The way you plan for feelings like that will be the difference in your level of success.

And that is how it all comes together. The svengalic properties of our habits make them cushy and safe, and without the belief another routine will yield similar rewards, we ultimately cling to bad habits with such vehemence, the tactician in our brain finds a way to validate them. We are all guilty of subjective validation, where if we want calzones to be healthy or a rabbit's foot to be lucky, we'll find a way to make it true. For this reason, habit change will not be fast, nor will it be easy. Yet, with the ability to recognize these traits in ourselves, and the wherewithal to identify cues and rewards, all habits can be reshaped. You are in control, and you can choose to do whatever you want. Sure, external forces such as social pressure or threats can get you to perform certain actions, but external forces won't instill in you the commitment to carry it forward.

Make these decisions for yourself, and you will own your future outcomes.

Acknowledge your bad behavior.
Determine the cue.
Discover the reward.
Experiment with new routines.
Believe in change.
Have a plan.

Five Major Points

- Habits are svengalic, often having more control over our behaviors than we are wont to believe.
- The more habitual an activity becomes, the less brain activity it requires.
- Cue, routine, reward is the habit loop, and if we can find a way to keep the cue and reward, we can alter the routine without disrupting our lives (as most of the time, we are incapable of giving up the entire habit loop).
- Teach yourself to make fewer decisions about your lifestyle each day, for the more willpower you have to use during the day, the less you have at night.
- Impelling habits are not only healthy habits in themselves, they can subconsciously promote other healthy activity throughout the rest of your day.

14

Balancing Your Future

This is Your Responsibility

THE BUBBLE OF COLLEGE GIVES us reason to wonder if college athletes are doomed to a declining standard of living in a steadily deteriorating environment. As our world gets more and more technologically advanced, it seems logical, even likely, we'll have an even greater departure from the basics, as we continue to be awestruck by the newest gadgets and tricks of training. Technology has changed us so much in the last century, it's hard to imagine what the future holds, and how quickly it will arrive. Just think that it took ten thousand years to get from the horse-drawn cart to an airplane, but only sixty-six years to get from powered flight on earth to a landing on the moon. For a couple thousand years we'd been communicating through messengers either carrying letters or simply carrying word, and not until the late 1800's did Alexander Graham Bell make his famous first telephone call. After that it only took about 100 years to get the first mobile telephone call, which was placed on April 3, 1973 on a phone weighing nearly two pounds, measuring ten inches long, three inches deep, and one and a half inches wide.[381] Only thirty-four years later did the first iPhone get released.

When your parents, and especially your grandparents were your age, they could fix their own cars, build essential items for their houses, and understand nearly every piece of technology that was on the market.

Even the plans for an AM radio could be explained in a paragraph (you only need five pieces: antenna, tuner, detector, amplifier, and speaker). Fast forward to today and you would be hard-pressed to find anyone, even those who work in the industry, that knows how to make a laptop computer. We have quickly constructed a radically more complex world where most of the information used is less than fifteen years old. The knowledge in certain fields of science, notably physics, is said to double every eight years! Ninety percent of all scientists who have ever lived on this Earth are working today![382]

The point is science and technology are going to continue to advance at these astronomical rates, often producing progress faster than we can understand it, but the body will remain virtually the same. The unpredictability of the future is astonishing, but we need not fear it. One may ask how we are going to prepare the future college athletes that are being born today to handle the world twenty years from now, given the assumed technological advances. The answer lies in the eternal simplicity of athletic preparation. Go back and revisit that excerpt from 2,000 years ago if you think otherwise. We already know what we need to do, it's just that we wish there was some new idea out there that could get us there faster. There will perpetually be something in the market-place advertised as the "breakthrough" of training; however, the basics will continually be more important. Too many of us have our heads down focusing on elements L-M-N-O-P, when we haven't yet conquered A-B- or C. Everyone wants to use a scalpel to fine tune specific characteristics of their training when we should be using an axe to get lifestyles in check.

Being a strength coach for college sports is quite an existential experience. When I think about the type of people that are willing to dedicate what they do to sports, but can't muster the willpower to drink water or sleep more, I quickly become confused. College strength coaching might be the most extreme form of psychology out there. Here is the ultimate paradox of college athletics: American college students are some of the most rational thinkers in the world, and by definition, are open to learning; yet, in the realm of athletics, they persistently show a resistance to learn new things and a lack of reasonable actions. This is as paradoxical and confusing as John Cage's three-movement composition *4'33"* — a four minute, thirty-three second piece of music that has *no music.* That's right, the entire composition is silence; you can even buy it from iTunes. Buying a song without music makes as much sense as the lifestyle of a typical college athlete, where one has the highest of goals but often the lowest forms of volition. Instead of taking free advice from their coaches, a lot of students turn to the diet and exercise industries to show them something different. Not surprisingly, fact is people are more likely to take advice when they've paid for it.[383]

Regardless of where you're getting your advice, realize your time to act is almost over. Most of you have merely four short years to compete before your athletic career is finished; you'll never have an opportunity like this again. What's incredible is that this final four year window of competition occurs at precisely the same time as the four year bubble you are the unhealthiest. The good news is that you can choose to be healthy if you wish. Believe it or not, it is a conscious decision you make every hour of every day.

While the psychological and technical characteristics of sport are certainly very challenging, the nutritional and physical aspects are ridiculously simple! Conceptualizing "real food" may be a struggle initially, but it can be found everywhere just as cheap as the food-like products. Water is free and ready to drink in almost every building in this country. Sleeping is the easiest mode for recovery, and even the more complicated ways to recover, such as stretching, can still be done with little or no prior experience. Yet still, people claim they can't figure it out.

The number one reason people can't pull it together to cook for themselves or stretch or drink water is because it requires responsibility, which, when you think about it, is not very surprising. We live in a society where restaurants are sued for making people fat, or, even better, when we spill coffee on ourselves. Somehow our nation has developed this environment in which it is common to not take responsibility of ourselves and to instead turn it all over to a doctor (or in our case a trainer or physical therapist), to which we can later pin our blame if things don't go our way. Our culture hasn't set the best example, but you can't let that be an excuse.   Your body is your responsibility.   You must assume responsibility of your athletic preparedness; it is on *you* to get better. *You* have to embrace the fact that your nutrition plays a huge role in your performance and begin to change your diet. *You* are obligated to listen to your body and rest when you need it, regardless of your prior convictions or what is on your schedule. *You* must accept the additional demands of being an athlete in order to succeed, and adopt the lifestyle of an omnitect to really get anywhere in this endeavor.   Fail to accept these res-ponsibilities, and you'll be acting in a paradoxical way: training hard for sport in the gym then throwing it away in the next 21 hours of the day.

To most of us, it's obvious that college is a miasmic environment. Students are needlessly and gratuitously unhealthy, and the surroundings are oppressive to athletes. Few people actually living in college would, or could, refute that claim. But it certainly doesn't have to be *this bad*. Adding some vegetables, water, and sleep could provide you with huge gains, but you may have to go it alone. Given your surroundings, it's going to be hard to break free and rise above your classmates. If history has taught us anything, it's that people that accomplish great things tend not to conform to what is popular during their given time. You have to be willing to branch out a bit from the deplorable situation in which you and your friends are entrenched; strive to be anachronistic, as this healthy way of living in college may not be popular now, but it is the wave of the future. The only question is if you're willing to do this *for* yourself, *by* yourself. As Ernest Shackleton, perhaps the best leader of the 20th Century, wrote, "Loneliness is the penalty of leadership."[384] This may be a lonely endeavor at first, but if you can stay true to yourself, people will want to follow you.

Lying to Yourself

Many books have been written that shed light on what it takes people to stay true to each other, and to themselves. Dan Ariely's *The (Honest) Truth About Dishonesty* is one of the best. Ariely explains how our behavior is driven by two conflicting motivations. On one hand, we want to be honest, honorable people, but on the other, we want to beg, borrow, and steal to ensure the most personal gain possible.[385] We all have a deeply ingrained propensity to lie to ourselves and others while desiring to think of ourselves as good people. If we know what we want, we'll go through all sorts of mental hoops, manipulating the criteria so we can both get what we want *and* keep up with the appearance that we're acting in a rational, moral way.[386] This might help explain why grand-mothers are ten times more likely to die before a midterm and nineteen times more likely to die before a final exam. In fact, students who are failing are *fifty times* more likely to lose a grandmother compared to nonfailing students![387] So we should either lock up our grandmothers in December and May, or we should agree there is a slight proclivity to cheat to get ahead in all of us.

The reason why this is important is because when people are attempting to change parts of their lifestyles, they are notorious for justifying what we can call "little cheats." The cigarette smoker will be cold turkey for a week then say, "I've been so good, I can have one." The dieter will be vegetarian for three days then say, "One burger won't ruin my diet." Unfortunately, what Dan Ariely found was thanks to the what-the-hell effect, a single act of dishonesty — one little cheat — can change a person's behavior from that point onward.[388] If we just slightly tarnish our self-image, we will have a much easier time doing so again in the future.

The first act of dishonesty might be particularly important in shaping the way people interpret their actions from then on, which is why we must have something or someone in place to help us turn our healthy decisions into healthy habits. Through his research, Ariely made two major discoveries: one, given the opportunity, most people will cheat, albeit not by a whole lot;[389] and two, many people need controls around them for them to do the right thing.[390] The mere hint that people were being monitored made them behave more honestly, and merely trying to recall moral standards was enough to improve moral behavior.[391] Signatures at the top of forms proved effective as moral prophylactic, and subtle suggestions of being watched worked well, too. But if we *really* want to rid ourselves of dishonesty, the only thing to do is to have some form of constant observation, as close supervision eliminated cheating altogether.[392]

The good news is, according to his research, although we will cheat up to a level that allows us to retain our self-image, we still want to be honest.[393] With this noble idea in mind, it seems the research is clear: we'll willfully be honest provided there is something in place to keep us honest! To do so, Ariely studied four main ways to decrease dishonesty: pledges, signatures, moral reminders, and the most effective of all, supervision.[394] And even small, seemingly inconsequential forms of supervision can be effective. Consider this: have you ever eaten an entire pizza? Or an entire jug of ice cream? It's a lot like riding a scooter or singing the Backstreet Boys: it's fun until somebody sees you. All you need is a little supervision to keep you honest, and while it would work to have one of your friends be on your case all the time about your eating habits, you could instead start a food journal (like the one in the back of the book or in the Healthy Habits Workbook) and track your nutritional decisions yourself. You could make a pact with your teammates to not drink in season, or you could post up a board in your room and keep a running tally on how many days in a row it had been without a drink or fried food or whatever your personal vice may be. What's important is to shut down our ability to make excuses or justify little cheats by creating moral reminders through some form of supervision.

While it may sound like you're being asked to go cold turkey on all your bad habits, you're not. No one is perfect, and no one should aspire to be, either. Even those that are already extremely healthy could still continue to improve. That is the essence of man: incapable of reaching absolute perfection. Especially if your lifestyle is exceptionally unhealthy, small changes will go a long way, and you're encouraged to do whatever you can whenever you can. You have the opportunity to make the right decision dozens of times every day. Whether it be at the buffet line in the dining hall, deciding to drink that extra glass of water, turning the TV off a half hour earlier, pushing yourself to do a little pleasure reading … no matter what the specific decision is, you will always know what is *right*. However, we all have an internal mechanism that allows us to bend the rules and still justify it as okay. Because "being healthy" is both excessively vague and extremely subjective, obtaining health can be frustratingly elusive. This is why you must be specific with your goals, and you must have a system in place that keeps you from backsliding.

The good news is that you've already covered the most important barometer of health: frequent exercise. And while the industry is chock-full of gadgets, technologies, and knowledge in regard to exercise, nothing is more meaningful and effective than an athlete making smart and simple lifestyle decisions. Luckily, it's getting easier every day to do the right thing. Especially on college campuses, water fountains are all over the place. Fruits and vegetables are served year-round in the dining halls, despite their seasonality. Easy cookbooks are becoming more readily-available via technology while fast food is becoming the newest social pariah. There is hope.

Hope

IT'S HARD TO BELIEVE THAT years ago smoking was the cool, normal, socially acceptable leisure activity. Everyone that was cool smoked in planes, hotel rooms, at the dinner table next to non-smokers, and at work. Today, in a much different time, those public smokers are more likely to be verbally accosted than welcomed inside to share their shameful habit. Laws were almost passed requiring packs of cigarettes to display labels, which depicted graphic images of diseased lungs or a man exhaling smoke through a tracheotomy hole, designed to detract smokers from their habit. What all started as a cool thing to do has transformed into a nearly illegal practice, thus morphing the trendy kids of the '50s to the scofflaws of the 21st Century.

This metamorphosis did not happen overnight, however. Quite the opposite. Slowly, as more and more scientists accepted tobacco was bad for one's health, the public began to view smoking as a faux pas. While the industry vehemently opposed labeling and refused to admit the health risks of their product, the public stood strong and demanded the truth. Finally, the government stepped in with the Surgeon General's Warning, forcing tobacco companies to face facts. One such company did so in a most interesting way.

In a fairly unknown story, Phillip Morris, one of the largest conglomerates of tobacco products, composed a study in 1999 that defies reason. When the Czech Republic was planning to raise taxes on cigarettes, Phillip Morris objected and consequently ran the numbers to show how the premature deaths from their products could actually generate economic growth for the state.[395] While this was certainly an ill-guided attempt to keep revenues high, the flood of criticism that came their way was unprecedented. In one quick act, the tobacco industry had admitted the truth about their products and revealed how low they were willing to stoop to save a buck. Without much surprise, even more people were turned off from smoking.

With the public in revolt, laws soon started to pass greatly limiting the world of tobacco. The lesson here is when the people refuse to tolerate an activity, eventually the government will act. Whether it be striking down out-of-date laws or creating up-to-date new ones, when the public is charged, actions soon follow. Happily, the wheels are in motion in regard to fast food and junk food, and although still in its infancy, the revolution against big business food companies is underway.

Whereas it used to be customary for adults to take in a meal at fast food establishments, now those same people are ashamed to be seen at one. Picketers march outside fast food restaurants demanding they serve healthier food and treat animals with more respect — proof that we're moving in the right direction. Another sign of optimism occurred recently when Hostess, the manufacturer of several once popular treats, filed for bankruptcy. (Although, their death was short-lived after all.) There are even commercials airing now promoting high fructose corn syrup, which is clearly a move of utter desperation by the soda, cookie, and junk food companies! There is no doubt that people all over America are beginning to make better decisions, or at the very least, *want* to make better decisions. Hopefully soon the government will contribute, as they did with smoking, and make it harder for Americans to do something so obviously detrimental to their health, such as eating junk food.

Where the government will never be able to step in, however, is in the face of overtraining. Today, athletes are demolishing themselves in the weight room and laying it all on the line several months before their first game. They're gorging themselves with supplements they can't even pronounce, and worst of all, their emphasis on recovery, the most important part of training, is dwindling. Studies done on former athletes have yielded some deplorable results. Former Division I athletes responded to questions in regard to sleep, anxiety, depression, fatigue, pain interference, physical function, and satisfaction with participation in social roles, and scored significantly worse on five of the seven scales, when compared to nonathletes. In addition, former athletes reported experiencing more chronic limitations in daily activities, and living with more major and recurring injuries than did the nonathlete controls.[396] But are college sports worth all that? After all, only six percent of the kids who play high school football go on to play in college, and only about one percent of those college players advance to the NFL.[397] The same is probably true for most sports: very few are going on to make the big bucks. However, these high school and college athletes that don't go on to play professionally still have grueling practices, still play in big games, and still want to succeed. Arguably, they work even harder than the professionals, as there are many examples to show that people will work more for a cause than for cash.[398]

Too often in these short eight years of high school and college do people injure themselves, forcing them to adhere to the phrase, "Oh it's an old football injury," for the rest of their lives without the cushion of money or Super Bowl rings. (Football is the most common, but there are nagging injuries in every sport, even distance running.) The scary thing is that athletic preparation back in the 1960s and '70s was nothing compared to what it is now. Weight rooms barely existed back then, supplements like creatine and protein powders were in their infancy if around at all, and a coach's idea of a tough workout would be a warm-up for most athletes in the twenty-first century.

Bob Goldman began asking elite athletes back in the 1980s whether or not they would take a drug that guaranteed them a gold medal but would also kill them within five years. The results have since become famous, and dubbed "The Goldman Dilemma." More than half of the athletes surveyed said yes, they'd take a drug to guarantee success and happily die within five years. Goldman repeated the survey biannually over the next decade, and the results were always the same. Nonathletes were asked the same question a few years ago, and precisely two of the 250 people surveyed said yes to the same question.[399]

All this data is a bit overwhelming and points to the fact that athletes want to succeed, and are willing to go to incredible lengths to do so. But! There is hope. There are ways to go about training and competing intelligently that won't kill you in five years. You're nearing the end of this book, which presumably means you've read everything before this. You have now learned how easy athletic preparation can be, and how important a healthy lifestyle is to your success. No longer will you let companies lead you down a hallway of confusion to buy their fad products or experiment with their ridiculous workouts. You are now on the front line of the battle that is ensuing against common sense, and you stand to gain a lot fighting for it. Not only will you experience more success on the field, but you're sure to lead a more fruitful life due to your newfound appreciation for healthy living and proper recovery.

All around you, it's getting easier to make the right choices. At this stage in history, it has never been more manageable to make the right decisions and become an omnitect. Ralph Keeney, a research professor at Duke University, once noted that our inability to make smart choices and overcome our own self-destructive behaviors is America's number one killer — not cancer, heart disease, smoking, nor obesity. Albeit morbid, most in the know would be inclined to agree. Keeney estimates about half of us will lead a life with at least one bad habit that will lead to a premature death, and that the real improvements in life expectancy and health are not going to be found through medical technologies, but rather improved decision making.[400]

This *perfectly* encapsulates the arena of college athletics. Neither better workouts, nor better supplements, nor better coaches are the answer; it all comes back to the decisions athletes make weekly, daily, and hourly. The challenge of athletic success isn't in the institution, it's in the individual — **it's not a policy problem, it's one of self-regulation.** We have to get control of ourselves and lead our lives based on the wisdom of those who have come before us.

David Brooks writes that, "Wisdom doesn't consist of knowing specific facts or possessing knowledge of a field. It consists of knowing how to treat knowledge: being confident but not too confident; adventurous but grounded."[401] Everyone possesses the knowledge of what is healthy and what is not, but few actually have the wisdom to do anything about it. There's no magic solution or secret knowledge to get you where you want to go, you just have to be wise and carry out your lifestyle as such. Have faith that you know everything you need to know, now just take responsibility, and act.

Five Major Points

- No matter where the future takes us, athletic preparation should remain the same. Balance the ineffables and the workouts, and you can't fail.
- We cannot change the college lifestyle with one single intervention; there must be a full-on, common sense counterculture in aggregate.
- We all have a proclivity to cheat and need structures in place to keep us honest. Use food journals, friends, coaches, or any other creative means to ensure there is always supervision.
- Collegiate sporting careers are ephemeral. Don't throw away your (better) future years on injuries you could avoid by living better now.
- In the end, this is your responsibility. This is not a policy problem, it's an individual, self-regulating issue.

Epilogue

FINISHING BOOKS ALWAYS MAKES ME want to pause and reflect on what I just learned. When I finished this book, I similarly reflected on the writing and concluded the most important thing in one's life is his or her environment — the people and things with which one chooses to surround him- or herself. How you perceive yourself and your environment is what ultimately shapes who you become, invariably controlling all the subjects of the chapters of this book.

When Daniel Coyle went around researching for his book about talent, he came across a thriving school that was once in a dilapidated state with little hope for renewal. The founders of the new, flourishing system accredited their success to focusing on every minute detail, even to the way in which students carried their binders around through the hallways.[402] By surrounding these kids with success and forcing them to respect their environment with excruciating attention to detail, they became success stories themselves.

We like to think that our character is stable and consistent, as if our behavior is based on inherent traits, but this is a mistake. Our circumstances and context play a much bigger role on our habits and tendencies than we realize.[403] This is why you need to find someone you look up to and try to spend the most amount of time with them possible. Studies show that even a brief connection with a role model can dramatically impact one's motivation.[404] Use pictures on your walls, change the background images on your devices, stand up proud and straight, write a note on your mirror, or bookmark some videos to watch every day before you head to the gym.   This attention to detail, this complete submersion into a winning environment, is ultimately what makes people successful.   We cannot withstand the associations that surround us.

And some of the strongest associations that we'll make in our entire lives are with our friends. The important question then becomes: who are your friends?   Are they a good mix of people from different backgrounds that help mold you into the person you want to be? Or are they all kind of homogenous with everyone sharing the same habits, beliefs, and preferences? Most believe the groups to which they do not belong are more homogenous than groups to which they do belong, but researchers have determined that most social groups are very homogenous and everything is contagious.[405]   We tend to think most lacrosse players look and act alike, most sorority girls look and act alike, and most wall street businesspeople look and act alike, but we are guilty of this in our own lives as well. In other words, we don't seek out friends, we merely associate with the people who share our small, physical space and do the things we do.[406]   Over time, we become the same people. If your friends are happy, you're more likely to be happy; if your friends eat healthy, you're more likely to eat healthy; if your friends are religious, you're religious; if your friends drink, you drink; if they stretch an hour each day, so do you. Before long, you will all feel a visceral loyalty to each other, and soon will be able to distinguish between members of your own group and members of another group in as little as 170 milliseconds.[407] In short, your relationships can be internecine conflicts or auspicious alliances.

Utilize this information for your own good and recognize we get healthier being around healthy people and we get smarter being around smart people. Cities are the single most important invention in human history for this reason.   What the numbers from experiments clearly show is that when people come together they exchange more ideas, generate more innovations, and become more productive per capita.[408] So here you are, a student at a college full of like-minded individuals; you have all the tools before you to generate an immense amount of success. You just need to find the *right* people that want what you want, or at the very least, convince those that share your space to join you.

Instill in others a sense of obligation that this movement of health is a necessity in order to thrive athletically.   Use that age old form of persuasion that's been effective since you were a little kid: peer pressure. Even if people don't *want* to initially participate, the social habits of your friendships and the strong ties between your other acquaintances have the power of creating something they'll be unable to ignore. All this movement needs is a leader in each university around the country. Because friendships are so strongly related to behaviors, your simple acts of healthfulness will be presented to your friends as a fait accompli. Eventually, they'll have to decide if they want to follow suit or get a new friend. At the core of it, everyone wants to be healthy, they just don't want to go it alone. We all need a community so that we can become followers of health in our normal social relationships with each other. A community of like-minded believers can maintain an unshakable faith in any proposition, however absurd, and even when people are unsure about themselves, a group can convince them to suspend disbelief.

And the best way to begin this campaign of health is to follow the advice of Alcoholics Anonymous with their slogan, "Fake it until you make it!" If you can fake it long enough, your mind will eventually accept it; or put more scientifically, behavior change often precedes changes in attitude and feelings.[409] Even if you don't like eating a lot of vegetables or drinking water or going to the grocery store, just force yourself to do it and before long your mind will begin to welcome the behavior as normal. **Short-term, forced compliance will give way to long-term, voluntary commitment.** Of course, we can't immediately believe our own lies that we're trying to sell to ourselves, but if we give it time, eventually we'll convince even ourselves! Even Aristotle once noted, "We acquire virtues by first having put them into action."

And if you think faking it will be hard, you must remember you lie every day. Ever notice how you, and nearly everyone else, behaves very differently when you are in a room full of girls, or a room full of guys, or with your family, or with your closest friends? During some interactions, you wear the mask of a scholar, whereas others you wear the mask of a fun-loving party-goer. Some situations have very clear-cut masks to wear, e.g. a job interview, while in other situations, we have no idea how to act, e.g. falling off a treadmill. Many sociologists have argued that the true self beneath all the masks doesn't exist, that it's masks all the way down, and we choose who we are depending on our current situation and immediate surroundings.[410] This is great news for college athletes amidst the typically regrettable environment in which they find themselves. Often times, in all of our lives, we sacrifice a certain pleasure in order to project the right image of ourselves to others, to present the right mask. All we have to do is choose to be the better mask more of the time. If you *choose* to be surrounded by the right atmosphere, you will adopt a lifestyle congruent with that ethos.

In the end, this receptiveness can only happen when you give it a shot — not when you think about it, nor when you study it, but only when you are actually immersed in it. Certainly, if you don't actually try it, you don't really know it. While it's easy to *think* healthy living in college is too challenging; or that buying nutritious food is too expensive; or drinking less is too off-putting; or stretching more is too inconvenient; you truly have no idea unless you venture out and do your damnedest. You've just got to go out there and get involved. Show up! Woody Allen famously declared that eighty percent of success is just showing up.[411]

All you've got to do is the right thing for yourself and people will gravitate toward you. The final question is if you're willing and ready. By now, maybe you've started thinking about your own training and lifestyle and you're saying, "You know what, I've gotten along just fine without this book. I know I'm not the healthiest, but I've been pretty successful in spite of that. And just about no matter what, I'm going to survive my college athlete experience and move on to bigger and better things." Well you know what, you're probably right.   Thinking purely rationally, of course people have survived athletically — won championships, made tens of millions of dollars — never heeding a word of this advice. And to be perfectly honest with you, it is possible; in fact, if you work hard, dare I say it's likely you'll do fairly well in sports. But, although that logic may be true for the most part, I know that you care too much to let that shape your decisions. You're here to do the right thing, and following the idea you're going to be just fine without living healthy is just a smug way to live. I know that you're above that, and you want to do what's right in the face of people that tell you it's unnecessary or inconvenient. Invest in the process, and you won't live with the regret of wishing, "If only I knew then what I know now."

Thanks Everybody!

Acknowledgements

As with any completed endeavor, one must look back and thank the people who got him there. First, foremost, and most importantly, I'd like to thank my parents, Peter and Nancy. Although their interest in this subject is minimal (in fact, I'd be surprised if they ever read this cover-to-cover), they were the biggest contributors to this book. With constant and endless support of my proclivity to go overboard, I must take the time to thank them for my college education and their encouragement throughout my upbringing. You guys are incredible, love you very much.

Now onto the knowledge emporium, otherwise known as Mike Pimentel. Mike is, has been, and will always be, my mentor. With an unbounded mastery of the subject, Mike has taught me nearly everything I know about training, but it goes even farther than that. He's taught, and continues to teach me, what it takes to be a good coach, where to invest my money, how to act mature and calm in any situation, and when the acceptable and not-so-acceptable moments are to burst into a diatribe. Anyway Mike, I certainly have no way of ever repaying you, which I think is the outcome of all protégé-mentor relationships, but my sincerest thank you.

Joe McManus was the perfect man to edit this book, or as he would call it, this "project." With an excessively high IQ, an ability to critique my writing without being condescending, and a jocular compadre with which to share a beer, I always looked forward to our time spent together, and still do. Joe has an uncanny ability to read what I have written, and deliver it back to me in a more concise, positive, and intelligent way. As I start a lot of my sentences with Joe, "I don't want this to sound too fawning" ... but my deepest thanks for your avidity in the work and your patience with me.

To Dan Kopcso, a man with whom I have shared more time than I care to admit, I owe a lot of gratitude. He has kept me employed and is always reaching out a helping hand. He even edited the hell out of this book with very little prodding. To the coaches at Tufts, especially Tina McDavitt, Cora Thompson, Courtney Farrell, Nancy Bigelow, and Bob Sheldon, thank you for allowing me the autonomy I craved to coach your teams through their off-seasons. I hope I haven't let you down. In this vast system of athletics where it is so hard to hack through all the nonsense, I'm starting to realize that although I can maybe write a mean strength and conditioning program, there are so many other vital components to training of which athletes must become aware. Thank you all for the continued support and for believing I know more than I actually do.

Thank you to Ethan Barron, award-winning track coach, Dan Simon (who came up with the title of this book), Jack McDermott, Jess Ingrum, Lindsey Walker, Sami Bloom, and Brian Williamson who were all chock-full of insight. They edited my early drafts, and helped shape this book into what it has become. I owe you all a lot of thanks. Thanks also to Brittany Norfleet, who was not embarrassed to be the sole athlete photographed for the book.

And as each draft neared the manuscript phase, I realized I was going to need a lot of help designing the cover and distributing this book out to my intended audience. The incredibly genuine, informative, and generous with his time Steve Gladstone did all the leg work to turn 106,000 words into a real book. We worked with Pixel Studio Banjaluka to design the cover, and a thank you goes out to them as well. Steve Gladstone is the paragon of generosity and I wish this paragraph could do justice to his munificence.

Steve Buckley put my own writing to shame with his panegyric foreword. I know he was working on that while on the road, and while I felt like I was being more than discommodious asking for it, I was overwhelmed when I got the finished product back late one Friday night. Steve's not the kind of guy that thinks he needs to be thanked gratuitously for anything, but I am so appreciative of his time, and I hope he knows it.

The authors of all the books in the bibliography have more to thank for my book than even I deserve. They were the ones carrying out the research, poring over the data, and devoting their lives to the science behind exercise, nutrition, and psychology; all I've done is poach their information for my own good! I hope, if they ever read my book, they can see their work has been quoted correctly and respectfully, and that I have reshaped their work to help a new body of people that may have never seen it otherwise. I like to think I'm taking their words and putting them in service of a new idea. Hopefully they think like Thomas Jefferson when he said, "He who receives an idea from me, receives instruction himself without lessening mine; as he who lights his taper at mine, receives light without darkening mine." And instead of putting another endnote there, I'll prove my point of how important these other authors are by telling you I read that on page 168 of Malcolm Gladwell's book *What the Dog Saw.*

Finally, I'd like to thank the Tufts community, first being the student-athletes. Since college, I have desperately wanted to be an athlete on a championship team, and all the hours I've spent with the Tufts athletes over the years has made me feel like I was. In time though, thanks to the respect they give me, and the opportunities I take from them, I've learned to become more concerned with studying them than becoming one. I owe a lot to the athletes at Tufts, and every day at work I try to give it back to them. In addition to the Tufts athletes, I also am indebted to the professors that taught me how to write and think critically, and the Athletic Department for keeping me employed. The professions that are typically the happiest are also the most social, according to David Brooks, so perhaps it should go without surprise that I love my job and am very happy within it. I owe my entire livelihood to the Hill, and it is my time spent with your athletes that wrote this book. Thank you to all.

Appendices

Appendix A — Seventy Major Points

Chapter One: Unnecessary Confusion
- The college environment can be oppressive to athletes, but you do not have to participate in the stereotype.
- The ineffable variables are just as important as the commercial variables — if not more.
- Omnitects need to follow the etymology of the word and work hard at everything, not just training.
- Being healthy is not complicated, nor expensive, merely abnormal in this, the fattest country ever.
- 21st Century athletes are no different than 1st Century ones, and need not overthink their training.

Chapter Two: 168 Hours
- There are 168 hours in a week, and whenever you aren't eating, sleeping, or training, you are still affecting those big three.
- Zoom out and look at the big picture more often.
- You have to *want* to be healthier in order to do so, otherwise you will simply be adding more stress to your already stressful life.
- Talent is not inbred. Everyone must work at least 10,000 hours to become an expert.
- Your surroundings matter, and you will inevitably become a product of them. Look around you.

Chapter Three: (Non-Religious) Faith
- Faith is not a reason; ensure your principles are based in scientific fact, not powerful emotion.
- We often start with a belief then find ways to justify it after the fact, not the other way around.
- There is no secret to health, no conspiracies.
- Do not accept what is popular. If you are interested in a topic, do the obligatory research to discover for yourself the truth.
- Delayed Gratification is one of the best predictors of future success, not only in athletics, but in regard to health, happiness, and business as well.

Chapter Four: Real Food

- Trust your instincts when choosing what foods to eat.
- Studying nutrition is very difficult, and most research is conducted by the food industry, so beware what you read.
- Learn more about the source of your foods by reading ingredients and shopping local.
- Focus more on the quality of your food than the quantities of nutrients within it. Cooking for yourself allows you to do this more regularly.
- "Real food" exists in nature, has a short shelf life, is worth money, and should be a conscious vote toward your improvement.

Chapter Five: Water's Significance

- There is no mechanism in the body to store water. This makes water consumption a daily task.
- Thirst signals arrive too late, so drink cold water frequently during exercise and games.
- All body signals (e.g. pain, soreness, tiredness) have immediate and direct connections to imbalances, many of which can be alleviated with water intake.
- Drink two glasses of water upon waking up and before every energy drink or coffee you may want.
- Attempt to find natural solutions to aches and pains before taking medications or seeking specialists.

Chapter Six: The Game of Nutrition

- Truly justify weight loss and gain. What is it you *really* want? Be specific.
- The RDA for protein will limit muscle growth. Refer to the tables and eat more food.
- Every athlete should own and use a bottle of protein powder every day. Between whey, soy, and plant, supplement the source your diet is lacking.
- A good post-workout meal should include both carbohydrates and protein, and should be eaten immediately.
- The only plausible supplements to take would be multivitamins, fish oils, and protein. Anything else is nearly unjustifiable.

Chapter Seven: Alcohol and College Athletics
- The "bubble" is not a good enough excuse to drink in excess. An alcoholic is an alcoholic.
- More athletes report experiencing alcohol-related "harms" than nonathletes.
- If you drink more than once every two weeks, you don't know how good the body *can* feel.
- Avoid alcohol as often as you can, especially during your competitive season.
- If you must drink, follow the rules:
    1. Don't drink within two hours post-workout.
    2. Keep caloric intake low, avoid congeners.
    3. Drink water as frequently as possible.
    4. Track your alcohol-related expenses.
    5. *Try*, just once, a short period (minimum two weeks) without one sip. See how good you can feel!

Chapter Eight: Energy Systems
- Identify your sport's energy system, then train within the confines of it as often as possible.
- Nearly every athlete could benefit from a short exposure to the CP and Glycolytic systems (roughly translating to lifting and running sprints).
- Endurance work not only fails to assist other physical qualities, it actually *hinders* them.
- Never perform long, slow distance unless you are that type of an athlete. Intervals may be the best alternative.
- Carbohydrates provide most of the energy for the majority of sports, so do not avoid them.

Chapter Nine: The Imbalance of Sport
- Sports are dangerous. Each one creates discrepancies in the body that can only be ameliorated by weight room training.
- The number one reason to lift weights should be in an attempt to rebalance the body between competitive seasons.
- A good posture aligns bones, muscles, and organs to work more effectively, and can even have dramatic effects on self-esteem and hormone levels.

- The four major ways to fix posture issues: stretch the tight muscle(s), strengthen the weak one(s), stand/sit/walk correctly, and find ways to exercise better posture throughout the day.
- The off-season is in place so you can recover from the season. Do not attempt to be in game-ready shape 12 months out of the year (no pro would even dream of that).

Chapter Ten: Exercise Specifics
- Be skeptical of new training methods. Remember the athletes of the First Century.
- Hard work and minimum recovery time (48 hours for same type of training) are the only real concepts athletes need to grasp about training. Recovery builds muscle, exercise only stimulates the change.
- Because college athletes do not have the luxury of choosing when to work out, lifestyle becomes ever more important to ensure they can keep up with their training.
- Try everything, *everything*, in practice before applying it to a competition.
- "Warm-ups" and "cool-downs" are not trite aphorisms, they are scientifically-proven mechanisms that prevent injury and aid recovery.

Chapter Eleven: Sleep
- Fit people need more sleep than the sedentary — scientists recommend 9 hours a night plus a nap.
- One should attempt to fall asleep at the same time every night and rise at the same time every morning, thus creating a healthy circadian rhythm.
- Eating practices, mood, and performance can all be directly related to- and affected by one's circadian rhythm.
- Increased sleep could improve performance overnight, and if one is required to be deprived of some sleep, it is preferable to lose it at night compared to forfeiting the auspicious morning hours.
- In relation to feelings of alertness, one hour of napping is roughly equivalent to one cup of coffee, but of course sleep is always preferable to drugs.

Chapter Twelve: 100% of Capacity

- In the scale of undertrained, optimally prepared, and overtrained, nearly all athletes playing a varsity sport are overtrained.
- Plateaus are almost always the first signs of overtraining. Rest when you experience them.
- Training at 100% of your capacity makes you much less susceptible to injury, is the only way to increase your 100% capacity, prepares you for game-like situations, reduces plateaus, keeps interests piqued, and can spotlight poor nutritional habits.
- If you are experiencing aches and pains, you cannot heal selectively. Focus on your lifestyle in aggregate.
- Non-contact injuries are not unlucky, random acts. They result from either over- or undertraining.

Chapter Thirteen: Healthy Habits How To

- Habits are svengalic, often having more control over our behaviors than we are wont to believe.
- The more habitual an activity becomes, the less brain activity it requires.
- Cue, routine, reward is the habit loop, and if we can find a way to keep the cue and reward, we can alter the routine without disrupting our lives (as most of the time, we are incapable of giving up the entire habit loop).
- Teach yourself to make fewer decisions about your lifestyle each day, for the more willpower you have to use during the day, the less you have at night.
- Impelling habits are not only healthy habits in themselves, they can subconsciously promote other healthy activity throughout the rest of your day.

Chapter Fourteen: Balancing Your Future

- No matter where the future takes us, athletic preparation should remain the same. Balance the ineffables and the workouts, and you can't fail.
- We cannot change the college lifestyle with one single intervention; there must be a full-on, common sense counterculture in aggregate.

- We all have a proclivity to cheat and need structures in place to keep us honest. Use food journals, friends, coaches, or any other creative means to ensure there is always supervision.
- Collegiate sporting careers are ephemeral. Don't throw away your (better) future years on injuries you could avoid by living better now.
- In the end, this is your responsibility. This is not a policy problem, it's an individual, self-regulating issue.

Appendix B — Impelling Habits Checklist

Week:	M	T	W	R	F	S	N
Record My Hours of Sleep from Last Night Here							
Make My Bed							
Eat Plants (fruit w/ bfast, salad w/lunch)							
Carry a Water Bottle Everywhere I Go							
Leave at Least One Thing Better							
Eat Something Immediately Post-Workout							
Stretch for 5 Minutes (before bed?)							
Pleasure Read for 5 Minutes (before bed?)							

Week:	M	T	W	R	F	S	N
Record My Hours of Sleep from Last Night Here							
Make My Bed							
Eat Plants (fruit w/ bfast, salad w/lunch)							
Carry a Water Bottle Everywhere I Go							
Leave at Least One Thing Better							
Eat Something Immediately Post-Workout							
Stretch for 5 Minutes (before bed?)							
Pleasure Read for 5 Minutes (before bed?)							

Week:	M	T	W	R	F	S	N
Record My Hours of Sleep from Last Night Here							
Make My Bed							
Eat Plants (fruit w/ bfast, salad w/lunch)							
Carry a Water Bottle Everywhere I Go							
Leave at Least One Thing Better							
Eat Something Immediately Post-Workout							
Stretch for 5 Minutes (before bed?)							
Pleasure Read for 5 Minutes (before bed?)							

Week:	M	T	W	R	F	S	N
Record My Hours of Sleep from Last Night Here							
Make My Bed							
Eat Plants (fruit w/ bfast, salad w/lunch)							
Carry a Water Bottle Everywhere I Go							
Leave at Least One Thing Better							
Eat Something Immediately Post-Workout							
Stretch for 5 Minutes (before bed?)							
Pleasure Read for 5 Minutes (before bed?)							

Week:	M	T	W	R	F	S	N
Record My Hours of Sleep from Last Night Here							
Make My Bed							
Eat Plants (fruit w/ bfast, salad w/lunch)							
Carry a Water Bottle Everywhere I Go							
Leave at Least One Thing Better							
Eat Something Immediately Post-Workout							
Stretch for 5 Minutes (before bed?)							
Pleasure Read for 5 Minutes (before bed?)							

Week:	M	T	W	R	F	S	N
Record My Hours of Sleep from Last Night Here							
Make My Bed							
Eat Plants (fruit w/ bfast, salad w/lunch)							
Carry a Water Bottle Everywhere I Go							
Leave at Least One Thing Better							
Eat Something Immediately Post-Workout							
Stretch for 5 Minutes (before bed?)							
Pleasure Read for 5 Minutes (before bed?)							

Appendix C — The Soy Debacle

This is a continuation from the discussion about soy on page 119. Everything you're about to read comes directly from the sources that were quoted in anti-soy articles, with my polemic peppered about:

• The first one worth mentioning is from the most-damningly titled article: *Nagata, Chisato et. al. "Inverse association of soy product intake with serum androgen and estrogen concentrations in Japanese men." Nutrition and Cancer 2000; 36(1):14-18.* What Nagata writes is, "Soy product intake was estimated from a semiquantitative food frequency questionnaire." Already, you can see how the data from this might be questionable. Anyway, he goes on to say, "Total and free testosterone concentrations were inversely correlated with soy product intake after controlling for the covariates." Admittedly, this sounds pretty bad, doesn't it? Well, wait, because here's the rest of the sentence: "but these correlations were of borderline significance (r = -0.25, p = 0.05 and r = -0.25, p = 0.06, respectively)." Good thing we got the numbers so we can assess just what "borderline significance" means. The "p" in the parentheses there attests to the probability of this result occurring by chance, and the term "statistically significant" is used to describe results for which there is a five percent — or p = 0.05 — or less probability that the results occurred by chance. So, looking at the numbers, not only are both findings barely significant, if at all, considering the soy product intake was estimated from a questionnaire, this one might be bust.

• *Löhrke, B et. al. "Activation of skeletal muscle protein breakdown following consumption of soybean protein in pigs." British Journal of Nutrition 2001; 85(4):447-457.* One anti-soy article used this quote from the study cited above: "Diets with protein of inferior quality may increase protein breakdown in skeletal muscle," but left out the rest of the sentence, "but the experimental results are inconsistent."

• *Kraemer, William et. al. "The effects of soy and whey protein supplementation on acute hormonal responses to resistance exercise in men." Journal of the American College of Nutrition 2013; 32(1):66-74.* Only <u>ten</u> people participated in this study which demonstrated "14 days of supplementation with soy protein does appear to partially blunt serum testosterone." Of course this study is quoted from way more regularly than another that took a cross-sectional analysis of 696 men with a wide range of soy intakes that found, "Soy milk intake was not associated with serum concentrations of testosterone, free testosterone, androstanediol glucuronide, sex hormone-binding globulin, or luteinizing hormone. These results suggest that soy milk intake, as a marker of isoflavone intake, is not associated with serum sex hormone concentrations among free-living Western men."[412]   As rational beings, we should be more apt to believe studies conducted with more than ten participants.

• *Habito, Raymundo et. al. "Effects of replacing meat with soyabean [sic] in the diet on sex hormone concentrations in healthy adult males." British Journal of Nutrition 2000; 84: 557-563.* This is a pretty interesting study in the sense that meat protein was replaced with tofu to investigate whether or not soy consumption influenced levels of sex hormones. Exactly what we're trying to find out, right? So the experimenters enlisted 42 men between the ages of 35 and 62 for the study, and they specifically excluded men who were regularly training for competitive sport. Anyway, this was a study conducted in the interest of one specific food on the human body, tofu, and as we discussed before, it's nearly impossible to study this due to all the inconsistent variables. The experimenters clearly try to compensate for the discrepancies in physical activity, alcohol consumption, fat consumption, etc. etc. but as we all know, this is very difficult. Okay, so what were the findings? Well, according to anit-soy articles the tofu diet yields a seven percent decrease in testosterone! AHH! Help us! Where these people are getting this quote comes from this section: "Serum testosterone, DHT, adiol-G and oestradiol did not differ significantly after the two diets." Those are all basically sex hormones, by the way. Moving on, "SHBG was 3% higher after the tofu diet than after the lean meat diet (P = 0.07), and the FAI was 7% lower on the tofu diet (P = 0.06). The mean serum oestradiol concentrations did not differ significantly after the two diets, although the testosterone: oestradiol tended to be higher on the meat diet (P = 0.06)." Okay, quick lesson: SHBG is short-hand for sex hormone-binding globulin, and FAI for free androgen index. While these two things, SHBG and FAI, *can* affect testosterone and oestradiol levels, what these scientists found was, "Serum levels of testosterone and its metabolites did not differ significantly between the two diets. The FAI had a slight tendency to be lower on the tofu diet; however, as FAI was calculated and is very sensitive to the SHBG measure, the actual changes in free hormone levels are not certain." Oh, and by the way, this study was really about prostate cancer risk among people who eat a lot of meat and not a lot of soy, and these researchers conclude their essay by saying that "soyabean [*sic*] intake may confer protection against prostate cancer, in combination with other dietary or lifestyle factors."

• One study, cited as: Zhong, et. al. "Effects of dietary supplement of soy protein isolate and low fat diet on prostate cancer." FASEB J 2000;14(4):a531.11 is quoted all around the bodybuilding community and allegedly claims that there is a 76 percent reduction of testosterone production in men after ingestion of soy protein over a brief period of time, according to T-nation.com's acrimonious article, "The Evils of Soy" written by Cy Willson. But you would be hard-pressed to find this article. Go to the Journal of the Federation of American Societies for Experimental Biology's website, www.fasebj.org, and search for it. Strangely, it doesn't exist there. But when you do keyword searches for soy protein, you'll find stuff like this:

▸ *Singhal, Rohit. "Is soy estrogenic? Hepatic gene expression in the presence or absence of endogenous estrogen." FASEB Journal 2007; 21:114.3.* "These data expand our understanding of the synergistic, additive and interactive effects of soy on estrogen-mediated signaling and suggest that even when soy protein isolate is the total dietary protein source, there is very little estrogenicity, especially in the presence of endogenous estrogens." In other words, even when soy is the *sole* dietary protein in one's diet, he does not become an estrogen-laden pansy.

▸ *Pasiakos, Stefan et. al. "High protein diets enhance body composition in rats: a comparative analysis of milk- and soy-based energy restricted diets." FASEB Journal 2013; 27:631.10.* "These data suggest consuming a high protein diet may spare fat-free mass and improve body composition independent of energy status, although skeletal muscle responses to milk- and soy-based diets are likely comparable."

▸ *Anthony, Tracy et. al. "Regulation of protein synthesis and translation initiation in skeletal muscle by feeding mixed meals containing soy or whey protein after endurance exercise." FASEB Journal 2006; 20:A854.* "Meals containing soy were similar to whey in promoting muscle protein synthesis … likewise, both soy and whey-containing meals stimulated phosphorylation of the translational repressor, rE-bp1, and formation of the mRNA cap binding complex … short-term recovery of general protein synthesis and the mRNA cap binding step is promoted comparably by soy vs. whey protein in the skeletal muscle of exercised rats."

▸ *Unknown Author. "Effects of soy and tea on hormone-induced prostate cancer in Noble rat model." FASEB Journal 2008; 22:311.2.* "Soy and tea also decreased prostate hyperplasia, increased Bax expression, and decreased gene expression of IL6 and IL1beta compared to control. These effects were not apparent in groups treated with soy or tea alone. The ongoing invivo studies thus far suggest that combination of foods, like soy and tea, may inhibit hormone-induced pro-inflammatory NFKB signals that contribute to prostate cancer development."

▸ *Wong, Julia et. al. "Effectiveness of a vegan based high soy protein diet on weight loss and serum lipids." FASEB Journal 2007;21:111.8.* "Under real-world conditions, a high soy protein vegan diet appears to improve the blood lipid profile compared to a [low-fat control] diet despite similar weight reductions."

When I found out that the aforementioned Zhong study did not exist on the FASEB website, I clearly went a little crazy searching for it and read all these studies instead. But I still wasn't satisfied. I mean, this Zhong article is being used all around the bodybuilding and athletic community as the *number one* reason to be anti-soy, containing seemingly the most damning evidence possible, and yet it cannot be found. So I redoubled my efforts. I contacted the FASEB Journal, I enlisted the help of reference librarians, and no one could find anything out about this study. The only thing we could find was an abstract, which mentioned the study was conducted with eleven participants (oh boy), only briefly explained the methods, and disclosed only some of the findings. Kind of a dead end.

After six weeks of searching, the FASEB finally got another lead and sent me a link to a professor in Hawaii with the note, "This may be one of the authors on the paper, Adrian A. Franke." I was so giddy with excitement, I just picked up the phone and dialed the number. A man picked up and said something but I was so nervous-excited I didn't hear a word, so I responded, "Is Adrian Franke there please?" To which the man replied, "That's what I just said."

I had finally found someone related to the study! I could hardly wait to ask him about it, and I had a million questions. After I explained who I was and what I was doing, I finally brought up the citation, and asked him why no one could find it. After a little rummaging around on his end, he told me it was only published as an abstract, nothing more. Damn. This meant two things: 1) the people using this as a source have cherry picked one sentence out of the abstract, and 2) I could get no further with this particular study. However, what Dr. Franke did next could not have helped us more: he sent me two more articles that he and his colleagues had published. Upon opening them, I found out the scientists involved in conducting the research were almost exactly the same as the ones from the Zhong study, and they were focusing on soy and prostate cancer as well! Next best thing! From *Zhou, Jin-Rong, et. al. "Inhibition of Orthotopic Growth and Metastasis of Androgen-Sensitive Prostate Tumors in Mice by Bioactive Soybean Components." The Prostate 2002;53: 143-153,* what I found were sentences like this, "Soy protein, genistin, and SPC did not significantly alter either the circulating levels of total testosterone or tumor AR expression."

After reading this and feeling pretty content that I had finally gotten to the bottom of this debacle, I asked Dr. Franke point blank what he thought about one of his studies being used as an anti-soy vehicle. I asked him in his professional opinion, as the man who conducted the study himself, if he thought athletes should be avoiding soy. His response was very typical of a man who governs his life by science: he simply went through his archives and found evidence. His response to me was simple, and to the point, "Dr. Mark Messina and coworkers did a thorough meta analysis on soy/isoflavones and male reproductive hormones and concluded, 'Neither soy protein nor isoflavones impact reproductive hormone levels in men.'" He then attached the slides Dr. Messina used during a conference in Vienna in 2008. A perfectly rational answer from a perfectly rational man.

I could go on with all this ridiculous anti-soy inanity, but I'll spare you. Remember, the articles from which I quoted above (not those random five from FASEB) were used as citations in anti-soy articles. If this is their evidence, they don't have a leg to stand on.

Appendix D — Cookbook

IN THE COMING PAGES, YOU will see six recipes for the college athlete. Each one takes several things into consideration:

- *Time:* For starters, this cookbook will take into consideration you do not have hours on end to cook. In fact, each recipe is designed to take the least amount of prep time as possible. Some are admittedly longer than others, but the longer the recipe is, the more food it will produce; therefore, you'll be able to have leftovers for days!

- *Equipment:* As a college student, it's likely you either live in a dorm room with a very limited kitchen, or you live in a house where the kitchen is far from "full," in the conventional sense. All these recipes will require is one pan, one pot, one knife, one spoon, and an occasional usage of an oven and/or a stovetop.

- *Budget:* None of these recipes will have a lot of ingredients in them (especially spices, as these are expensive and hard to come by in college), and the ingredients you are asked to buy will be cheap! What would be advisable is to have some Extra Virgin Olive Oil on hand, however.

- *Experience:* If you're anything like the average college student, it can be assumed you don't have a ton of experience cooking. Because of that, the recipes that follow will talk you through things that more advanced cookbooks would glaze over. You won't read anything without an exact description of how to do it.

Cooking for yourself comes with a large number of benefits, namely the fact you can control what ingredients are being used, thereby controlling your intake of unnecessary food products (e.g. butter, high-fat cuts of meat, etc.). Developing your skills as an amateur chef in college will certainly give you a leg up as you enter adult life in a few months/years. Have fun with the recipes!

Lemon Feta Chicken

Ingredients:

- Two chicken breasts
- Small amount of feta cheese (quarter-pound should be plenty)
- One lemon
- Oregano (optional)

Equipment Needed:

- Oven
- Knife
- Oven-safe dish (ideally a small square or round glass dish)
- Aluminum foil (optional, but highly recommended)

Preparation:

Very, very easy. First, preheat the oven to 400 degrees. Next, look over the chicken to see if it's got any large hunks of fat on it (white strips typically along the ends); if it does, cut those off. Now, put the raw chicken breasts on a dish ready for the oven. In an ideal world, you'd first coat the dish with aluminum foil. If you don't have this, coat the pan with some olive oil to try to keep the chicken from sticking to pan. Once chicken is on a coated pan, crumble up the feta cheese and place it on top of the chicken. You want to kind of push it hard into the chicken so it will stay in place. Once you've topped the chicken with the feta, cut the lemon in half and squeeze the juice from one half of the lemon all over the chicken and feta. If you have any oregano, now is the time to sprinkle some on top of everything; if not, no big deal. Now you're ready for the oven. Place in the preheated oven for about 30 minutes. Maybe after 15 minutes, depending on how much you like lemon, you might want to squeeze the other half out on top of everything. To see if chicken is ready for consumption, cut it open and if it's no longer pink/raw inside, it's ready to eat!

Texas Caviar

Ingredients:

- One can of black eyed peas
- One can of corn
- One can of pinto beans
- One can of kidney beans
- One red pepper — chopped
- Four green onions (scallions) — chopped
- Quarter cup of olive oil
- Quarter cup of sugar (optional)
- Quarter cup of apple cider vinegar (optional)

Equipment Needed:

- Can opener
- Knife
- Medium- to large-sized bowl
- Measuring cup(s) would be helpful, but not necessary

Preparation:

Open all cans, then drain and rinse the contents of each one by first pouring out all excess water within the cans, then flushing all the contents with water. This can be done with a colander or just by keeping the opened lid over the top of the can while you run it under the sink. Now mix all ingredients together minus the olive oil, sugar, and vinegar. If you only have olive oil, pour that over the top. If you have all three dressing ingredients (olive oil, sugar, and vinegar), boil them in a small pot until blended together nicely, just a few minutes, then pour this over the top of beans, etc. Stir well then chill in refrigerator. Once it's cold, this goes great as a snack to be eaten plain with a spoon, or to be used as a dip for pita chips. As a meal, you could use it with whole wheat wraps and just add some hummus and/or spinach to make a delicious Mediterranean-style wrap!

Tuna or Chicken Salad Panini

Ingredients:

- Two chicken breasts **or** two cans of tuna
- One red onion — chopped into half-inch pieces
- One large green pepper — chopped into half-inch pieces
- One large tomato — chopped into half-inch pieces
- Two avocados — chopped into half-inch pieces
- Slices of favorite cheese (optional)
- Mustard (optional)

Equipment Needed:

- Pan (ideally a panini machine)
- Knife
- Large bowl
- Depending on chicken/tuna, an oven-safe dish or a can opener

Preparation:

If using chicken, bake it for half hour at 400, or until done, then cut into half-inch pieces. If using tuna, simply open and drain the cans. Add whatever protein you're using in with the vegetables. To make a great panini, put the salad you've just created between two pieces of whole wheat bread and place in a panini grill! If you do not own one of these, place the sandwich on a pan and cook each side over medium heat until the bread starts to toast. Using cheese (not within the salad, but on the sandwich) will act as an adhesive for the sandwich and the whole thing will stay together better.

Black Bean Vegetable Chili

Ingredients:

- One onion — chopped
- Two carrots — chopped
- Two celery stalks — chopped
- Two garlic cloves — chopped
- 3 cans of black beans with chili spices — no need to drain or rinse
- One can of corn
- One can of stewed tomatoes
- One tablespoon of vegetable oil
- Two and a half cups of vegetable stock
- Spices (optional): teaspoon of garlic, two teaspoons of chili powder, two teaspoons of cumin, half-teaspoon of black pepper

Equipment Needed:

- Knife
- Can opener
- Large pot with lid
- Stove-top

Preparation:

Although a little laborious, this is well worth the effort. In a large pot, heat the oil, then add the onions, carrots, celery and garlic. Sauté until the onion softens — about five minutes. If you have the spices, add them now, and stir for another minute. Now add the vegetable stock, beans, corn, and tomato. Bring this entire thing to a boil over medium-high heat, then reduce the heat to a simmer. Cover the pot and let it simmer another 10 to 15 minutes longer, or until the carrots become tender. This could be served with regular chili accoutrements such as raw red onion, sour cream, blue corn tortilla chips, and/or grated cheese.

Roasted Chickpea Snack

Ingredients:

- One can garbanzo beans (i.e. chickpeas) — drained and rinsed
- Olive oil
- Spices (optional): garlic salt, garlic pepper, or just garlic powder

Equipment Needed:

- Oven
- Oven-safe dish (ideally a cookie sheet with aluminum foil)
- Can opener

Preparation:

Preheat the oven to 400. Once garbanzo beans are drained and rinsed, spread chickpeas out one-layer thick onto your cookie sheet (or whatever you've got) that is ideally coated with aluminum foil. From here, spray or drizzle your olive oil lightly on top, and sprinkle with the spices if you've got them. Bake at 400 for about 20 minutes, then pull them out of the oven and let them cool. After a few minutes, enjoy the very high fiber, high protein snack!

Enchiladas (enough for several days)

Ingredients:

- Chicken (optional) — two large breasts (1+ pound)
- One can of black beans
- One or two cans of mild, diced green chiles
- One can of corn
- Three large jalapeño peppers — diced (throw out seeds)
- One sweet onion — diced
- Four roma tomatoes — diced
- Garlic powder
- Cumin powder (optional)
- Mexican shredded cheese
- Whole wheat tortillas

Equipment Needed:

- Knife
- Can opener
- Large pot
- Large bowl
- To make quesadillas, need a panini machine
- To make enchiladas, need an oven and a baking dish

Preparation:

Boil large pot of water, then throw in chicken for thirty minutes. During the half hour, open and drain cans of beans, corn, and chiles, and chop/dice all other vegetables. Place everything in a large bowl with some garlic. Once chicken is done, shred it by using two forks and tearing chicken into manageable, bite-sized pieces. If you have cumin, add it to chicken then put chicken in with the vegetables. Add some cheese (half a handful), and now you are ready to make whatever you want! To make quesadillas, simply fill half a tortilla with the mix then place in panini machine. To make enchiladas, roll tortillas with mix inside, top with some cheese, then bake at 350 degrees for about 30-40 minutes.

Appendix E — Qualitative Food Journal

IN THE COMING PAGES, YOU will see a week-long food journal dedicated to the *quality* of your food choices, not the quantitative values of what is in those food choices (there is a 12-week version online found in the "Beneath the College Jersey Healthy Habits Workbook"). The goal of this journal is to get you to focus on what types of foods you're eating, which should result in two outcomes: 1) you'll be more focused on eating plants and animals instead of *x* grams of protein or *x* grams of whatever supplement, and 2) the quantities will take care of themselves because your focus is in the right place. The first thing you'll have to understand is how to mentally break up your food into categories. A limited guide can be found on the following pages, but let's start with brief descriptions here.

- *V for Vegetables:* Although it's easy to recognize broccoli and carrots as vegetables, for our intents and purposes, we're also going to include almost all plant life outside of fruit. This includes nuts, legumes, beans, seeds, seaweed, and mushrooms. Yes, of course, these foods are not technically vegetables, but each one of these items is nutrient-dense without negative side effects the way vegetables are.

- *F for Fruit:* On top of apples and bananas, don't forget about avocados, berries, melons, lemons, limes, and any fruit juice or jam that is actually made from the fruit itself.

- *W for Whole Grains:* Whole wheat bread, bagels, english muffins, pasta, certain breakfast cereals, whole wheat flour products (if you are baking them yourself), brown rice and any variety of quinoa or other healthy pasta alternative (e.g. farro, satan). Again, some of these are not technically whole grains, but the idea is just to separate your mind from the standard American diet of white pasta, white bread, and pizza.

- *Fi for Fish:* Basically this category includes anything that is not a plant that comes from a water source. This would be including, but not limited to, tuna, salmon, lobster, mussels, oysters, clams, crab, shrimp, mackerel, scallops, shark and octopus meat.

- **A** *for* **A**nimal: In addition to beef and pork and chicken, don't forget to add animal products, which include milk, cottage cheese, yogurt, cheese, butter, and eggs. Also include in this category any non-traditional meat source such as duck, rabbit, and insects ... if you should ever find yourself eating those foods.

- **O** *for* **O**ther: If what you are eating does not fit into one of the aforementioned categories, you can consider it an "other," and you probably want to abstain from as much "otherness" as possible. Products that could be categorized as other would include anything processed or that doesn't exist in nature, for starters, but then also would have to include white breads, white pastas, most breakfast cereals, coffee (room for debate here, but it is a drug, so I'm cate-gorizing it as an "Other"), donuts, ice cream, most processed condiments, pizza, calzones, french fries, soda, sports drinks, candy, alcohol of any sort, etc.

- **H** *for* **H**$_2$O: Record how much water you drink throughout the day in this section. For athletes, nearly 80 ounces is recommended.

Now of course, not everything you eat will fit neatly into one of these categories. In fact, for most of the food Americans eat, they'd have to use more than one category for each thing they put in their mouth. While a nice piece of chicken would obviously belong in *A*, if you top it with swiss cheese, tomato, and wrap it up with wheat bread, you'd have to add an additional *A*, a *V*, and a *W*. Ordering a veggie lover's pizza, and plan to eat the whole thing? Use your intelligence to determine how many servings you're consuming, but remember to add *O* because it's pizza, and *A* because of all the cheese in addition to the *V*. Having an apple turnover? Well unless you or a family member made it with *real* apples, don't add an *F* to that *O*.

You can also use the columns to keep track of certain food-related goals. Say you want to cut down on the amount of coffee you drink. Track and record all of the coffee beverages you have with a big "C" in the journal and total it up each day and week.

Trust your instincts with this, and don't let the decision-making consume you. Focusing too long on which foods belong where is a short route to irascibility, and you will be missing the point of this exercise. To be successful with this, you have to edit: make snap decisions.

Finally, you might be asking what is "good" according to this journal. First, it should be said that more than anything, this journal is about self-awareness. Step one in every habit change is determining the problem, and unless you know how you've been eating as of late, how will you know where you need to improve? Second, if one were to read specific health claims or recommendations about which food is best, it leaves him or her extremely limited to try anything else. For this reason, you will not find explicit instructions here. What can be said about this style of food journaling is that if one were living healthy, the sum of their V and F columns would be greater than any other column (maybe even more than all the others combined?). The O column would be extremely limited, and the W column would be around the sum of the Fi and A columns. In a very broad sense, athletes need more fruits and vegetables than anything else (especially if that is including beans and nuts and seeds, as in our case), then need more servings of carbohydrates than they do protein (which is of course important too). But, most carbo-hydrate-rich foods have far more carbohydrates than protein-rich foods have protein, respectively. For this reason, you don't need the W column to be double the Fi and A columns. Check out the *Macronutrients* section of this book to rediscover the specificities of athletes' needs.

On the following page, you'll see a brief guide to assist you in categorizing your food, then a sample day. Finally, on the succeeding pages, a week-long journal starts, and seven days later a page is reserved for calculating your week's totals. Enjoy it, and learn from it.

FOOD	V	F	W	Fi	A	O
Alcohol - any variety						X
Almond Butter - only allowed to check *V* if ingredients are solely almonds.	?					?
Bars - read nutritional label, as each bar is made quite differently. You are likely to check more than one category.	?	?	?	?	?	?
Beans - black, pinto, garbanzo, soy, etc.	X					
Breads - whole wheat or rye			X			
Breads - all other varieties						X
Breakfast Cereals - vast majority will be *O*, although possible to get a *W* also			?			X
Butter					X	
Cheese - all varieties					X	
Chips - depends on the variety	?		?			X
Coffee - both regular and decaf						X
Crackers - depends on the variety			?			X
Donuts						X
Eggs					X	
Ice Cream - all varieties					X	X
Jellies and Jams - check ingredients, only check *F* if it's an elitist brand		?				?
Juice - same rules as jellies and jams		?				?
Ketchup						X
Mayonnaise					X	X
Milk - from cows, goats, or sheep					X	
Milk - from soy, almonds, or coconuts	X					

FOOD	V	F	W	Fi	A	O
Muffins - no alternate checks unless they are homemade	?	?	?		?	X
Mushrooms - although really fungi	X					
Mustard - gourmet varieties	X					
Mustard - standard yellow						X
Nuts - including legumes	X					
Pasta - whole wheat varieties			X			
Pasta - of other varieties						X
Peanut Butter - only check the *V* if the ingredient list is solely "peanuts"	?					?
Pizza - baseline is *O* and *A*, then add ingredients	?	?	?	?	X	X
Potatoes - baked or roasted (including sweet potatoes and other varieties)	X					
Potatoes - french fries, chips, etc.						X
Protein Powders - whey					X	X
Protein Powders - soy and plant	X					X
Quinoa			X			
Rice - brown			X			
Rice - all other varieties, including pilaf						X
Salsa - check ingredients	?	?			?	?
Seeds	X					
Soda, Sports Drinks, and Energy Drinks						X

EXAMPLE DAY OF FOOD	V	F	W	Fi	A	O	H
Meal 1		X	X		X		16
Two packets of oatmeal with blueberries		X	X				
Small serving of plain greek yogurt with			X				
granola and raspberries							
Two glasses of water							
Meal 2			X		X	X	8
Homemade breakfast sandwich with whole			X		X		
wheat bagel, 3 eggs, slice of cheese					X		
Coffee with cream					X		
Glass of water							
Meal 3	X	X					16
Carrots with Hummus	X	X					
Two bananas	X						
	X						
Two glasses of water							
Meal 4	X	X	X		X		16
Turkey in wheat wrap with carrots,	X				X		
hummus, spinach, and cucumbers	X						
One pear	X						
Two glasses of water							
Meal 5	X	X					16
POST-WORKOUT:	X	X					
Two handfuls of raisins	X						
Two apples with peanut butter and							
cinnamon							
Two glasses of water							
Meal 6	X		X	X			8
Grilled shrimp with brown rice and roasted	X		X	X			
summer squash and zucchini							
One glass of water							
TOTALS FOR TODAY	_13_	_7_	_8_	_2_	_7_	_1_	_80_

DATE:	V	F	W	Fi	A	O	H
Meal 1							
Meal 2							
Meal 3							
Meal 4							
Meal 5							
Meal 6							
TOTALS FOR TODAY							

DATE:	V	F	W	Fi	A	O	H
Meal 1							
Meal 2							
Meal 3							
Meal 4							
Meal 5							
Meal 6							
TOTALS FOR TODAY							

DATE:			V	F	W	Fi	A	O	H
Meal 1									
Meal 2									
Meal 3									
Meal 4									
Meal 5									
Meal 6									
TOTALS FOR TODAY									

DATE:	V	F	W	Fi	A	O	H
Meal 1							
Meal 2							
Meal 3							
Meal 4							
Meal 5							
Meal 6							
TOTALS FOR TODAY							

DATE:	V	F	W	Fi	A	O	H
Meal 1							
Meal 2							
Meal 3							
Meal 4							
Meal 5							
Meal 6							
TOTALS FOR TODAY							

DATE:	V	F	W	Fi	A	O	H
Meal 1							
Meal 2							
Meal 3							
Meal 4							
Meal 5							
Meal 6							
TOTALS FOR TODAY							

DATE:	V	F	W	Fi	A	O	H
Meal 1							
Meal 2							
Meal 3							
Meal 4							
Meal 5							
Meal 6							
TOTALS FOR TODAY							

Weekly Totals	V	F	W	Fi	A	O	H
Monday							
Tuesday							
Wednesday							
Thursday							
Friday							
Saturday							
Sunday							
TOTALS							

Bibliography

Alano, Ryan et. al. *"The associations between sleep quality and eating patterns in young adults."* FASEB Journal 2010; 24:lb361.

Allen, Naomi. "Soy milk intake in relation to serum sex hormone levels in British men." Nutrition and Cancer 2001; 41(1-2): 41-46.

Ambrose, Stephen. 1996. *Undaunted Courage: Meriwether Lewis, Thomas Jefferson, and the Opening of the American West.* Simon & Schuster: New York, NY. Procured through Apple's iBooks for iPad.

Anthony, Tracy et. al. "Regulation of protein synthesis and translation initiation in skeletal muscle by feeding mixed meals containing soy or whey protein after endurance exercise." FASEB Journal 2006; 20:A854.

Ariely, Dan. 2009. *Predictably Irrational Revised and Expanded Edition: The Hidden Forces that Shape Our Decisions.* Harper Collins Publishers, New York, NY. Procured through Apple's iBooks for iPad.

Ariely, Dan. 2012. *The (Honest) Truth About Dishonesty: How We Lie to Everyone - Especially Ourselves.* Harper Collins Publishers, New York, NY. Procured through Apple's iBooks for iPad.

Baechle, Thomas and Roger Earle. 2000. *Essentials of Strength and Conditioning.* Human Kinetics: Champaign, IL.

Bascomb, Neal. 2004. *The Perfect Mile: Three Athletes, One Goal and Less than Four Minutes to Achieve It.* Houghton Mifflin Company: Boston, MA.

Batmanghelidj, Fereydoon. 2003. *Water: for Health, for Healing, for Life.* Wellness Central: New York, NY.

Baty, Jacob et. al. *"The Effect of a Carbohydrate and Protein Supplement on Resistance Exercise Performance, Hormonal REsponse, and Muscle Damange."* Journal of Strength & Conditioning Research 2007; 21(2).

Benedetti, Fabrizio. 2007. *The Placebo and Nocebo Effect: How the Therapist's Words Act on the Patient's Brain.* No. 69 Mind & Body. Pages 7-9. Karger Gazette.

Bittman, Mark. 2011. "What's Wrong with What We Eat." TEDTalks: Chew on This. Retrieved from Netflix on 9 September 2013.

Bonnet, Michael et. al. *"The Use of Caffeine Versus Prophylactic Naps in Sustained Performance."* Sleep 1995; 18(2):97-104

Brooks, Amber and Leon Lack. *"A Brief Afternoon Nap Following Noctural Sleep Restriction: Which Nap Duration is Most Recuperative?"* Sleep 2006; 29(6): 831-840.

Brooks, David. 2011. *The Social Animal: The Hidden Sources of Love, Character, and Achievement.* Random House: New York, NY. Procured through Apple's iBooks for iPad.

Brown, Charles. 1942. *The Contribution of Greek to English.* Vanderbilt University Press: Nashville, TN.

Bugliosi, Vincent. 2007. *Reclaiming History: The Assassination of President John F. Kennedy.* W.W. Norton & Company, Inc.: New York, NY.

Butler, George and Robert Fiore. 1977. "Pumping Iron." Cinegate & Almi Cinema 5.

Butts, Frank B. 2009. "Problematic Drinking Among College Athletes." The Journal of Coaching Education, 2(1).

Callahan, Steven. 2002. *Adrift; Seventy-Six Days Lost at Sea.* Houghton Mifflin Company, a Mariner Book: Boston, MA. Procured through Apple's iBooks for iPad.

Callner, Marty. 1998. "Jerry Seinfeld: 'I'm Telling You for the Last Time' – Live on Broadway." Home Box Office.

Campbell, T. Colin and Thomas M. Campbell II. 2006. *The China Study: Startling Implications for Diet, Weight Loss and Long-Term Health.* BenBella Books, Inc: Dallas, TX.

Carmichael, Chris. 2004. *Food for Fitness: Eat Right to Train Right.* Berkley Books: New York, NY.

Cialdini, Robert B. 2009. *Influence: The Psychology of Persuasion.* HarperCollins e-books: New York, NY. Procured through Apple's iBooks for iPad.

Clark, Nancy. 2008. *"Alcohol, Athletes and Pressure to Drink."* Active.com. www.active.com/nutrition/articles/alcohol-athletes-and-pressure-to-drink?page=1

Colgan, Michael. 1993. *Optimum Sports Nutrition: Your Competitive Edge.* Advanced Research Press: New York, NY.

Colquhoun, James. 2008. "Food Matters." Aspect Film.

Colquhoun, James. 2012. "Hungry for Change." Permacology Productions.

"Cooper, Martin." 2008. *Encyclopedia of World Biography.* Retrieved November 12, 2012 from Encyclopedia.com: http://www.encyclopedia.com/doc/1G2-25063000048.html

Coyle, Daniel. 2009. *The Talent Code: Greatness Isn't Born. It's Grown. Here's How.* Bantam Books: New York, NY. Procured through Apple's iBooks for iPad.

Crispim, Cibele Aparecida et al. *"The influence of sleep and sleep loss upon food intake and metabolism."* Nutrition Research Reviews 2007; 20(2):195-212.

Crowe, Cameron. 1996. "Jerry Maguire." TriStar Pictures.

Cuddy, Amy. 2012. "Your Body Language Shapes Who You Are." TEDTalks: Life Hack. Retrieved from Netflix on 14 September 2013.

Diamond, Jared. 1999. *Guns, Germs, and Steel: The Fates of Human Societies.* W. W. Norton & Company: New York, NY. Procured through Apple's iBooks for iPad.

Diamond, Jared. 2011. *Collapse: How Societies Choose to Fail or Succeed.* Penguin Books: New York, NY.

Detienne, Marcel. 1972. *The Gardens of Adonis: Spices in Greek Mythology.* Princeton University Press: Princeton, NJ.

Drake, Christopher et. al. *"Effects of rapid versus slow accumulation of eight hours of sleep loss."* Psychophysiology 2001; 38(6):979-987.

Duhigg, Charles. 2012. *The Power of Habit: Why We Do What We Do in Live and Business.* Random House: New York, NY.

Economos, et. al. 2008. *College Freshman Stress and Weight Change: Differences by Gender."* American Journal of Health Behavior. 32(1): 16-25.

Epictetus. Translated by Tad Brennan and Charles Brittain. 2002. *Simplicius: On Epictetus' Handbook 27-53.* Cornell University Press: Ithaca, NY.

Evans, Melissa and Allen Jackson. 1992. "Applied research psychological factors related to drug use in college athletes." The Sports Psychologist, Volume 6, Issue 1.

Francis, Charlie. 1991. *Speed Trap: Inside the Biggest Scandal in Olympic History.* St. Martin's Press: New York, NY.

Frazer, James George. 1935. *The Golden Bough.* Third Edition. Volume Two. The Macmillan Company: New York, NY.

Frontiera, Joe and Daniel Leidl. 2012. *Team Turnarounds: A Playbook for Transforming Underperforming Teams.* Jossey-Bass: San Francisco, CA. Procured through Apple's iBooks for iPad.

Fulkerson, Lee. 2011. "Forks Over Knives." Monica Beach Media.

Fussell, Samuel Wilson. 1991. *Muscle: Confessions of an Unlikely Bodybuilder.* Avon Books: New York, NY.

Gartner, James. 2006. "Glory Road." Walt Disney Pictures.

Georgakilas, Evangelia et. al. *"College students' midpoint sleep time and dietary intake."* FASEB Journal 2013: 27:lb421.

Gladwell, Malcolm. 2002. *The Tipping Point: How Little Things Can Make a Big Difference.* Hachette Book Group: New York, NY. Procured through Apple's iBooks for iPad.

Gladwell, Malcolm. 2005. *Blink: The Power of Thinking Without Thinking.* Back Bay Books: New York, NY. Procured through Apple's iBooks for iPad.

Gladwell, Malcolm. 2008. *Outliers: The Story of Success.* Back Bay Books: New York, NY. Procured through Apple's iBooks for iPad.

Gladwell, Malcolm. 2009. *What the Dog Saw.* Hachette Book Group, Inc: New York, NY. Procured through Apple's iBooks for iPad.

Goldacre, Ben. 2010. *Bad Science: Quacks, Hacks, and Big Pharma Flacks.* Faber and Faber, Inc: New York, NY.

Goldstein, Jonathan. 2012. *I'll Seize the Day Tomorrow.* Penguin Books: New York, NY. Procured through Apple's iBooks for iPad.

Gordon, Douglas and Philippe Parreno. 2006. "Zidane: A 21st Century Portrait." Anna Lena Films.

Grandjean, Ann. "Diets of Elite Athletes: Has the Discipline of Sports Nutrition Made an Impact?" American Society for Nutritional Sciences 1997; 127(5): 874s-877s.

Green, Tamara. 1994. *The Greek and Latin Roots of English.* Ardsley House Publishers Inc.: New York, NY.

Greenstreet, Steven. 2008. "Killer at Large." ShineBox Media Productions.

Habito, Raymundo et. al. "Effects of replacing meat with soyabean [sic] in the diet on sex hormone concentrations in healthy adult males." British Journal of Nutrition 2000; 84: 557-563.

Hard, Robin. 1997. *Apollodorus: The Library of Greek Mythology.* Oxford University Press: Oxford.

Hill, DW et. al. *"Effect of time of day on aerobic and anaerobic responses to high-intensity exercise."* Canadian Journal of Sport Science 1992; 17(4):316-319.

Holford, Patrick. 2004. *The New Optimum Nutrition Bible.* The Crossing Press: Berkeley, CA.

Hu, Frank B. et al. Journal of the American College of Nutrition 2001; 20(1): 5-19.

Iyengar, Sheena. 2010. *The Art of Choosing.* Twelve; Hachette Book Group: New York, NY. Procured through Apple's iBooks for iPad.

Jackson, Phil. 2001. *More than a Game.* Simon & Schuster: New York, NY.

Jacobson, Bert and Steven Aldana. *"Current Nutrition Practice and Knowledge of Varsity Athletes."* Journal of Strength and Conditioning Research 1992; 6(4).

Kahneman, Daniel. 2011. "The Riddle of Experience vs. Memory." TEDTalks: Head Games. Retrieved from Netflix on 22 August 2013.

Kahneman, Daniel. 2011. *Thinking Fast and Slow.* Farrar, Straus and Giroux: New York, NY. Procured through Apple's iBooks for iPad.

Kaida, Kosuke et. al. *"Indoor Exposure to Natural Bright Light Prevents Afternoon Sleepiness."* Sleep 2006; 29(4):462-469.

Kenner, Robert. 2009. "Food, Inc." Magnolia Pictures.

Kim, Sangmi et. al. *"Eating patterns and nutritional characteristics associated with sleep duration."* Public Health Nutrition 2010; 14(5):889-895.

King, Don Roy. 2008. "The Michael Phelps Diet." *Saturday Night Live.* National Broadcasting Company. 13 September.

King, Ian. 1998. *How to Write Strength Training Programs.* King Sports Publishing: Reno, NV.

King, Ian. 2000. *Foundations of Physical Preparation.* King Sports Publishing: Reno, NV.

Kiyosaki, Robert. 1998. *Rich Dad, Poor Dad.* Warner Books: New York, NY.

Klopfer, Brono. 1957. *Psychological Variables in Human Cancer.* Pages 331-340. Journal of Prospective Techniques.

Kluth, Andreas. 2011. *Hannibal and Me: What History's Greatest Military Strategist Can Teach Us About Success and Failure.* Riverhead Books: New York, NY. Procured through Apple's iBooks for iPad.

Kraemer, William et. al. "The effects of soy and whey protein supplementation on acute hormonal responses to resistance exercise in men." Journal of the American College of Nutrition 2013; 32(1):66-74.

Krakauer, Jon. 2009. *Where Men Win Glory.* Anchor Books: New York, NY.

Lehrer, Jonah. 2012. *Imagine: How Creativity Works.* Houghton Mifflin Harcourt: Boston, MA. Procured through Apple's iBooks for iPad.

Löhrke, B et. al. "Activation of skeletal muscle protein breakdown following consumption of soybean protein in pigs." British Journal of Nutrition 2001; 85(4):447-457.

Lowitt, Bruce. 1999. *Bannister Stuns World with Four-Minute Mile.* 17 December. St. Petersburg Times. Retrieved 11 November 2010. <http://www.sptimes.com/News/121799/Sports/Bannister_stuns_world.shtml>

Mah, Cheri et. al. *"The Effects of Sleep Extension on the Athletic Performance of Collegiate Basketball Players."* Sleep 2011; 34(7):943-950.

Maher, Bill. 2012. *"Real Time: with Bill Maher."* Episode #234. 20 January. Home Box Office.

Maher, Bill. 2013. *"Real Time: with Bill Maher."* Episode #287. 21 June. Home Box Office.

Maraniss, David. 1999. *When Pride Still Mattered: A Life of Vince Lombardi.* Simon & Schuster Paperbacks: New York, NY.

Martens, Matthew et. al. 2006. "Brief report comparing off-season with in-season alcohol consumption among intercollegiate athletes." Journal of Sport and Exercise Psychology, Volume 28, Issue 4.

Martens, Matthew et. al. 2006. "A systematic review of college student-athlete drinking: prevalence rates, sport-related factors, and interventions." Journal of Substance Abuse Treatment, 31:305-316.

McDougall, Christopher. 2009. *Born to Run: A Hidden Tribe, Superathletes, and the Greatest Race the World Has Ever Seen.* Random House / Vintage Books: New York, NY.

McRaney, David. 2011. *You Are Not So Smart: Why You Have Too Many Friends on Facebook, Why Your Memory is Mostly Fiction, and 46 Other Ways You're Deluding Yourself.* Penguin Books: New York, NY. Procured through Apple's iBooks for iPad.

Metcalf, Allan. 2002. *Predicting New Words: The Secrets of their Success.* Houghton Mifflin Company: Boston, MA.

Millman, Dan. 2000. *Way of the Peaceful Warrior.* HJ Kramer & New World Library: California.

Moore, Kenny. 2006. *Bowerman and the Men of Oregon: The Story of Oregon's Legendary Coach and Nike's Cofounder.* Rodale Books: Emmaus, PA. Procured through Apple's iBooks for iPad.

Montgomery, Iain et. al. *"Energy Expenditure and Total Sleep Time: Effect of Physical Exercise."* Sleep 1982; 5(2):159-168.

Murphy, Alistair et. al. 2013. "The effect of post-match alcohol ingestion on recovery from competitive rugby league matches." The Journal of Strength and Conditioning Research, 25(5):1304-1312.

Nagata, Chisato et. al. "Inverse association of soy product intake with serum androgen and estrogen concentrations in Japanese men." Nutrition and Cancer 2000; 36(1):14-18.

Nelson, Toben and Henry Wechsler. 2001. "Alcohol and college athletes." Medicine and Science in Sports and Exercise, 33(1):43-47.

O'Brien, C. and F. Lyons. 2000. "Alcohol and the athlete." Sports Medicine, 29(5):295-300.

Pasiakos, Stefan et. al. "High protein diets enhance body composition in rats: a comparative analysis of milk- and soy-based energy restricted diets." FASEB Journal 2013; 27:631.10.

Perkins, H. Wesley and David W. Craig. *"A Successful Social Norms Campaign to Reduce Alcohol Misuse Among College Student-Athletes."* Journal of Studies on Alcohol and Drugs 2006; 67(6):880-889.

Pierce, Charles P. 2009. *Idiot America: How Stupidity Became a Virtue in the Land of the Free.* Doubleday: New York, NY.

Pollan, Michael. 2006. *The Omnivore's Dilemma: A Natural History of Four Meals.* Penguin Books: New York, NY.

Pollan, Michael. 2008. *In Defense of Food: An Eater's Manifesto.* Penguin Books: New York, NY.

Reilly T. and Piercy M. *"The effect of partial sleep deprivation on weight-lifting performance."* Ergonomics 1994; 37(1):107-115.

Reynolds, Gretchen. *"Phys Ed: Will Olympic Athletes Dope if They Know It Might Kill Them?"* The New York Times 2010; January 20.

Robbins, John. 2011. *The Food Revolution: How Your Diet Can Help Save Your Life and Our World.* Conari Press: San Francisco, CA.

Robbins, John. 2012. *No Happy Cows: Dispatches from the Frontlines of the Food Revolution.* Conari Press: San Francisco, CA.

Robergs, Robert and Scott Roberts. 1997. *Exercise Physiology: Exercise, Performance, and Clinical Applications.* Mosby-Year Book Inc: St. Louis, MO.

Rousmaniere, John. 2000. *Fastnet Force 10: The Deadliest Storm in the History of Modern Sailing.* W. W. Norton & Company: New York, NY.

Sacheck, Jennifer et. al. 2010. "Physical fitness, adiposity, and metabolic risk factors in young college students." Med. Sci. Sports Exerc., 42(6):1039-1044.

Salatin, Joel. 2011. *Folks, This Ain't Normal: A Farmer's Advice for Happier Hens, Healthier People, and a Better World.* Center Books: New York, NY. Procured through Apple's iBooks for iPad.

Schlosser, Eric. 2002. *Fast Food Nation: The Dark Side of the All-American Meal.* Harper Perennial: New York, NY.

Schwartz, Barry. 2004. *The Paradox of Choice: Why More is Less.* Harper Collins e-books: Pymble, Australia. Procured through Apple's iBooks for iPad.

Schwarzenegger, Arnold. 1998. *The New Encyclopedia of Modern Bodybuilding.* Simon and Schuster: New York, NY.

Shackleton, Sir Ernest. 2004. *South: The Endurance Expedition.* Penguin Books: New York, NY. Originally published in Great Britain by William Heinemann in 1919. Procured through Apple's iBooks for iPad.

Shermer, Michael. 2011. *The Believing Brain: From Ghosts and Gods to Politics and Conspiracies - How We Construct Beliefs and Reinforce Them as Truths.* Times Books: New York, NY. Procured through Apple's iBooks for iPad.

Simon, Janet and Carrie Docherty. 2014. "Current health-related quality of life is lower in former Division I collegiate athletes than in non-collegiate athletes." American Journal of Sports Medicine, Volume 42, Number 2, pp. 423-429.

Singhal, Rohit. "Is soy estrogenic? Hepatic gene expression in the presence or absence of endogenous estrogen." FASEB Journal 2007; 21:114.3.

Smith, Carlyle and Danielle Smith. 2003. "Ingestion of ethanol just prior to sleep onset impairs memory for procedural but not declarative tasks." Sleep Journal, 26(2): 185-191.

Smith, RS et. al. *"Circadian rhythms and enhanced athletic performance in the National Football League."* Sleep 1997; 20(5):362-365.

Souissi, Nizar et. al. *"Effects of Time-of-Day and Partial Sleep Deprivation on Short-Term Maximal Performances of Judo Competitors."* Journal of Strength and Conditioning Research 2013; 27(9):2473-2480.

Steel, Carolyn. 2011. "How Food Shapes Our Cities." TEDTalks: Chew on This. Retrieved from Netflix on 26 August 2013.

Stephan, Andrew and John Dorsey. 2011. "The Marinovich Project." ESPN Films Presents.'

Tarnopolsky, Mark. "Building muscle: nutrition to maximize bulk and strength adaptations to resistance exercise training." European Journal of Sport Science 2008; 8(2):67-76.

Tavris, Carol and Elliot Aronson. 2007. *Mistakes Were Made (but not by me): Why We Justify Foolish Beliefs, Bad Decisions, and Hurtful Acts.* Harcourt, Inc: Orlando, FL. Procured through Apple's iBooks for iPad.

"Ten Vegetarian Athletes." 2011. Spanfeller Media Group: TheDailyMeal.com. Viewed 10 July 2013. <www.thedailymeal.com/10-vegetarian-athletes>

This American Life. 2011. "Million Dollar Idea." National Public Radio. WNYC, New York. 7 August.

This American Life. 2012. "Take the Money and Run for Office." National Public Radio. WNYC, New York. 30 March.

Thygerson, Alton L. 2005. *Fit to Be Well.* Jones and Bartlett Publishers: Sudbury, MA.

Unknown Author. "Effects of soy and tea on hormone-induced prostate cancer in Noble rat model." FASEB Journal 2008; 22:311.2.

United States District Court Eastern District of New York. *Ackerman et. al. against The Coca-Cola Company.* Filed July 21st, 2010. Case 1:09-cv-00395-JG -RML Document 44. Procured at <cspinet.org/new/pdf/order_on_m-dismiss_doc_44.pdf>

University of California San Diego. *"Alcohol and Athletic Performance."* Athletic Performance Nutrition Bulletin. Procured at <www.nmnathletics.com/attachments1/507.htm>

University of Georgia. *"Alcohol and Athletic Performance."* University Health Center, Student Affairs 2014.

University of Notre Dame. *"Alcohol and Athletes."* Office of Alcohol and Drug Education, Division of Student Affairs 2008. Procured at <oade.nd.edu/educate-yourself-alcohol/alcohol-and-athletes/>

U.S. Census Bureau. 2010. *The 2010 Statistical Abstract: Expectations of Life at Birth, 1970 to 2006, and Projections 2010 and 2020.* <http://www.census.gov/compendia/statab/2010/tables/10s0102.pdf>

Wadler, Gary. *"Alcohol."* Drugs and Sport. ESPN.com Special Section 2010; September 6th.

Whitney, Ellie and Sharon Rady Rolfes. 2005. *Understanding Nutrition.* Tenth Edition. Thomson Wadsworth: Belmont, CA.

Wikipedia.com. 2010. *"Mile Run World Record Progression."* Retrieved August 11. Wikimedia Foundation, Inc. <http://en.wikipedia.org/wiki/Mile_run_world_record_progression>

Williams, Melvin. 2005. *Nutrition: for Health, Fitness, and Sport.* Seventh Edition. McGraw Hill High Education: Boston, MA.

Williams, Roger. 2010 (1643). *A Key into the Language of America.* Cosimo Classics: New York, NY.

Wong, Julia et. al. "Effectiveness of a vegan based high soy protein diet on weight loss and serum lipids." FASEB Journal 2007;21:111.8.

Wright, Lawrence. 2012. *Going Clear: Scientology, Hollywood, and the Prison of Belief.* Alfred A. Knopf: New York, NY. Procured through Apple's iBooks for iPad.

Vanderkam, Laura. 2012. *What the Most Successful People Do Before Breakfast.* Penguin Publishers: New York, NY. Procured through Apple's iBooks for iPad.

[1] 2010:20
[2] Diamond 2011:349
[3] Shermer 2011:305
[4] Gladwell 2009:197
[5] 2009:197
[6] Brooks 2011:230
[7] Maraniss 1999:348
[8] Iyengar 2010:133
[9] Iyengar 2010:222
[10] Brennan 2002:52-3
[11] Grandjean 1997
[12] Brooks 2011:124
[13] Economos 2008:16-21
[14] Crowe 1996
[15] 2000:72
[16] Brooks 2011:154
[17] Holford 2004:259
[18] Brooks 2011:284
[19] 2000:56
[20] McRaney 2011:16
[21] Holford 2004:258
[22] Gladwell 2008:27
[23] Gladwell 2008:27
[24] Coyle 2009:46
[25] 2008:15
[26] Coyle 2009:99
[27] Baechle 2000:20
[28] Gladwell 2008:145
[29] Coyle 2009:58
[30] 2001:290
[31] Coyle 2009:116
[32] Gladwell 2009:260
[33] Brooks 2011:113
[34] According to David Maraniss' 1999 book When Pride Still Mattered: A Life of Vince Lombardi.
[35] 1998:57
[36] Gladwell 2002:108
[37] Gladwell 2002:111
[38] 2002:117
[39] Coyle 2009:90
[40] Gladwell 2005:38
[41] Simple Wikipedia.com search
[42] Bascomb 2004:161
[43] Bascomb 2004:156
[44] Bascomb 2004:190
[45] Bascomb 2004:161
[46] Bascomb 2004:211
[47] Lowitt 1999
[48] Another simple Wikipedia.com search
[49] Bascomb 2004:160
[50] McRaney 2011:69
[51] Cialdini 2009:60
[52] 2007:28
[53] 2007:30
[54] McRaney 2011:35
[55] McRaney 2011:227
[56] Brooks 2011:24
[57] Wright 2012:18
[58] Kahneman 2011:22
[59] Shermer 2011:395
[60] Shermer 2011:305
[61] 2011:10
[62] 2011:68
[63] Tavris 2007:30
[64] Kahneman 2011:111
[65] Tavris 2007:7
[66] Tavris 2007:28
[67] Kahneman 2011:97
[68] 2011:129
[69] Tavris 2011:288
[70] 2011:124
[71] Robergs 1997:566
[72] Robergs 1997:570
[73] Whitney 2005:263
[74] 2011:77

[75] Shermer 2011:91
[76] Ariely 2012:113
[77] Kahneman 2011:485
[78] Cialdini 2009:154
[79] Kahneman 2011:294
[80] Kahneman 2011:146
[81] Shermer 2011:158
[82] Kahneman 2011:406
[83] Cialdini 2009:77
[84] 2011:192
[85] Kahneman 2011:15
[86] Bugliosi 2007:xiv
[87] Episode #234
[88] Gladwell 2002:73
[89] Robbins 2012:35
[90] Robbins 2011:103
[91] Robbins 2011:101
[92] Robbins 2011:103
[93] Robbins 2011:104
[94] Schlosser 2002:142
[95] Robbins 2012:105
[96] Robbins 2011:335
[97] Robbins 2011:335
[98] Holford 2004:283
[99] Robbins 2012:37
[100] Campbell 2006:6
[101] Campbell 2006:5-6
[102] Robbins 2011:107
[103] Robbins 2011:99
[104] Kahneman 2011:94
[105] Kahneman 2011:16
[106] 2011:155-6
[107] 2009:92
[108] McRaney 2011:75
[109] Schlosser 2002:242
[110] Holford 2004:287
[111] 2010
[112] McRaney 2011:165
[113] Robbins 2012
[114] Ambrose 1996:25
[115] Bittman TedTalk:2011 What's Wrong with What We Eat
[116] 2002:5
[117] 2008:106-132
[118] Hungry for Change
[119] Goldacre 2010:152
[120] Greenstreet 2008 Documentary "Killer at Large"
[121] Robbins 2011:xxiv
[122] Schlosser 2002:240
[123] Forks Over Knives
[124] Robbins 2012:140
[125] Holford 2004:269
[126] Steel TEDTalk: 2011 How Food Shapes Our Cities
[127] Schlosser 2002:120
[128] Robbins 2012:78
[129] Robbins 2011
[130] Kenner Food, Inc. 2009
[131] Robbins 2011:122
[132] Brooks 2011:218
[133] Michael Pollan on Bill Maher Episode #287
[134] Schlosser 2002:204
[135] Schlosser 2002:195
[136] Schlosser 2002:202
[137] Robbins 2011:91
[138] Robbins 2012:71
[139] Holford 2004:169
[140] Robbins 2011:85
[141] Schlosser 2002:196
[142] Brooks 2011:209
[143] Brooks 2011:210
[144] McRaney 2011:49
[145] Holford 2004:169
[146] Holford 2004:104
[147] Diamond 1999:120
[148] Diamond 1999:184-5
[149] Brooks 2011:27
[150] Diamond 2011:391

[151] McDougall 2009:225
[152] Pollan 2008:145
[153] Holford 2004:50
[154] McDougall 2009:182
[155] Holford 2004:171
[156] Holford 2004:170
[157] Pollan 2008:34
[158] Kahneman 2011:387
[159] 2008:80
[160] Brooks 2011:360
[161] 2011:32
[162] Iyengar 2010:111
[163] 2005:120
[164] Gladwell 2005:220
[165] Robbins 2012:141
[166] Kahneman 2011:550
[167] Ariely 2009:66
[168] Gladwell 2005:139
[169] Pollan 2006:243
[170] Schlosser 2002:4
[171] Lehrer 2012:106
[172] Whitney 2005:41,49
[173] Batmanghelidj 2003:4
[174] Batmanghelidj 2003:128
[175] Batmanghelidj 2003:17
[176] Holford 2004:166
[177] Robbins 2012:148
[178] Batmanghelidj 2003:61
[179] Holford 2004:93
[180] Batmanghelidj 2003:61
[181] Colgan 1993:19
[182] Batmanghelidj 2003:34
[183] Colgan 1993:19
[184] Holford 2004:18
[185] Holford 2004:40
[186] Holford 2004:159
[187] Whitney 2005:397
[188] Whitney 2005:396
[189] Batmanghelidj 2003:225
[190] Whitney 2005:493
[191] Colgan 1993:32
[192] U.S. District Court Document 44. Page 35
[193] Moore 2006:290
[194] Batmanghelidj 2003:65
[195] Iyengar 2010:131
[196] Shermer 2011:94
[197] Cialdini 2009:226
[198] Jacobson et. al. 1992:6(4)
[199] Colgan 1993:144
[200] King SNL 2008
[201] Whitney 2005:252
[202] Whitney 2005:257
[203] Whitney 2005:256
[204] Whitney 2005:263
[205] Whitney 2005:115
[206] Colgan 1993:105
[207] Williams 2005:122
[208] Williams 2005:124
[209] Williams 2005:124
[210] Tarnopolsky 2008
[211] Holford 2004:387
[212] Whitney 2005:201
[213] 2005:218
[214] Colgan 1993:149
[215] Baty 2007: 21(2).
[216] Colgan 1993:151
[217] Holford 2004:45
[218] Holford 2004:79
[219] Colgan 1993:80
[220] Williams 2005:173
[221] Williams 2005:135
[222] Williams 2005:217
[223] Williams 2005:135
[224] Baechle 2000:100
[225] Baechle 2000:153
[226] Holford 2004:287

[227] Colquhoun. Food Matters. 2008
[228] Holford 2004:98
[229] Holford 2004:427
[230] Holford 2004:100-101
[231] Holford 2004:126
[232] Holford 2004:387
[233] Holford 2004:266
[234] Holford 2004:258
[235] Brooks 2011:386
[236] Brooks 2011:375
[237] Holford 2004:55
[238] Butts 2009:2(1)
[239] Wadler's ESPN.com "Alcohol"
[240] Butts 2009:2(1)
[241] Clark 2008: "Alcohol, Athletes and Pressure to Drink"
[242] Kahneman 2011:485
[243] Evans 1992:6(1)
[244] Nelson 2001:33(1)
[245] O'Brien 2000:29(5)
[246] Martens 2006:31
[247] Brooks 2011:254
[248] McRaney 2011:159
[249] Perkins and Craig 2006:67(6)
[250] Whitney 2005:242-3
[251] Baechle 2000:105
[252] University of Notre Dame's "Alcohol and Athletes"
[253] University of Notre Dame's "Alcohol and Athletes"
[254] UC San Diego's "Alcohol and Athletic Performance"
[255] Clark 2008: "Alcohol, Athletes and Pressure to Drink"
[256] Batmanghelidj 2003:17
[257] McRaney 2011:142
[258] Batmanghelidj 2003:61-68
[259] Cialdini 2009:42
[260] Martens 2006:31
[261] Robergs 1997:225
[262] Williams 2005:124
[263] Baechle 2000:75,83
[264] Baechle 2000:65
[265] Robergs 1997:226
[266] King 2000:54-57
[267] Robergs 1997:432
[268] King 1998:71
[269] Carmichael 2004:22
[270] Baechle 2000:22,103
[271] Robergs 1997:357
[272] Baechle 2000:20
[273] Holford 2004:19
[274] McRaney 2011:187
[275] Baechle 2000:155
[276] Moore 2006:136
[277] Moore 2006:136
[278] Shermer 2011:333
[279] Gladwell 2009:52
[280] Tavris 2007:300
[281] Shermer 2011:331
[282] Shermer 2011:308
[283] Thygerson 2005:61
[284] Amy Cuddy 2012:TEDTalk Your Body Language Shapes Who You Are
[285] Coyle 2009:77
[286] Goldacre 2010:17
[287] Lehrer 2012:272
[288] Ariely 2009:196
[289] Gladwell 2008:153
[290] McRaney 2011:32
[291] Rousmaniere 2000:76
[292] 2009:78
[293] Baechle 2000:401
[294] Baechle 2000:11
[295] Baechle 2000:10
[296] Baechle 2000:41
[297] Duhigg 2012:276
[298] Moore 2006:304
[299] 2004
[300] Kahneman 2011
[301] Schwarzenegger 1998:140
[302] Brooks 2011:288

[303] Baechle 2000:322
[304] Baechle 2000:323
[305] Baechle 2000:322
[306] Baechle 2000:51
[307] Whitney 2005:478
[308] 1993
[309] Baechle 2000:11
[310] Whitney 2005:474
[311] Fussell 1991
[312] Reilly 1994: 37(1):107-115
[313] Drake 2001: 38(6):979-987
[314] Crispim 2007: 20(2):195-212
[315] Mah 2011: 34(7):943-950
[316] Kim 2010: 14(5):889-895
[317] Alano 2010: 24:lb361
[318] Georgakilas 2013: 27:lb421
[319] Hill 1992: 17(4):316-319
[320] Smith 1997: 20(5):362-365
[321] Kaida 2006: 29(4):462-469
[322] Souissi 2013: 27(9):2473-2480
[323] Montgomery 1982: 5(2):159-168
[324] Colgan 1993:74
[325] Brooks 2006: 29(6):831-840
[326] Bonnet 1995: 18(2):97-104
[327] 2011:509
[328] Baechle 2000:514
[329] Baechle 2000:514
[330] Moore 2006:13
[331] Moore 2006:17
[332] Baechle 2000:534
[333] Francis 1991:107
[334] Duhigg 2012:12
[335] Duhigg 2012:42
[336] 2012: 42-3
[337] Duhigg 2012:213
[338] Kahneman 2011:208
[339] McRaney 2011:52
[340] Lehrer 2012:414, 382
[341] Gladwell 2009:207
[342] Duhigg 2012:36
[343] Coyle 2009:96
[344] Duhigg 2012:31
[345] Duhigg 2012:81
[346] Brooks 2011:288
[347] Duhigg 2012:218
[348] McRaney 2011:22
[349] Brooks 2011:303
[350] Duhigg 2012:66
[351] Duhigg 2012:159
[352] Duhigg 2012:70
[353] Ariely 2012:72
[354] Ariely 2012:80
[355] Duhigg 2012:153
[356] Coyle 2009:129
[357] Gladwell 2009:255
[358] McRaney 2011:200
[359] McRaney 2011: 201
[360] McRaney 2011:208
[361] Iyengar 2010:86
[362] Ariely 2012:57
[363] Duhigg 2012:130
[364] Pollan 2008:164
[365] Shermer 2011:98
[366] Shermer 2011:98
[367] Duhigg 2012:174
[368] Duhigg 2012:134
[369] 1999:333
[370] 1999:334
[371] Duhigg 2012:37
[372] Duhigg 2012:95
[373] 2012:314
[374] Duhigg 2012:97
[375] Duhigg 2012:113
[376] Duhigg 2012:232
[377] Duhigg 2012:106
[378] McRaney 2011:210

[379] Duhigg 2012:303
[380] 2011:54
[381] Encyclopedia.com 2008
[382] Cialdini 2009:238
[383] Goldacre 2010:71
[384] Shackleton 1919:127
[385] 2012:22
[386] 2012:115
[387] 2012:73
[388] 2012:94
[389] 2012:101
[390] 2012:10
[391] 2012:31
[392] 2012:38,155,157
[393] 2012:33
[394] 2012:170
[395] This American Life "#412: Million Dollar Idea" 8/7/11
[396] Simon 2014:42(2)
[397] Krakauer 2009:85
[398] Ariely 2009:91
[399] Reynolds New York Times article
[400] Ariely 2009:278
[401] 2011:206
[402] Coyle 2009:128
[403] Gladwell 2002:123
[404] Coyle 2009:204
[405] 2011:102
[406] 2011:234
[407] Brooks 2011:341
[408] 2012:218
[409] Brooks 2011:161
[410] Brooks 2011:434
[411] Lehrer 2012:268
[412] Allen 2001

28133978R00179

Made in the USA
Middletown, DE
04 January 2016